Tennessee
Treasure

Heirloom
Recipe Collection

Tennessee Treasure

Copyright 1985
Pearlie B. Scott
DBA/MC Art Co., Inc.
Printed in United States of America

Nashville, TN 37207

1st Printing May 1985
2nd Printing April 1989
3rd Printing Nov. 1992
4th Printing Dec. 2005

INTRODUCTION

Webster defines heirloom as "something of special value handed on from one generation to another."

With this in mind, I have dedicated this book to my granddaughters, Jamie and Ashley. When the next century dawns my granddaughters and their peers will be homemakers; mothers and wives. Just like housewives of today they will have their own specialties but they may wish for recipes from their past that tasted so great when they were children. This book is a collection of recipes not only from their past but from the past of their mothers and grandmothers. We hope to provide a link to the past and a bridge to the future with memories of good food and warm kitchens.

Most of us can remember dishes our mothers or grandmothers cooked that we would love to taste again, but the recipes seem to have vanished into thin air. My search for some of our culinary roots turned up an interesting look at by-gone days. Friends and relatives contributed recipes that had been hand-written so long ago they were dark yellow with age and ready to crumble; some had personal notes to other family members that made me feel like I really know them; some came in unusual containers such as a fifty year old Crystal Wedding Oat box ragged from use and yellow with age. A few gems were given to me verbally by older people who said they had never been "put down on paper" before. Most of these had to be tested to determine just how much a dab of salt; a pinch of pepper; or a scoop of lard really is.

Since my roots are in the south this book contains mostly southern recipes, some known to be at least 150 years old. We have been fortunate in collecting recipes that have represented this region at gatherings such as family reunions, church suppers and state fairs over the years. We are just as proud of the ones that are just plain good "down home" cooking.

It has been a pleasure to collect, test and assemble these recipes. We hope you will enjoy using them and making these time tested recipes part of your daily life. Four pages have been added in back for you to add your own personal additions. By doing so the book will become part of your heritage and something of value that can be passed on to the next generation as your family heirloom.

Pearlie Baise Scott

3

Tennessee Treasures

Memories of the
Past

Dedicated to the
Future

DEDICATION

This book is dedicated with much love, to my grandaughters;

ASHLEY SCOTT
4 years

JAMIE WOODARD
11 years

May you always be happy and enjoy cooking as much as you have enjoyed "helping" in the kitchen these early years of your lives.

Love,
Nana

TABLE OF CONTENTS

MEAT SAUCES

What to serve with:

Roast Veal — Tomato sauce or horseradish.
Roast Pork — Cinnamon apples, sherberts, tart jelly.
Roast Pork — Apple or cranberry sauce. Apple or pineapple rings.
Roast Beef — Tomato sauce, grated horseradish, cranberry sauce.
             Yorkshire pudding.
Roast Mutton — Currant jelly, caper sauce.
Chicken — Cranberry sauce or peaches, sherbert.
Roast Lamb — Mint sauce, mint pears or jelly.
Roast Turkey — Cranberry sauce, currant jelly or sherbert.
Venison or Wild Ducks — currant jelly.

Seasoning is fundamental to the success of meat sauces. Finely chopped onions and green peppers added to a brown sauce is excellent for certain meats. Mushrooms, berries, curry mustard and nutmeg are highly important when added to meat sauces.

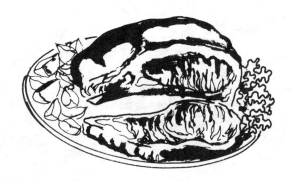

CHICKEN DIVAN

1 pkg. broccoli, cooked &
  drained
2 cup cheddar Cheese

4 chicken breast, broiled and
  boned

SAUCE:
1 can cream of chicken soup
½ cup mayonnaise
1 tsp. lemon juice
½ tsp. curry powder

Grease casserole dish. Layer broccoli, chicken and sauce. Grate cheese and pour on top. Sprinkle ½ cup bread crumbs, cheese and 3 tablespoons butter. Bake 350 degrees for 30 to 40 minutes.

Mary Ann Shacklett
Nashville, Tenn.

CREAMED CHICKEN

3 Tbs. butter
½ cup diced pimento
3 Tbs. flour
¾ cup mushrooms, cut
1½ cups milk
½ cup hot chicken stock

4 cups diced cooked chicken
Salt
Celery Salt
Few drops lemon juice

Melt butter, stir in flour and seasoning. Slowly pour on milk and stock, stirring constantly. Bring to boiling point. Add diced chicken seasoned with celery salt. Let stand in double boiler over boiling water 20 to 30 minutes. Serve hot.

SOUTHERN CHICKEN STEW

4 lb. stewing chicken	2 large onions
⅓ cup flour	2¼ tsp salt
1 tsp. salt	¼ tsp peppers
⅓ cup fat	1 lb tender okra
3 cups water	1 Tbs. flour
1½ lb tomatoes, 4 medium	¼ cup water

Choose chicken for stewing. Singe, clean and wash. Dredge with flour and the 1 tsp salt mixed. Brown slowly in hot fat in a large heavy skillet or Dutch oven. Add 3 cups water, cover, reduce heat. Simmer gently for 1 hour. Add peeled, sliced tomatoes, sliced peeled onions and remaining salt and pepper. Continue to simmer until chicken is nearly tender enough to serve. Twenty minutes before chicken is to be served, add trimmed, sliced okra pods on top of stew and cook uncovered for remaining time. Add flour to the ¼ cup cold water and blend until smooth; stir gently into stew, stirring constantly and cook until stew thickens slightly. Serve at once. 6 servings.

SAVORY FRIED CHICKEN

1 frying chicken, cut up	3 cups milk
½ cup shortening	¼ tsp. sage
½ cup onion, chopped	1 tsp. salt
½ cup celery, chopped	pepper to taste
6 Tbs. flour	

Preheat oven to 325-350 degrees. Salt and pepper pieces of chicken. Heat shortening in heavy skillet and brown chicken. Remove chicken to casserole dish. To shortening in skillet, add onions and celery, cook over low heat, until soft and lightly browned. Stir in flour, slowly add milk and stir over low heat until thick and smooth. Add seasonings. Pour gravy over chicken. Cover casserole and cook for about 1 hour, until chicken is tender.

CHICKEN AND DRESSING

3 lbs. frying chicken, cut in serving pieces
5 tsp. regular flour
½ cup butter
1 cup chopped onions
1 cup chopped celery
½ tsp. salt
⅛ tsp. pepper
4 chicken bouillon cubes
2 cups boiling water

Coat chicken with ¼ cup flour. Place ¼ cup butter and chicken in a 3 quart casserole. Bake at 350 degrees for 30 minutes. Lightly brown onion and celery in ¼ cup butter until tender. Blend 1 tsp. flour, salt, pepper. Place around chicken. Spoon topping over casserole. Dissolve bouillon cubes in boiling water; pour over topping. Bake 30 minutes.

Corn Bread topping:

1 cup flour
1 tsp. baking powder
½ tsp. salt
¼ tsp. sage
1 tsp. shortening
¾ cup milk

½ cup corn meal
2 tsp. sugar
⅛ tsp. pepper
¼ tsp. thyme
3 eggs beaten

Combine in mixing bowl: flour, corn meal, baking powder, sugar, salt, sage, thyme and pepper. Cut in shortening. Add eggs, milk; blend well.

NOTE: If using self-rising flour, decrease baking powder to 1 tsp. and omit salt.

CHICKEN AND DUMPLINGS

1 Stewing hen
3 cups flour
1 egg
1 heaping Tbs. shortening

1 tsp. salt
½ cup cold water

Cut chicken for stewing. Barely cover with water and cook until tender for about 2 to 3 hours. Remove chicken from stock and remove bones. Put flour in mixing bowl. In center of flour put egg, shortening and salt. Gradually add cold water. Work plenty of flour into the dough. Roll thin and cut in 2 x 3 inch strips. Drop into fast boiling broth one at a time. When all dumplings are added, lower heat and simmer about 12 to 15 minutes. Place chicken back in the stew. A little butter may be added if chicken is lacking in fat.

FARMERS SMOTHERED CHICKEN

2 broilers, 2½ lbs. each
½ tsp. salt
½ cup flour
Shortening for frying
2 cups sliced onions

2 cups diced carrots
½ cup chicken stock
Pepper

Wash, clean, split broilers, wipe dry. Rub salt into chicken and rub with flour. Fry in deep hot shortening, drain on paper to remove excess shortening. Place the onions and carrots in heavy pan. Place chicken over the vegetables, pour in stock, cover pan and bake in fairly slow oven about 2 hours. Serve on a hot platter.

* Long slow cooking necessary. Serve with hot corn bread.

CHICKEN NOODLE CASSEROLE

½ tsp. salt
⅛ tsp. pepper
½ tsp. celery salt
1 cup English peas
¼ cup pimiento
1½ cups cheese, grated
1 can mushroom soup
⅓ cup onion, finely chopped

1 chicken, cut up and cooked
6 cups chicken broth
3 ounce can mushrooms
1 cup olives sliced
12 oz. medium wide noodles
⅓ cup bell pepper, minced

Preheat oven to 350 degrees. Cook noodles in 6 cups broth. Lightly brown onion and pepper until limp. Add sliced olives. Add soup and seasonings to undrained noodles. Mix all together. Bake for about 45 minutes. Sprinkle cheese on top when almost done. Serves 12.

CHICKEN ALMOND RICE CASSEROLE

1 large hen, cooked
1 onion, diced
½ bunch celery chopped fine
½ large green pepper, cut up
  fine
1 cup uncooked rice

2 packages chicken noodle
  soup
4 cups chicken broth
1 cup almonds
½ tsp. curry powder

Preheat oven to 350 degrees. Lightly brown vegetables in small amount of oil until tender. Add uncooked rice and the chicken noodle soup mix. Add 4 cups boiling chicken broth. Add cooked, diced chicken, slivered almonds and curry powder. Bake in covered casserole for 1 hour. Remove cover the last few minutes.

CHICKEN RAVIOLI

1 hen
1 onion, chopped
1 green pepper, cut fine
5 stalks of celery, chopped
1 package wide noodles
1 can sliced mushrooms

1 lb. cheddar cheese, grated
1 stick margarine
1 small jar pimiento
1 can cream of mushroom soup
Salt and pepper to taste

Preheat oven to 350 degrees. Cook chicken. Remove bones and cut in bite sized pieces. Reserve stock. Lightly brown green pepper, onions and celery in margarine. Cook noodles in chicken stock. Mix together cheese (save a little for topping) pimiento, mushrooms, mushroom soup, one cup chicken stock, salt and pepper. Add to noodles. Put in large pan and top with cheese. Bake for 30 minutes or until hot and bubbly.

CHICKEN SUPREME

½ cup shredded cheese
1 Tbs. lemon juice
1 can sliced mushrooms
1½ cups milk
2 Tbs. flour
¼ cup flour

¼ cup butter
Dash pepper
3 large chicken breasts, halved
1 tsp. salt
1 tsp. paprika

Pre heat oven to 350 degrees. Combine ¼ cup flour, paprika, salt and pepper. Coat chicken breasts with flour mixture. Brown in butter. Add 2 tablespoons water. Simmer, covered 25 to 30 minutes. Remove chicken to a large baking dish. Save drippings. Combine 2 tablespoons flour, salt and milk. Stir into drippings in skillet. Cook and stir until thick and bubbly. Drain mushrooms, add with lemon juice to sauce. Pour over chicken. Bake about an hour. Sprinkle with cheese. Bake, uncovered, till cheese melts. About 1 to 2 minutes. Serves 6.

CHICKEN SPAGHETTI

1 package spaghetti, cooked
½ cup chicken broth
4-6 chicken breasts, chopped
and deboned
1 medium onion, chopped
1 green pepper, chopped
1 stick celery
1 can tomatoes

1 can tomato soup
Butter
Cracker crumbs
1 can cream of mushroom soup
2 cups cheddar cheese, grated
1 can chicken soup
1 can mushrooms, drained

Preheat oven to 350 degrees. Cook onion, pepper and celery in chicken broth until tender. Add chicken, tomatoes, soups and mushrooms. Season with salt and pepper. In large casserole, layer ½ spaghetti, ½ sauce and ½ cheese. Repeat. Top with cracker crumbs and dot with butter. Bake in oven for 40 minutes.

CHICKEN N CHEESE

3½ cups macaroni
1 green pepper, chopped
1 can asparagus tips, drained
2 Tbs. onion
2 Tbs. melted butter
1 cup cottage cheese
2 cups cooked chicken
½ tsp. salt

2 Tbs. flour
½ cup cream cheese
½ cup milk
¼ tsp. pepper
½ tsp. salt
½ cup sour cream
1 can sliced mushrooms,
drained
1 Tbs. blue cheese

Preheat oven to 350 degrees. Place half of macaroni in lightly greased 4 quart casserole dish. Cover with asparagus tips. Lightly brown green pepper and onion in butter in small skillet. Add flour, stirring until vegetables are coated. Remove from heat, stir in cottage cheese, cream cheese and sour cream. Spread over asparagus. Spoon chicken over cheese mixture and top with remaining macaroni and mushrooms. Sprinkle with blue cheese, cheddar cheese, salt and pepper. Pour milk overall. Bake for 30-40 minutes.

15

BEER BATTERED FRIED CHICKEN

1 cup all purpose flour sifted
½ tsp. salt
1 cup beer
1½ tsp. finely chopped parsley
2 Tbs. finely chopped onions

12 chicken drumsticks
Salt and freshly ground pepper
Peanut oil for frying.

To make batter, combine flour and salt in bowl. Add in beer until batter is smooth and let stand for about 30 minutes. Stir in parsley and onions. Wash chicken drumsticks. Pat dry. Use heavy knife or cleaver to cut off the knuckle of each leg. Remove tendon and push skin and meat away from bone. Sprinkle both sides with salt/pepper. In large skillet, heat 2 inches of oil to 350 degrees. Dip drumsticks in batter, allowing excess to drip off. Carefully place drumstick in oil and cook about 20 minutes, turning occasionally, until golden brown. Allow oil to return to right temperature before frying each batch. Remove drumsticks from pan and drain on paper towel. Keep cooked chicken on baking sheet in preheated 180 degree oven until all chicken is done. Makes 3 to 5 servings.

BROILERS - SOUTHERN STYLE

2 broilers, 2½ lbs. each
2 small onions
3 stalks celery

1 tsp. salt
¼ cup rice, wash well and
    cooked
Pepper

Wash, split broilers, place cut side down in iron skillet. Add onions and celery. Add boiling water to half cover chicken. Cover tightly and cook slowly for 50 minutes. Add the cooked rice and continue cooking until chicken is tender, about 20 minutes longer or more. Remove onion and celery and serve rice with the chicken.

CRUNCHY CHICKEN CASSEROLE

3 cups chopped cooked chicken
½ cup slivered almonds
1 8½ oz. can water chestnuts, sliced
¼ cup chopped pimento
¼ tsp. celery salt
⅛ tsp. paprika
1 Tbs. chopped parsley
½ cup chopped mushrooms, canned
1 10¾ 4 oz. can of cream of mushroom soup-undiluted
½ cup French fried onion rings, crumbled
½ cup shredded sharp cheddar cheese

Combine all ingredients except onion rings and cheese. Pour into a greased 1½ quart casserole. Sprinkle onion rings and cheese over top. Bake at 350° for 30 minutes. Serves 6.

Freezes well—add onions and cheese after thawing.
   ****Prize winning recipe. Always a favorite at family reunions and Church dinners.

                    Lynda Woodard
                    Goodlettsville, Tenn.

CHICKEN AND WILD RICE CASSEROLE

2 fryer chickens
1 cup dry sherry
1½ tsp. salt
½ tsp. curry powder
Onion
½ cup sliced celery

2 packages long grain wild rice
   w/seasonings
1 pound mushrooms
¼ cup margarine
1 cup sour cream
1 can cream of mushroom soup

Cook chicken in water, sherry, salt, curry, onion, and celery. Simmer until done. Strain broth and reserve; debone chicken. Using broth, cook rice according to directions for firm rice. Slice mushrooms and saute in margarine. Reserve a few mushrooms for topping and combine the rest with the chicken and rice. Blend sour cream and soup. Combine with Chicken mixture. Arrange mushrooms on top. Bake covered at 350 degrees for 1 hour. Serves 10 to 12.

SAVORY CHICKEN CASSEROLE

6 chicken breasts
1 cup chopped green pepper
1 cup chopped onion
1 cup chopped celery
½ cup butter
½ pound Velveeta cheese
1 can cream of mushroom soup

1 can mushrooms, sliced
1 jar stuffed olives, sliced
1 package green noodles

Boil chicken in salted water; drain and reserve chicken stock. Bone and dice chicken. Blend green pepper, onion, and celery in butter. Add Velveeta and melt. Blend in soup, mushrooms, and olives. Add chicken and 1 cup of reserved stock. Boil noodles in remaining stock until done; add to chicken mixture. Bake at 350 degrees for 30 minutes in a large casserole dish. Serves 8 to 10.

MACARONI WITH CHICKEN

1½ cups boiled macaroni
3 cups cold cooked chicken cut
  in pieces
1 can mushrooms

2 cups cream sauce
⅛ tsp. Celery Salt
⅛ tsp. Onion Seasoning

Butter baking dish, place layer of diced chicken, add mushrooms then layer of cooked macaroni, then chicken. Repeat. Pour over mixture rich cream sauce, set in pan of hot water. Bake 45 minutes in moderate oven.

CHICKEN LUNCHEON DISH

2 chickens each 2½ lbs. cut in
   pieces
½ lbs. sliced bacon, fried
1 can peas
1 can mushrooms

2 potatoes
2 carrots
1 turnip
2 onions

Fry the bacon. Lightly flour the chicken and fry in hot bacon grease until brown on both sides. Then fry sliced vegetables in bacon grease to a light brown. Place chicken, bacon in center, surround with vegetables, mushrooms on top, in a buttered casserole, cover with a gravy made of 2 tablespoons of butter, 2 tablespoons of flour and cook in the frying pan in which bacon was prepared adding enough hot water to make a thin gravy. Bake in covered casserole 2 hours. Remove cover last 20 minutes to brown.

CHICKEN A LA CREME

2 cups sour cream
8 chicken breasts
1 Tbs. Worcestershire sauce
1½ tsp. paprika
1 Tbs. salt

3 Tbs. lemon juice
1 Tbs. celery salt
½ clove garlic, minced
½ tsp. pepper
4 cups dry bread crumbs, fine
1 stick margarine

Preheat oven to 300 degrees. Mix sour cream, lemon juice, worcestershire sauce, celery salt, paprika, garlic, salt and pepper. Add chicken and coat well. Let stand in refrigerator overnight. Remove chicken and roll in bread crumbs. Place on baking sheet meaty side up. Spoon melted butter over chicken and bake for 1½ hours.

CHICKEN BISQUE

2 tbsps. buter
2 tbsps. flour
3 cups chicken stock
1 cup top milk

1 cup cooked ground chicken
salt and paprika

Melt butter, blend in flour, add chicken stock gradually, then top milk and ground chicken.
Season to taste. Heat well and serve—luscious preceding a salad main course at luncheon when topped with whipped cream, sprinkled with paprika. Amount: about 5 cups.

SAUSAGE SCRAPPLE

1 pint corn meal
½ lb. seasoned sausage

2 tsps. salt
2 quarts water

Add meal gradually to boiling salted water. Stir constantly for 10 minutes. Then cook in double boiler for 30 minutes, add sausage and beat well. Pour into greased baking pan. When cold, slice, dip in flour and fry slowly until golden brown. For breakfast, serve with maple syrup, for luncheon with apple sauce.

HOMEMADE SAUSAGE

3¼ lbs. lean pork, ground	2 Tbs. salt
1¼ lbs. fat pork, ground	½ Tbs. black pepper
½ Tbs. sage	Poultry seasoning to taste

Mix the meat together thoroughly and stir in the seasoning. Place in the refrigerator 10 to 12 hours to flavor. Will make 5 lbs.

* It is important to cook all pork thoroughly.

SAUSAGE ROLLS

2 cups flour	⅔ cups milk
1½ tsp. salt	1 pound sausage, at room
3 tsp. baking powder	temperature
5 Tbs. shortening	

Sift flour with salt and baking powder. Cut in shortening until mixture resembles coarse meal. Add milk all at once and mix well. Divide dough into two parts. Roll half of dough out ¼-inch thick. Spread thinly with sausage. Roll as for a jelly roll. Repeat with remaining dough. Wrap in waxed paper and chill in refrigerator. When ready to serve slice ⅓ inch pieces and bake for 10 to 15 minutes in a preheated 400 degree oven. Uncooked rolls freeze well.

21

SAUSAGE STROGANOFF

1 or 2 cloves garlic
2 pounds sausage
3 Tbs. flour
2 cups milk
2 large onions, chopped
2 4 oz. cans mushrooms or 1
   pound fresh mushrooms
   sliced

4 Tbs. butter
2 tsp. soy sauce
2 Tbs. Worcestershire
Paprika to taste
1 pint sour cream
½ tsp. salt
⅛ tsp. pepper

Rub large skillet with garlic and heat. Brown sausage well, pouring off grease as it accumulates. Degrease sausage as well as possible after frying, dredge with flour. Add milk and simmer until slightly thickened. Set aside. Lightly brown onions and minced garlic cloves in butter, adding sliced mushrooms the last couple of minutes. To the sausage cream sauce mixture, add soy sauce, worcestershire, onions, mushrooms, and seasonings. When mixture bubbles, add sour cream. Keep hot in chafing dish as the stroganoff should not boil after the sour cream has been added. Excellent served as a brunch, luncheon, or supper dish with white, brown or wild rice. May also be heaped upon biscuits or pastry shells or used as a dip with Doritos. When served as an appetizer for 50 people or over, double receipe, but add only 3 onions. May be made in advance and frozen, eliminating sour cream. On day of party, thaw and heat in large skillet, adding sour cream as called for in receipe.

ITALIAN SAUSAGE

1 lb. pressed ham sausage or
   bologna
2 onions
1 tbsp. salad oil
2 cups tomatoes

1 tsp. salt
½ tsp. pepper
2 tsps. Worcestershire sauce
2 cups egg noodles

Brown onions, chopped, in salad oil. Add ham sausage or bologna, chopped. Combine seasoning with tomatoes. Pour over meat. Add cooked noodles to meat mixture and cook in moderate 350° oven 30 minutes. Serve surrounded with 1 cup of grated cheese.

TURKEY AMANDINE

½ cup chopped onion
6 Tbs. butter
6 Tbs. all purpose flour
½ tsp. curry powder, optional
⅛ tsp. paprika
2 cups milk

1 can cream of chicken soup
2 cups grated sharp Cheddar
   cheese
2 cups cooked, diced turkey
1 cup slivered blanched
   almonds, toasted
1 cup cooked rice
2-4 ounce cans sliced
   mushrooms, drained
1 cup buttered bread crumbs

Cook onion in butter until tender. Blend in flour, curry powder and paprika. Gradually add milk and soup. Cook over medium flame stirring constantly until thickened. Blend in cheese; stir until melted. Add turkey, almonds, rice and mushrooms. Turn into 2 quart cassrole dish. Sprinkle top with bread crumbs. Bake in 350 degree oven 45-50 minutes. Makes 8 servings.

TURKEY HASH

¼ cup chopped onion
¼ cup chopped green pepper
2 Tbs. butter
2 cups chopped leftover turkey
   with some skin

1½ cups rich turkey broth made
   from bones
Salt and pepper to taste
1½ cups leftover dressing
3 cups cubed cooked potatoes

Saute onion and green peppers in butter for 10 minutes until yellow and transparent. Add remaining ingredients and mix lightly. Heat thoroughly and serve immediately. 4 to 6 servings.

23

TURKEY A LA KING

¼ cup butter	1½ cups cubed cooked turkey
¼ cup flour	1 cup sliced mushrooms
1½ cups milk	½ tsp. salt

Melt butter in top of double boiler over direct heat. Blend in flour, add milk gradually, stirring constantly. Cook over boiling water until mixture thickens. Stir to keep smooth. Add next 3 ingredients, cover and cook 15 minutes. Serve at once over toast, Chinese noodles or in patty shells. 4 to 5 servings.

MEAT CROQUETTES

2 cups cooked cold meat	1 egg
1 to 2 Tbs. flour	Salt to taste
2 Tbs. butter	Pepper
1 cup milk	Celery Salt
Fine bread crumbs	

Make cream sauce of flour, butter and milk. Add seasoning, moisten meat with sauce. Form into croquettes. Chill 30 minutes. Roll in flour, dip in beaten egg with 1 tablespoon milk or water, then roll in bread crumbs. Fry in deep hot fat until brown. Drain on unglazed paper. Serve with tomato sauce.

HAMBURGER CORN PONE

1 cup canned kidney beans,
  drained
1 cup corn bread batter
1 cup canned tomatoes
1 tsp. Worcestershire sauce

1 lb. ground beef
⅓ cup chopped onion
1 Tbs. shortening
2 tsp. chili powder
¾ tsp. salt

Brown meat and onion in melted shortening. Add seasoning and tomatoes. Cover and simmer over low heat for 15 minutes. Add kidney beans, pour into greased casserole dish. Top with corn bread batter and bake in hot oven at 425 degrees for 20 minutes.

SOUPER STEW

2 lbs. stew meat, cut into cubes
1 envelope onion soup mix
1 can cream of mushroom soup

⅔ cup sherry
2 tsp. pepper
Dash nutmeg
Cooked noodles

Preheat oven to 325 degrees. Combine all ingredients except noodles in 4 quart casserole. Cover and bake 3 hours, adding small amount of water if mixture becomes too thick. Serve on bed of noodles.

CORNED BEEF

1 corned beef
1 bay leaf
1 sliced onion
1 tsp. peppercorns
1 carrot cut in lengths

2 ribs celery, cut into lengths
2 cloves garlic
Water

Put corned beef in pan and cover with water. Add bay leaf, onion, pepper corns, carrot, celery and garlic. Cover, bring to a boil and boil for 2 to 3 hours until tender. Remove meat from broth and cut off excess fat. Remove from broth 30 minutes before serving and let firm up before slicing. Cook cabbage in broth. Serves 12.

PEARLS BAKED COUNTRY HAM
(Lard Stand Method — very old receipe)

16-22 lb. country ham   1 c. vinegar
2 cups sorghum   Cold Water to cover

Pour vinegar and sorghum over ham. Cover with water. Slowly bring to full boil. Boil for one hour.

Remove ham and container from stove and wrap tight in quilts or blankets. Let stand for 12 hours. Take ham out of water, cover with brown sugar and bake in medium oven — 350 degrees — until brown. Cool before slicing.

*In the old days lard was bought in 10 gal. metal containers called "lard stands." When empty they were used for all sorts of things, cooking ham just being one of them. If you don't have a lard stand handy, use a large canner or any other pot with cover large enough to accommodate a 20 lb. ham and enough water to cover.

                    Annie Pearl Matthews
                    White House, Tenn.

HAM LOAF

2 cups ground ham (raw or
   cooked), 1 lb.
2 cups ground pork, beef or
   veal, 1 lb.
2 tbsps. chopped green pepper

1 tbsp. minced onion
1 egg, beaten
1 cup milk
1 cup bread crumbs
Salt and pepper to taste

Combine all ingredients in order listed. Blend thoroughly and shape
into loaf. Fit into greased bread pan. Bake in moderate 350° oven
until done, for about ¾ to 1¼ hours. Slice and serve hot with mushroom or tomato sauce. Or serve cold. Amount: 8 servings.

HAM-BAKED BACON

4 lb. piece bacon
Cold water
1½ tsps. dry mustard

1½ cups vinegar
2½ cups boiling water
Brown sugar

Wash bacon, place in large kettle of cold water. Bring to boil for 10
minutes. Then simmer 45 minutes. Pour off water, return meat to
kettle and cover with hot water. Cook slowly 1½ hours. Take bacon
from water, remove rind and place fat side up in baking pan. Bake
slowly about 20 minutes to ½ hour, basting with mixture of dry
mustard, vinegar and boiling water. Remove from oven, sprinkle
surface of bacon with brown sugar and continue baking ½ hour or
until done. Serve with spinach, cabbage, sauerkraut or any winter
vegetable.

BEEF STEW WITH DUMPLINGS

1½ lbs. short ribs, shank, neck,
   flank, plate, rump or brisket
¼ cup flour
1½ tsps. salt
¼ tsp. pepper

1 small onion
⅓ cup cubed carrots
⅓ cup cubed turnips
4 cups potatoes, cut in quarters

Wipe meat, remove from bone, cut in 1½ inch cubes. Mix flour with salt and pepper and dredge cubes of meat with it. Heat some of fat from meat in frying pan. Add cubes of meat and brown.

Put meat with browned fat into stew kettle. Add boiling water to cover, or a pint of tomatoes, stewed and strained. Simmer until tender (about 3 hours). Add carrots and turnips for last hour of cooking. Add potatoes 20 minutes, and dumplings 15 minutes, before serving.

IRISH STEW

2 lbs. mutton or lamb, breast,
   neck or shoulder
6 medium potatoes
6 medium carrots
6 small onions
1 cup sliced celery or peas

3 sprigs parsley, if desired
2 tsps. salt
¼ tsp. pepper
2 tsps. sugar
Flour to thicken

Cut meat into inch cubes, add cold water to cover (measuring it), and bring to boil. Add potatoes cut in ⅛ths, carrots in strips, small whole onions, celery or peas, parsley, salt, pepper and sugar. Cover closely. Simmer slowly for 2 hours or until meat is tender. For each cup of water, stir in 1 tbsp. of flour mixed smoothly with an equal quantity of cold water. Stir gently until it simmers. Cook closely covered for about 10 minutes.

HAMBURGER LOAF

1½ lbs. chopped meats, beef or
   pork
1 tsp. salt
1 tsp. onion seasoning
Black Pepper
½ cup tomato soup

Celery Salt
1 beaten egg
½ cup bread crumbs
Cooked rice or macaroni
1 Tbs. butter, melted

Mix well, make a loaf. Add little pepper and onion seasoning. Bake in moderate oven about an hour.

HAMBURGER SCRAMBLE

1 lb. 12 oz. lean ground beef
2 Tbs. butter
2½ c. fresh mushrooms or
1½ cups chopped green pepper
1½ cups sliced onions

1 Tbs. salt
½ tsp. pepper
¼ lb. fine noodles (uncooked)
1½ cup crushed tomatoes
1 cup grated cheddar cheese

Cook the meat in the butter in a skillet until nicely browned, stirring frequently. Add the vegetables and salt and pepper and cook just until tender. Meanwhile cook the noodles until tender in boiling salted water. Drain, and add to the meat-vegetable mixture. Add crushed tomatoes. Pour into a two-quart casserole, sprinkle with the grated cheese, and bake at 275 degrees for one hour. Serves 8 to 10.

  * Good with Potato Salad and toasted buns.

MEAT LOAF

1½ lbs. ground beef
1 egg, well beaten
1 cup milk
1¼ tsp. salt

1 cup coarse soft bread crumbs
⅛ tsp. pepper
Parsley

Combine all ingredients thoroughly, and pack into a lightly oiled glass bread loaf pan (8¾ x 2¾ inches). Turn out onto a greased shallow baking pan, and bake in a moderate oven (350F) for about 1 hour or until done. Serve hot with tomato sauce and a parsley garnish. The meat loaf mixture may be baked in custard cups for individual loaves, in which case the baking time should be reduced to 45 minutes. 5 servings.

SLOPPY JOES

1 tsp. beef drippings or cooking
   oil
1 pound ground beef
1 med. onion finely chopped
½ cup ketchup
½ cup chili sauce

1 Tbs. Worcestershire sauce
1 tsp. salt
⅛ tsp. pepper
⅓ cup water
6 hamburger buns, warmed

Brush skillet with drippings and warm over moderate heat ½ minute. Add beef and onion and cook 10 minutes stirring frequently. Add all remaining ingredients except buns and simmer, uncovered, 10 minutes. Spoon mixture between split buns and serve. Serves 6.

HAMBURGER TURNOVERS

1 Tbs. butter
½ cup onion, chopped
½ pound ground beef
2 Tbs. Bisquick
¼ tsp. sugar
½ tsp. oregano
½ tsp. salt

¼ tsp. garlic salt
½ cup tomato sauce
2 Tbs. sour cream
1½ cups Bisquick
½ cup milk
1 Tbs. butter, melted

Heat oven to 400 degrees. Melt 1 tablespoon butter. Brown onions and beef in butter. Add 2 tablespoons biscuit mix, sugar, oregano, salt and garlic salt; mix well. Stir in tomato sauce and sour cream. Place 1½ cups biscuit mix in a bowl; add milk and form soft dough. Beat 15 strokes. Knead dough 8 to 10 times. Roll into 12-inch square. Cut into 4x6-inch squares. Place meat on half of each square. Moisten edge of dough with water and fold over. Seal with fork. Brush with melted butter. Make slits in top of each turnover. Bake 20 minutes. Yield: 4 servings.

HAMBURGER STROGANOFF

2 Tbs. minced parsley
¼ tsp. pepper
1 cup sour cream
1 lbs. fresh mushrooms
1 can cream chicken soup
2 Tbs. flour

2 tsp. salt
½ cup minced onion
1 clove garlic, minced
¼ cup butter
1 lb. ground beef

Lightly brown onion and garlic in butter. Stir in ground beef and brown. Stir in flour, salt and pepper and mushrooms, cooking 5 minutes. Stir in undiluted soup. Simmer, uncovered, 10 minutes. Stir in sour cream. Heat through then spinkle with parsley.

GOULASH

2 cups diced cooked leftover
   roast beef or pot roast
1½ lbs. potatoes, 3 or 4
1 cup beef broth or water

No. 2 can tomatoes
1 lb. small white onions
Salt to suit taste

Combine meat with potatoes which have been pared and cut into 1-inch dice. Add broth and tomatoes, cover, and cook until potatoes are tender. Meanwhile, peel onions, leave whole and boil in enough water to cover until just tender. Add to meat and vegetable mixture. Season to suit taste and serve piping hot. 5 servings.

LAMB SHOULDER CHOPS WITH DRESSING

5 shoulder arm or blade lamb
   chops
2 tsp. bacon drippings
3 cups coarse dry bread crumbs
½ cup cold water
1 egg

1 medium onion, grated
2 Tbs. chopped parsley
½ to 1 tsp. poultry seasoning
½ tsp. salt
5 slices bacon

Brown chops slowly in bacon drippings. Meanwhile soak crumbs in the water until they take it all up; squeeze out any excess. Sprinkle onion, parsley, and seasonings over crumbs, add beaten egg and mix very lightly to distribute well. Put dressing in bottom of a buttered baking dish; cover with the browned chops. Cover dish and bake in a moderate oven (325F) about 1 hour. Remove cover, place a slice of bacon on each chop and bake 15 minutes longer to crisp bacon. Serves 5.

HOMINY AND PORK CHOPS

4 medium pork chops, 1¼ lbs.   Salt
No. 2½ can hominy   Parsley

Cook pork chops. Remove chops from skillet to a plate to keep warm. Turn the undrained hominy into the skillet containing the hot pan gravy from the chops. Cook the hominy over low heat, crushing it well with a potato masher, then stirring it occasionally until thoroughly heated through and the gravy has been absorbed. Add more salt if desired. Crushing the hominy permits it to acquire much more flavor than if the grains are left whole. Turn hominy into a heap in center of a hot platter and arrange hot chops around it. Garnish with parsley. 4 to 5 servings.

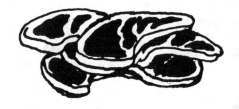

CASSEROLE PORK CHOPS

5 thick loin or rib pork chops   No. 2 can cream style corn
1½ Tbs. salt   ⅓ cup diced green pepper
Pepper   2 Tbs. hot water

Brown chops slowly in a skillet in the hot fat, and sprinkle with the salt and enough pepper to suit taste. Mix corn and green pepper, and arrange in buttered casserole in alternate layers with browned chops. Add the water, cover, and bake 45 minutes in a moderate oven (350F); then remove cover and bake 15 minutes longer. 5 servings.

"PAN-BROILED" PORK CHOPS AND POTATOES

4 loin pork chops, inch-thick,
   1½ lbs.
2 baking potatoes, 1¼ lbs.
1¾ tsp. salt

2 Tbs. water
1 Tbs. flour
½ cup milk
¼ cup water

It is important that the chops be thick and uniform in thickness. Heat skillet until hot, sprinkle a little salt over bottom, lay in chops. Lift chops immediately, then let them drop back into place to keep them from sticking to the skillet. Cook moderately fast until chops are nicely browned on under side, turn and brown other side. Sprinkle with 1¼ tsp. of the salt. Cover skillet, reduce heat and cook so that fat sizzles gently in skillet about 10 minutes. Meanwhile pare potatoes thinly, cut into 3 lengthwise, uniformly thick slices. Turn pork chops again and push together compactly. Lay potato slices flat around chops, sprinkle with remaining salt; cover and cook another 30 minutes; turn potatoes and chops once again. Add the 2 tbsp. water last 15 minutes of cooking. When potatoes and chops are tender and a tempting brown, remove to a hot platter. Pour off all but 1 tbsp. of fat from skillet. Add flour to skillet, then the milk and ¼ cup water. Boil gently and scrape all the brown residue from the bottom and sides of the skillet. Cook until smooth and thick. Serve with the chops. Serves 4.

PORK CHOPS WITH CLING PEACHES

6 rib chops
2 Tbs. salad oil
1 tsp. salt
¼ tsp. pepper

¼ cup chili sauce
3 Tbs. lemon juice
1 16-ounce can cling peach
   slices

In large skillet over medium high heat, brown chops on both sides. Sprinkle with salt and pepper. Add chili sauce, lemon juice and ⅓ cup syrup drained from peaches. Cover and cook over low heat 50 minutes or until chops are fork tender. During last 5 minutes of cooking time, add peach slices. Serves 6.

STUFFED SALMON

1 Tbs. onion
4 boneless salmon steaks
1 tsp. green pepper
6 spinach leaves
1 tsp. pimiento
1 ounce grated cheese, cheddar
Dash of salt and pepper

2 Tbs. sliced mushrooms
2 Tbs. baby shrimp
2 Tbs. butter
½ cup chicken broth
½ cup cream
2 Tbs. flour

Lightly cook onions, green pepper, pimiento, and mushrooms in butter, until soft. Add salt and pepper. Add flour, and blend. Pour in chicken broth and cream, and cook until thick. Add shrimp, cheddar cheese and spinach. Stir to blend, and cook for one minute. Let cool, then form into four balls. Place the stuffing in the center of the salmon steak between the two "tails." Fasten tails together with toothpicks, and place salmon steaks into a shallow buttered pan. Bake 18 to 20 minutes at 350 degrees. Baste two or three times with pan juices.

MOBILE SHRIMP

2 eggs beaten
½ cup grated cheese
⅓ cup fine bread crumbs
1 cup peas (cooked)
¾ cups cut carrots
¾ tsp. salt

1 can shrimp
1½ cups milk
Onion Seasoning
Celery Salt
Pepper
Paprika

Mix all ingredients, place in well greased baking dish and bake about one hour in moderate oven. Set baking dish in a little hot water to cool.

BAKED FISH

1 choice fish
1½ ounces butter
1 Tbs. stale bread crumbs
2 Tbs. water

1 tsp. lemon juice
¼ tsp. salt
¼ tsp. pepper
Paprika
Onion seasoning

Remove fins from fish, clean carefully, wash and dry. Place in dish, pour water and lemon juice over fish. Sprinkle onion, salt, pepper and bread crumbs, drop pieces of butter on fish. Bake about 30 minutes according to thickness.

BAKED FISH WITH TOMATO SAUCE

2 cups tomatoes
1 cup water
1 slice onion
3 Tbs. flour
¾ tsp. salt
Pepper

1 Tbs. butter
2 pounds white fish, clean
  carefully
Onion seasoning

Cook these ingredients until thick, stirring constantly. Strain. Place fish in greased baking pan, pour sauce over fish, bake about 40 minutes basting often. Have hot platter and serve immediately.

BEEF KABOBS

2 pounds tender steak
 juice of 1 lemon
2 teaspoons oregano
1 bay leaf, crushed
½ teaspoon salt

1 med. tomato
½ green pepper
1 onion
1 cup wine vinegar
½ cup cooking oil
1 tablespoon Worcestershire
 sauce

Cut steak into 1½-inch cubes. Pour lemon juice over meat. Cut tomato, pepper, and onion into eight pieces. Alternate meat, tomato, pepper, and onion on 4 skewers. Combine remaining ingredients. Marinate kabobs for about 2 hours. Broil 15 to 20 minutes or until beef is desired doneness. Makes 4 kabobs.

BEEF BEAN POT

½ lb. dried kidney beans or No.
 2 can canned kidney beans,
 2½ cups
⅛ lb. salt pork, sliced thin
¼ cup chopped onion
½ lb. diced or ground beef
No. 2½ can, 3½ cups canned
 tomatoes

3 tsp. salt
¼ cup chopped green pepper, if
 desired
Liquid from beans plus water to
 make 1¼ cups
Crackers or toast

If dried kidney beans are used, wash and drain, then simmer in enough boiling salted water to cover, until tender, 1½ to 2½ hours. Heat pork until some fat accumulates on bottom of skillet or dutch oven. Add chopped onion and ground beef, and cook until grayish in color. Stir in drained beans, tomatoes, salt, green pepper and liquid. Cover and simmer for ½ hour or until meat is thoroughly cooked and flavors well-blended. Serve hot on crisp crackers or toast. 5 to 8 servings. If any is left over, it will keep well in a covered jar in the refrigerator.

SALMON CROQUETTES

1 cup boned salmon	⅛ tsp. pepper
1 Tbs. butter	½ tsp. salt
1 Tbs. flour	Paprika
½ cup milk ·	½ tsp. black pepper
1 tsp. lemon juice	

Make cream sauce with butter, flour, milk, salt and pepper, cooking until thick. Put salmon into bowl, add sauce and lemon juice; mix well with fork until salmon is well broken. Set aside, when cold, mold into desired shape, roll in bread crumbs, dip in egg beaten with 1 tablespoon cold milk, then in bread crumbs. Let dry an hour. Fry in deep hot fat. Serve with butter sauce.

* Ground cooked chicken may be used instead of salmon.

SUNDAY SALMON LOAF

1 tsp. chopped parsley	1 pound can salmon
1 Tbs. lemon juice	½ cup bread crumbs
½ cup hot milk	⅛ tsp. pepper
2 egg whites	½ tsp. salt
2 Tbs. melted butter	2 egg yolks

Remove skin and bones from salmon, add all ingredients except egg whites. Fold in stiffly beaten egg whites, bake in buttered mold in moderate oven for one hour. Sprinkle with paprika.

LOBSTER, CRAB OR SHRIMP NEWBURG

4 tbsps. butter
2 cups lobster meat, diced
Salt
Paprika

Nutmeg
3 egg yolks
1 cup cream
¼ cup cooking sherry

Melt butter in double boiler, add lobster and cook 3 minutes, stirring constantly. Add seasoning and cook 1 minute longer. Beat egg with cream, add to lobster. Cook for 2 minutes, add sherry and serve at once on hot buttered toast.

Nancy Hempel
Largo, Fla.

SHRIMP CREOLE

2 lbs. boiled shrimp
1 can tomatoes
1 large white onion

2 green peppers
Salt, pepper, bay leaf

Place shrimp in buttered casserole with tomatoes, chopped onion and green peppers, and bake about ½ hour in moderate 350° oven.

SHRIMP WIGGLE

4 tbsps. butter
2 tbsps. flour
1¼ cups milk
1 cup boiled shrimp
1 cup peas, drained

Salt, paprika, celery salt
1 egg yolk
1 tsp. lemon juice or cooking
    sherry

Make sauce of first three ingredients. When boiling, add shrimp and peas. Add egg yolk, cook for 1 minute over low heat and then add lemon juice or sherry. Serve Wiggle on rounds of buttered toast or in hot patty shells. To reheat it, place over hot fire.

TAMALE PIE

1 cup cooked meat
1 cup gravy, stock or water
1½ cups tomato soup or purée

½ small clove garlic(optional)
1½ tsps. chili powder
4 cups boiling water
1 cup cornmeal
½ tsp. salt

Cook cornmeal and salt in boiling water until mush is thick. Stir to prevent sticking. Line buttered baking dish with ¾ of mush. Pour in ground or finely chopped meat, gravy, tomato, garlic, chopped fine if used, and chili powder. Dot top with remaining mush, rolled into 1-inch balls. Bake in a moderate 350° oven until brown, about 25 to 45 minutes. Amount: 6 servings.

SHORT RIBS en CASSEROLE

3 lbs. beef short ribs
3 medium onions, chopped
1 carrot
3 tbsps. fat

¼ tsp. pepper
1½ tsps. salt
1 tsp. sugar
2 cups canned tomatoes
½ cup rice

Melt fat in frying pan, add onions and meat, and brown well. Put into casserole. Mix tomatoes, sliced carrot, rice and seasonings and pour over beef and onions. Add enough hot water to cover all ingredients, cover and cook in slow 275° oven for about 3 hours, or cook on top of stove in Dutch oven. Add more water if necessary.

BARBECUED SPARERIBS

3 lbs. spareribs	½ tsp. prepared mustard
1 medium onion, chopped	½ cup water
1 tsp. butter or bacon fat	½ cup chopped celery
1 tsp. vinegar	2 tsp. salt
1 tsp. sugar	Dash of cayenne
3 tsp. lemon juice	1 to 2 tsp. Worcestershire sauce

Wipe spareribs with damp cloth; cut in serving-size pieces. Place in a shallow baking pan and bake uncovered in a moderate oven (350F) for 30 minutes. Meanwhile cook onion in butter or bacon drippings for 5 minutes; then add remaining ingredients, mix well, and simmer 5 minutes. Pour over the spareribs and continue baking for an hour longer, basting the ribs from time to time with the sauce in the bottom of the pan. 5 servings.

Maggie Nola Sloan
Goodlettsville, Tenn.

FRUITED SPARERIBS

1 lb. dried prunes	1½ tsp. salt
3 lbs. spareribs	2 or 3 apples, sliced

Soak prunes in warm water for 1½ to 2 hours. Remove pits. Wipe spareribs clean with damp cloth. Cut in serving portions. Lay half in baking dish; add half the salt. Cover with soaked and pitted prunes. Put apples on top of the prunes. Cover fruit with the remainder of the spareribs and sprinkle on rest of salt. Cover, bake in a moderate oven (350F) until meat is tender, from 1½ to 2 hours. Cover may be removed for last half hour of baking to brown top. 5 servings.

SMOTHERED SPARERIBS

4 lbs. spareribs, lean
1 tsp. salt
¼ tsp. pepper
1 Tbs. bacon drippings
1 Tbs. flour
Onion seasonings

1 can tomato soup
3 or 4 potatoes
Salt
Pepper
Celery salt

Wipe the spareribs with a clean cloth and cut into pieces for serving. Sprinkle with salt and pepper. Place the bacon fat in the frying pan and heat, but do not brown. Cook the spareribs to a golden brown and remove to a hot platter. Add the flour and chili powder to the hot fat and stir until well blended. Stir in the boiling water and bring to the boiling point. Stir in the tomatoes and the cooked meat. Cover and simmer over a low heat for one hour.

ROAST SPARERIBS

Season spareribs with salt and pepper. Make bread stuffing of dry bread crumbs, moisten with melted butter, salt to taste, little pepper, sage. Fill ribs, roll, fasten ends together so bone will stand up. Place in roasting pan, sprinkle with little flour, add water, bake 2 hours.

  * Serve with stuffed potatoes, and a green salad.

STUFFED STEAK

1½ lbs. round or flank steak
3 medium onions
½ cup minced suet
2 cups stale bread crumbs

1 egg
1 tsp. sage
¼ tsp. pepper
Hot water
2 tbsps. drippings
Flour

Cut meat into two slices ½ inch thick. Peel onions and pour boiling water over them; let stand 15 minutes; drain and chop fine. Add to onions, suet, bread crumbs, seasoning and egg and mix well. Add hot water to make moist enough to spread. Lay steaks flat, spread bread mixture evenly over both, roll each separately and skewer or tie securely. Roll in seasoned flour and sear quickly in hot frying pan in which drippings have been melted. Place in casserole and add ½ cup hot water; cover and cook in moderately slow 275° oven for about 1 hour. Remove to hot platter, take off skewers or strings. Thicken gravy in pan and serve. Serves six.

BREADED VEAL STEAK

1 slice of round, ¾ inch thick
1 egg
bread crumbs

½ tsp. salt
1 tsp. paprika
Butter
Cream

Pound meat well with edge of plate. Cut surface lightly with criss-cross gashes. Cut meat into pieces for serving. Season, dip in bread crumbs, in egg to which 1 tbsp. water is added, and again in crumbs. Sauté in butter until brown. Half cover with cream and cook covered for one hour over very low heat. Serve with mushroom sauce or gravy made with drippings.

STUFFED VEAL BREAST OR SHOULDER

4 lbs. breast or shoulder of veal
½ cup melted butter
1 small onion, minced
3 cups dry bread crumbs
3 tsps. salt

½ tsp. pepper
⅓ cup boiling water
1 tsp. each sage and chopped
 parsley
½ cup chopped celery

Have deep "pocket" made in the breast of veal, or have shoulder boned. Make dressing as follows: Slightly cook onion in melted butter or fat. Add bread crumbs, seasonings, water. Mix and stuff into veal. Sew up or fasten edges securely. Dredge with flour, salt and pepper. Place in slow 300° oven. Roast according to general rules.

PIG IN A BLANKET

1 round steak
5 slices bacon

Salt, pepper, garlic salt to taste
1 onion

Cover the steak with 5 slices uncooked bacon. Roll and tie with a string. Brown in oil on all sides. Add 2 cups water, season with salt, garlic salt and pepper to taste. Simmer for 1½ to 2 hours on low heat. Remove meat. Thicken gravy with cornstarch. Remove string from meat and cut 1½ inch slices.

* Serve with baked potato and french fries.

ROUND STEAK PARMESAN

1 pound round steak or veal
Salt and pepper
⅓ cup Parmesan cheese
⅓ cup dry bread crumbs
1 egg, beaten
¼ cup oil

1 onion, minced
1 cup tomato paste
2 cups hot water
½ tsp. marjoram
Sliced Mozzarella cheese
2 Tbs. butter

Cut meat into serving pieces; salt and pepper. Combine Parmesan cheese and bread crumbs. Dip meat into egg, and then coat with cheese mixture. Heat oil in a skillet and fry meat pieces until brown. In another pan, fry onion in butter until soft; add all the Mozzarella cheese. Boil a few minutes. In a casserole layer one half of sauce with meat; then add all the Mozzarella cheese. Top with rest of sauce and bake uncovered at 350 degrees for 30 minutes. Serves 6.

STEAK SHORT CAKE

2 Tbs. butter or margarine
½ lb. ground beef
1 medium onion, chopped
½ cup fine dry bread crumbs
½ tsp. salt
⅓ cup milk
¼ cup chopped green pepper

1 recipe of Baking Powder
  biscuits
11 oz. can cream of mushroom
  soup
½ cup water or milk
1 Tbs. chopped parsley

Melt butter in a skillet, add beef and brown lightly, breaking up with fork. Add onion, crumbs, salt, the ⅓ cup milk and green pepper. Stir well. Meanwhile turn biscuit dough out onto lightly floured board and knead about 8 times, then roll or pat out into rectangle 6 x 12 inches and ¼ inch thick. Cut into eight 3-inch squares. Divide meat mixture on four of the squares. Then place remaining squares on top to form shortcakes. Crease top with back of knife to form pattern, then brush with milk. Place on greased baking sheet and bake in a hot oven (425F) for 15 minutes. Meanwhile place soup in saucepan, add water, stir until blended and heat to boiling. Remove from stove, add parsley. Transfer shortcake to platter, serve immediately with mushroom sauce. 4 servings.

SWISS STEAK

2 lb. round steak at least 1-inch
  thick
⅓ cup flour
2 tsp. salt
Dash of pepper

3 Tbs. shortening
2½ cups water or No. 2 can
  tomato juice

Wipe steak thoroughly with clean damp cloth. Rub flour, salt and pepper into steak; Do not pound with heavy saucer or mallet. Melt shortening in heavy skillet and brown the steak slowly on both sides. Add ½ cup of the water or tomato juice, cover tightly and place in a slow oven (300F) for about 1½ hours or until very tender. Add remaining water or juice gradually to prevent skillet from going dry. If preferred, cooking may be finished on top of the stove over low heat, rather than in the oven. Serve meat in its own gravy. 5 or 6 servings.

BROILED LIVER STEAK

1½ lbs. beef liver sliced 1 inch
  thick
3 Tbs. butter, melted

1 tsp. salt
Pepper, if desired
2 tsp. chopped chives or parsley

Have liver sliced evenly, the same thickness all through for even cooking. Remove the skin and tubes from liver. Brush liver on both sides with melted butter, and place on the pre-heated broiler rack. Adjust broiler rack so surface of liver is 3 inches below the source of heat (electric heating element or tip of gas flame.) Cook for 6 minutes on one side; then turn and cook about 6 minutes on other side, or until just cooked through. Remove to a hot platter. Brush with more butter and sprinkle with salt, pepper and chopped chives or parsley. Garnish and serve immediately. A pleasing accompaniment is French-fried onions and Sour-cream gravy. 5 servings.

SAVORY VEAL STEAKS

1½ lbs. veal shoulder steaks	2 tsp. shortening
2 tsp. flour	2 medium onions
1½ tsp. salt	½ cup water
1½ tsp. dry mustard	1 cup top milk

Buy 3 shoulder arm steaks. Wipe clean with a damp cloth. Mix dry ingredients and pound into meat with edge of a sturdy saucer or back of heavy knife blade. Brown slowly on one side in hot lard. Sprinkle with remaining flour mixture. Turn and cover with sliced onions. When second side is brown, add water, cover and simmer gently for 45 minutes, or until tender. Remove meat to platter. Blend milk with drippings, heat thoroughly and serve as sauce with meat. 5 or 6 servings.

PEPPER STEAK

1½ lb. inch-thick round steak	½ tsp. sugar
¼ cup salad oil	1 tsp. salt
½ clove garlic	Dash of pepper
3 egg-size onions, sliced	1½ cups cold water or bouillon
Pinch of thyme or basil	2½ to 3 medium size green
⅓ cup tomato sauce or puree	peppers

Cut meat into inch cubes on cutting board. Heat oil in 10-inch heavy skillet, add garlic and meat. Brown slowly, about 20 minutes, stirring often. Add onion last few minutes of browning. Now add next 5 ingredients and ½ cup of the water. Cover and simmer until meat is tender, from 50 to 60 minutes, stirring occasionally. Add remaining water in 2 or 3 portions as liquid evaporates. Remove stems, seeds and cores from peppers and cut into inch squares; add to meat, cover and cook 15 minutes longer. When done, there should be about ¾ cup rich gravy to serve with the meat. Serve hot with potatoes, rice or noodles. 4 to 5 servings.

SAVORY VEAL STEW

1 lb. boneless veal cut for stew	Few dashes pepper
3 Tbs. margarine or shortening	½ cup coarsely diced celery
3 Tbs. flour	¼ tsp. thyme, optional
½ egg-size onion	1 cup water or more
1 tsp. salt	Fluffy hot rice

Wipe veal pieces with a damp cloth and put on waxed paper. Sift flour over meat, then shift paper back and forth to coat all pieces evenly. Heat margarine in a 2-quart heavy saucepan until sizzling hot. Add veal with flour remaining on paper. Brown richly but slowly on all sides, about 20 minutes. Add sliced onion last 5 minutes of browning. Now add salt, pepper, celery and thyme, and enough water to almost cover meat. Cover pan and simmer until meat is tender, from 2 to 2½ hours. Serve piping hot over rice, mashed or boiled potatoes. 3 to 4 servings.

POT ROAST OF VEAL

2½ lbs. veal shoulder	⅓ cup chopped celery
3 tsp. bacon drippings	2 tsp. salt
1 medium onion, chopped	

Wipe veal with a damp cloth. Brown slowly on one side in bacon drippings in heavy skillet or Dutch oven. Turn meat over, add onion and celery and stir occasionally until meat is well browned on other side. Sprinkle meat with salt. Add about ½ cup hot water, cover tightly and simmer until meat is tender, about 1½ hours; add more water as needed. Serve with gravy which may be thickened if desired. 5 servings.

VEAL FRICASSEE

2 lbs. veal shoulder-boneless
¼ cup butter or shortening
1½ tsp. salt
Water

4 carrots, diced
3 onions, sliced
2 tsp. finely cut parsley
4 potatoes, sliced

Wipe meat with damp cloth and cut in 1½ inch dice. Brown in butter in heavy skillet. Sprinkle salt on meat and add water to just half cover meat. Cover skillet tightly and simmer slowly until meat is tender, or about 1 to 1½ hours. Prepare vegetables and add them ½ hour before end of cooking time. Just before serving, thicken gravy if desired with flour and water paste, stirring over direct heat until it boils and thickens. 5 servings.

* This is good with beef or chicken used instead of veal.

GOOD OLE-TIME ROAST PORK AND POTATOES

3¾ lb. pork loin, from ham end
2¼ tsp. salt

Pepper
½ cup water
2½ lbs. potatoes, pared, halved

Have ready a small roaster with trivet and cover. Start oven 10 minutes before roasting, set to moderate (350F).

Have butcher saw backbone free from ribs but leave in place for roasting. Wipe meat with a damp cloth. If there is a thick layer of fat on top, slice some of it off, then crisscross the top into ¼ or ½-inch squares so fat will cook out. Rub salt and pepper well into meat, under severed backbone as well as all over outside. Place meat fat-side up on trivet in roaster. Add water, cover and place in oven. Roast 2 hours, then lay potatoes around roast, cover and continue roasting 1 hour longer, or until meat is tender and nicely browned and potatoes are done. Remove from oven. Loosen and remove backbone carefully. Lift roaster and potatoes to platter, cover with roaster lid while making gravy. 6 servings.

ROAST DUCK WITH ORANGE SAUCE

1 young duck, 5 lbs.
1 Tbs. salt to rub duck
Pepper
3 cups soft bread crumbs
5 Tbs. melted butter
1 orange rind, chopped

2 oranges, peel, remove seed
 and white pulp
2 tart apples, peel, cut cubes
1 tsp. salt for dressing
½ cup orange juice

Clean duck carefully; singe, wash inside and out. Dry, stuff with blended ingredients. Sew opening. Place duck on a rack breast up in roasting pan, allow 20 to 25 minutes to a pound and place in a hot oven 450 degrees. Baste every 5 minutes using drippings in the pan or orange juice to keep duck moist. Serve on a hot platter. Garnish with glazed orange slices. Will serve 4 to 5.

ORANGE SAUCE:

4 Tbs. butter
4 Tbs. flour
1 cup stock, from cooking
 neck, tips of wing and giblets

1 cup strained orange juice
Few grains red pepper
Strips of orange rind

Melt the butter, blend in the flour, slowly stir in the hot stock. Stir constantly and cook until mixture thickens, then stir in orange juice. Cook orange rind in boiling water for 5 minutes. Drain. Add rind to sauce and cook 5 minutes.

LIVER IN BAKED ONIONS

½ lb. calves liver
10 slices bacon
1 cup chopped celery
½ tsp. salt

Paprika
6 or 8 med. sized onions
Celery Salt
Onion Seasonings

Scald liver in boiling water about 2 minutes. Remove skin and put through food chopper. Cut bacon in small pieces and fry until crisp. Add liver, celery and seasoning to bacon. Remove outer skin of onions, remove center and leave firm shell. Fill with liver, bacon mixture, sprinkle top with buttered bread crumbs and bake in slow oven using baking pan with little water. Bake about 1 hour.

BONNIE'S SWISS STEAK

3 pounds round steak, 2 inches
  thick
Salt and pepper
2 cups cooked tomatoes

1 cup all-purpose flour
½ cup shortening
2 onions, sliced

Season steak with salt and pepper. Place on well-floured cutting board. Cover steak with flour. Pound with meat hammer or edge of heavy saucer. Continue to turn, flour, and pound meat until all flour is taken up by steak. Melt shortening in skillet. Brown onions in hot fat. Remove onions. Brown steak on both sides. Drain excess fat. Place onions on top of steak. Add tomatoes. Cover and cook slowly over low heat for 2½ to 3 hours, or until fork-tender, or bake in 350° F. oven. Remove steak to hot platter. Serve with gravy made from drippings in skillet. Makes 6 to 8 servings.

Bonnie Sloan
Hendersonville, Tenn.

51

BEEF BURGUNDY

3 lbs. cubed beef
¼ lb. diced slab bacon
1 large garlic clove, chopped
1 carrot, chopped
1½ c. chopped onion

1 Tbs. dried parsley
1 bay leaf
½ tsp. thyme
½ bottle burgundy
1-2 cans beef bouillon

Cook beef in bacon drippings until brown. Transfer to stew pot. Brown diced bacon, garlic, carrot, onion and parsley. Cook until bacon is crisp, transfer this to stew pot, add bay leaf and thyme. Deglaze frying pan with ½ bottle of burgundy, scraping up all the pieces of meat and vegetables left in the bottom of the pan. Bring to a quick boil and pour into stew pot. Add enough beef bouillon to cover meat. Cover pot tightly and bake 1-3 hours. Fresh mushrooms and small baby onions can be added the last 15 minutes of cooking time.

* Very tasty served with rice.

CHRISTMAS ROAST GOOSE WITH POTATO STUFFING

5 lbs. potatoes
¼ cup butter
1½ cups milk
2 tsp. salt
¼ tsp. pepper
½ tsp. poultry seasoning

1 egg, beaten
¼ cup finely chopped parsley, lightly packed
12 lb. goose
1 Tbs. salt

Pare, boil and wash potatoes. Add next seven ingredients and beat until light and fluffy. Prepare goose for roasting as described in recipe above. Rub the tbsp. of salt on inside. Fill goose with stuffing, skewer, lace together. Place breast-side up on rack in an open roasting pan, bake uncovered in moderately slow oven (325F) 4½ to 5 hours or until tender. Do not prick skin to release excess fat during baking. Boil giblets in a small amount of salted water until tender. Chop and add giblets to drippings along with their cooking broth for gravy.

WESTERN STYLE BAR B Q BRISKET

Brisket, 4 pounds or larger
1 Tbs. salt
1 Tbs. garlic salt
1 Tbs. black pepper

2 Tbs. celery seed
1 Tbs. liquid smoke
2 Tbs. Worcestershire sauce

SAUCE:
1 cup your favorite barbeque
  sauce
1 cup catsup

¼ to ½ cup brown sugar

Place meat fat side up in a pan lined with heavy foil. Mix marinade ingredients and put on top of meat. Wrap tightly with foil; refrigerate for 24 hours. Bake brisket at 300 degrees, 1 hour per pound. Mix sauce ingredients together and bring to a boil. Open foil and drain off juice. One hour before serving, put sauce over meat; rewrap with foil and cook for 1 more hour at 300 degrees. Serves 8 to 10.

BEST EVER BRISKET

Beef brisket, about 10 to 11
  pounds
Salt and pepper
1 cup water

3 medium onions, sliced
¼ to ½ cup flour

Place meat fat side up in a large deep pan. Add water to ½-inch depth in pan bottom. Salt and pepper meat freely. Arrange onion slices on top; cover with foil and bake at 300 degrees for 8 to 9 hours. When done, remove brisket to warm platter, skim off fat from pan drippings and add mixture of flour and water. Boil, stirring constantly for 3 to 5 minutes. Remove from heat and serve on top of meat.

OVEN BRAISED BRISKET OF BEEF

2¼ lb. boned brisket
1½ tsp. salt
Dash of pepper
1 onion, egg size, sliced
¼ cup water

4 medium potatoes
½ tsp. salt
1½ tsp. flour mixed with 2 Tbs.
 water

Start oven 10 minutes before baking; set to moderately slow (325F). Wipe meat with damp cloth. Place in casserole or roasting pan with tight fitting cover. Sprinkle with salt and pepper. Top with onion slices. Pour water around meat, cover and bake 2½ hours or until almost tender. No more water is needed. Now pare potatoes, cut in half and place around meat; sprinkle them with salt, cover and continue baking until potatoes and meat are done, about 1 hour longer. Now drain meat juice from casserole into saucepan, add the flour-water paste and cook and stir until gravy thickens. Serve hot. 6 servings.

QUICK BAR-B-QUE

1 lb. ground beef
1 Tbs. green pepper, chopped
1 Tbs. brown sugar
Dash of salt and pepper

3 Tbs. onion, chopped
1 cup tomato sauce
½ tsp. cinnamon
4 hamburger buns

Brown beef in skillet, add onion and green peppers. Stir in sugar, cinnamon, and tomato sauce. Season with salt and pepper. Let mixture bubble for a few minutes, then serve on buns. Serves 4.

  * Great for a quick snack.

TENNESSEE FARM BOILED DINNER

5 lbs. corned beef
1 cabbage, cut in pieces
3 turnips
4 carrots

4 potatoes
Pepper
Onion seasoning
Celery salt

Wash meat carefully, place in pan, cover with cold water. Skim. Come to a boil. Place over low heat, cook 3 hours. About 45 minutes before serving, remove all fat. Take part of liquid, strain, and in separate pan cook vegetables until tender. Add to meat after being placed on hot platter.

BRISKET WITH ONION SAUCE

3 lbs. beef brisket
1½ cups chopped onions
2 tbsps. fat
2 tbsps. flour
1½ cups meat stock

1 tbsps. vinegar
2 tsps. salt
Whole cloves and peppercorn
  (optional)

Cover meat with boiling water. Add vinegar, salt, cloves and peppercorn; cover and simmer slowly three hours, or until meat is very tender. When done, remove to hot platter. Brown onions in fat, add flour and stir until well blended. Then pour over stock in which meat was cooked. Cook slowly, stirring constantly, until smooth and thickened. One tbsp. chopped parsley may be added. Pour hot sauce over meat and serve. Vegetables may be cooked in water with meat for last hour.

SPAGHETTI WITH MEAT BALLS

1 lb. mixed ground beef and
  pork
¼ cup grated sharp cheese
1 tsp. caraway seed
1 Tbs. finely chopped parsley
2 Tbs. chopped green pepper
Dash of pepper
1 egg, well beaten
2 tsp. salt
3 strips of bacon cut in small
  pieces

¼ cup chopped onion
2 Tbs. butter or additional
  bacon fat
1 qt. canned tomatoes or No. 3
  can
1 can tomato paste, about ⅓
  cup
¼ tsp. sugar
1 lb. spaghetti, freshly cooked
Parmesan cheese

Combine first 7 ingredients with 1 tsp. of the salt, and shape into
small balls. Saute bacon in heavy skillet or large Dutch oven until fat
melts out into bottom of pan. Add meat balls and brown slowly on all
sides. Add onion and additional butter if pan is dry and saute onion
until soft, about 5 minutes. Add remaining salt, tomatoes, tomato
paste and sugar. (Tomatoes may be sieved if desired to remove seeds,
but it is not necessary.) Reduce heat as low as possible and simmer
very slowly for 1½ to 2½ hours, stirring occasionally until sauce is
the desired thickness. Pour over hot, rinsed, drained spaghetti and
serve at once with additional cheese to be sprinkled over top if
desired. 4 to 6 servings.

Beth Scott
Goodlettsville, Tenn.

BACON-BROWNED MACARONI

1 cup macaroni	¼ cup bacon drippings
1 cup bacon	Nutmeg
1 cup stock	Salt and pepper to taste

Break macaroni into small pieces, put into slightly salted water, boil rapidly for 5 minutes, then drain well. Have some stock boiling in saucepan, put in macaroni, and stew until tender, but not too soft. Cut bacon into small dice, fry lightly in pan, then add well-drained macaroni, bacon drippings, a good pinch of nutmeg and salt and pepper to taste. Stir gently over fire until macaroni acquires a nice brown color, turn on hot dish and serve.

CREOLE POT ROAST

5 lbs. beef chuck	2 tsps. allspice
¼ cup salad oil	2½ tsps. salt
2 bay leaves	¼ tsp. pepper
1 onion, minced	2 tbsps. flour
Juice 1 lemon	2 tbsps. fat

Mix together oil, lemon juice and seasoning. Rub well into each side of meat. Sprinkle flour over meat. Brown in hot fat. Add boiling water to half cover the meat. Cover closely and cook about 2 hours until done in a moderately slow 325° oven, or cook on top of stove in Dutch oven for 3 hours. Serve with liquid in which meat was cooked, thickening it if preferred.

COUNTRY POT ROAST

Fold in a double thickness of aluminum foil large enough to wrap a 4 pound chuck roast. Sprinkle a package of onion soup in center of foil and another package over roast. Wrap smugly. Cook 4 to 5 hours at 300 degrees. If frozen roast is used, cook 8 to 10 hours at 225-250 degrees.

BEAN STEW WITH HAM

½ lb. dried navy beans
2 tsp. salt
½ cup chopped onion
2 tsp. butter

2 cups cooked tomatoes
Dash of pepper
½ lb. boiled ham sliced thin
3 Tbs. chopped parsley

Wash beans and soak overnight in cold water. Drain, cover with fresh cold water (about 2 cups) add salt and boil gently for 15 minutes or until tender. Cook onion in the butter in a large skillet. Add beans with their cooking water, tomatoes and pepper; cook at moderate rate for 15 minutes. Turn into a heated serving dish. Arrange overlapping slices of delicately browned pan-fried ham around edge and a sprinkling of chopped parsley in the center. 5 servings.

NOODLES WITH HAM

½ lb. noodles
1 slice raw ham
3 Tbs. olive oil
2 onions, chopped
1 carrot, diced

½ cup tomato puree
Salt
Pepper
1½ cups meat stock

Cut ham in thin strips, cook. Cook onions and carrots in hot olive oil but do not brown. Heat stock and tomato sauce thoroughly. Cook noodles in boiling salted water 12 minutes, drain. Place on hot platter, in center leave space for hot sauce. Blend well and serve with grated parmesan cheese and ham.

LYNDA'S HAMBURGER CASSEROLE

1½ pounds ground beef
1 chopped onion
1 can corn drained
1 can cream of mushroom soup
1 can cream of chicken soup
1 carton sour cream
1 package egg noodles, cooked

Mix all of the above together. Pour into large casserole dish and bake in 350 ° oven for 30 minutes. Top with grated cheddar cheese and return to oven for 5-7 minutes.

Lynda Woodard
Goodlettsville, Tenn.

COLD WEATHER MEAL

1 lb. hamburger steak
2 Tbs. butter
2 qts. boiling water
1 can red kidney beans
Paprika

1 can tomatoes
½ cup macaroni
1 tsp. chili powder
Salt to taste

Place hamburger and butter in large cooker, add little water, cook until meat separates. Add remainder of water, salt, tomatoes, and macaroni which has been washed and broken into pieces. Cook until well done or about one hour. Add chili powder and beans. Serve very hot with hot corn bread.

ROCKY TOP VENISON BARBEQUE

4 lbs. venison roast
6 Tbs. white vinegar
3 Tbs. fat
Salt and pepper

2 cloves, garlic, minced
3 Tbs. catsup
1 stalk celery
3 Tbs. Worcestershire sauce

Season roast with salt and pepper. Melt fat in heavy pan; add roast and brown slowly on all sides. Add garlic and celery. Combine vinegar, catsup and Worcestershire sauce in a cup measure. Add water to make one cup liquid. Pour over roast, cover, and cook at 350 degrees until tender.

VENISON POT PIE

2 slices round steak, 2 lb., cut
    ¾-inch thick
3 Tbs. flour
2½ tsp. salt
⅛ tsp. pepper
⅓ cup shortening
3½ cups water
¼ cup thickly sliced carrots

½ cup coarsely cut celery
¾ lb. shelled peas, 2 cups,
    frozen may be used
2 Tbs. chopped onion
¼ tsp. sugar
Rich biscuit dough
Butter, melted

Wipe steaks clean with a damp cloth. Trim off any strong-smelling fat. Cut into 1½-inch pieces and dredge thoroughly with the combined flour, salt, and pepper. Slowly brown meat and any remaining seasoned flour in the hot shortening. Reduce heat, add 1 cup of the water, cover and simmer for 1½ hr. or until meat is nearly tender. Add remaining water gradually as needed, then the vegetables and sugar and continue cooking covered for ½ hr. or until vegetables and meat are tender. Pour boiling stew into two casseroles (4½-cup capacity each). Immediately top with biscuit dough rolled to ½-inch thickness. Flute edge and brush with butter. Cut vents in the center. Bake in a hot oven (450 degrees F) for 12 to 15 minutes or until crust is cooked through and richly browned. Serve immediately. 8 to 10 servings.

PAN BROILED VENISON

1 lbs. venison steak	Salt
2 Tbs. cooking oil	¼ tsp. Tabasco sauce

Season steak and place in heated oil in skillet. Pan broil on one side until nicely browned. Turn and brown on other side. Serve at once with melted butter.

VENISON POT ROAST

3 to 4 lbs. of venison	8 whole small potatoes
6 whole carrots	6 small whole onions
¼ to ½ cup water	2 stalks celery

Flour meat. Add salt and pepper, and brown in fat. Add water and cover tightly. Cook over low heat 2 or 3 hours. Add the vegetables ½ hour before the meat is done. Make a gravy of the liquid in the pan and pour over the venison and vegetables.

SMOTHERED VENISON CHOPS

4 Tbs. cooking oil	¼ tsp. Tabasco sauce
2 lbs. vension chops	3 Tbs. flour
¼ cup onion flakes	½ cup currant jelly
1¼ tsp. salt	
½ cup beer	

Brown chops on both sides in hot oil in a heavy skillet. Add onion, tabasco, salt, pepper and beer. Cover tightly and cook over low heat until chops are tender. Place chops on warm platter and keep warm. Combine flour and jelly and stir into sauce in pan. Cook over low heat, stirring constantly until sauce has thickened slightly. Pour over chops on platter and serve at once.

BEEF AND VEGETABLE PIE

1½ lbs. beef, chuck or round
2 Tbs. bacon drippings
1½ tsp. salt
4 medium potatoes
5 medium carrots

1 medium onion
Salt and pepper to taste
Plain pastry for single crust
(or biscuit dough)

Cut beef in 1-inch dice, brown slowly in bacon drippings and add boiling water to just barely cover meat. Add salt and simmer, covered for 30 to 60 minutes, until almost done (or have meat ground, brown in bacon drippings, add water and salt and cook 15 to 20 minutes). Wash, pare and dice potatoes; scrape and slice carrots, and peel and slice onion; add to meat (with more boiling water to just cover if needed) and simmer until all are tender, about 20 minutes longer. To thicken the gravy stir in flour and water paste, to give the desired thickness. Add salt and pepper to taste. Heat to boiling and pour into an 8-cup buttered casserole. Cover with pastry which has been rolled thin and has a design cut in center for the steam vents, or arrange biscuits over the top. Bake in a moderately hot oven (425F) about 15 minutes, or until golden brown. 5 servings.

CASSEROLE OF BEEF

4 cups cold cooked beef
2 cups meat stock
½ cup celery, cut in pieces
1 cup carrots
1 onion sliced
1 cup tomatoes

⅛ tsp. Pepper
½ tsp. salt
1 can peas
1 cup beans
1 cup cooked macaroni
1 tsp. Worcestershire sauce
Celery Salt

Mix all ingredients except peas, beans. Cover, bake in moderate oven one hour. Add above vegetables, cook.

LASAGNA CASSEROLE

TOMATO SAUCE-First Step

1 lb. ground beef	1 large onion, chopped
1 clove garlic, minced	6 sprigs parsley minced
¼ cup salad oil	1-2½ can tomatoes
1 small can tomato paste	2 bay leaves

Cook onion, garlic and parsley in oil over low heat. Add canned tomatoes coarsely chopped and tomato paste. Then stir in one pound of lean ground beef. Break into small bits. Add ½ cup water, 1 tsp. salt, ¼ tsp. pepper, and 2 bay leaves. Mix well, cover and simmer about 45 minutes stirring as needed.

CHEESE SAUCE-second step

1 small onion, minced	¼ cup butter
3 tsp. flour	¾ cup grated cheese
2 cups milk	2 egg yolks, beaten

Cook minced onion in melted butter over low heat for one minute. Stir in flour, grated parmesan or American cheese, dash of salt, and milk. Cook over low heat stirring until thick and smooth as rich cream. Pour a little of the hot mixture into beaten yolks, stirring briskly. Then pour egg mixture slowly into remaining sauce while beating constantly. Cover over low heat about 10 minutes, watching closely.

LASAGNA NOODLES-third step

Cook lasagna noodles as directed on package and drain. Rub large 9 x 13 inch baking dish with butter. Arrange layer of noodles on bottom, pour enough tomato sauce over noodles to cover and then top with cheese sauce. Continue these layers until all ingredients are used. Top of casserole should be cheese sauce. Bake in moderate oven (325F) about 20 minutes if all ingredients were hot. Then broil until top is bubbly golden.

Dot Casteel
Madison, Tenn.

OLD-FASHIONED HASH

1½ cups lean cooked roast beef
  or pot roast
2¼ cups chopped cold boiled
  potatoes
⅓ to ½ cup chopped onion
1¼ tsp. salt

¾ tsp. monosodium glutamate,
  optional
⅛ tsp. pepper
2½ tsp. butter or margarine
1¼ cups boiling water

Chop or cut meat into ¼ inch cubes. Combine with potatoes and onion. Potatoes cooked in jackets, cooled and peeled are best. Sprinkle with seasonings, and toss lightly with fork until well mixed. Melt butter in skillet, preferable a heavy iron one, pour in boiling water and heat to boiling; add meat mixture, spread evenly; cover and cook over medium heat until browned on under side. This requires about 15 minutes. Turn carefully with spatula or pancake turner, and, if necessary add a little more butter, cover and brown but do not cook hash too dry. Entire cooking time requires 20 to 25 minutes. Serve with broiled tomatoes or chili sauce. 3 servings.

BEEF LOAF — SOUTHERN STYLE

4 pounds beef, ground
¼ pound pork, ground
3 eggs, well beaten
4 Tbs. cream
8 crackers rolled fine
¾ cup milk

Salt
Butter size of egg, melt over hot
  water
Pepper
Onion Seasoning
Celery
Poultry seasoning to suit taste

Blend all ingredients. Roll in beaten egg and cracker crumbs, baste with hot water into which little butter has been dissolved. Will make 2 loaves. Serve with hot tomato sauce. Bake in 375 degree oven about 1 hour for one half of receipe, to serve 6 to 8.

BEEF STEW

1½ lbs. boneless beef for stew
3 Tbs. bacon fat or shortening
1¾ tsp. salt
Few dashes of pepper
Onion size of large egg, peeled
⅓ cup water, and more as
　needed

4 or 5 six-inch long carrots
4 or 5 medium size potatoes
Gravy:
⅓ cup water
3 Tbs. flour

Wipe meat with damp cloth; cut into 1½-inch cubes. Heat fat until sizzling in a heavy 3-quart saucepan or Dutch oven; add meat, turning it often until a fine rich brown. Add thickly sliced onion to meat last five minutes of browning. When brown, sprinkle with 1 tsp. of the salt and pepper. Add water, cover, heat to boiling, then reduce heat and simmer until meat is almost done, from 1½ to 2 hours. After simmering 1 hour if more water is needed, stir it in ¼ cup at a time. Half hour before serving time, add scraped washed carrots cut in 2-inch lengths and the pared halved potatoes. Sprinkle with remaining ¾ tsp. salt. Cover and cook until vegetables are just done. There should be enough liquid in kettle to almost cover meat and vegetables.

To make gravy: Measure water into a slender glass; sprinkle flour over it, then place hand over top of glass to cover tightly and shake hard until mixture is smooth. Now push meat and vegetables gently to one side; pour flour mixture, while stirring, in a thin stream into broth. Cook and stir 2 or 3 minutes longer until thickened and smooth. To serve, lift meat into center of hot platter; arrange vegetables around it, then pour gravy over all, or serve separately.

BEEF STEW AND LIMA BEANS

¾ lb. dried lima beans
1 lb. boneless chuck stewing
　　meat cut in pieces

1 bunch carrots,
Salt
Pepper
Celery Salt

Soak beans overnight, drain. Add meat and cook 1½ hours in boiling water. Add carrots and cook until tender. Season with salt, pepper, celery. Serve with tomato sauce.

OLD SOUTH GUMBO

1 fat hen
1 small ham hock
1 large onion
1 large can tomatoes
Salt
Pepper
Celery
2 Tbs. butter

1 pint chopped oysters
1 cup okra
2 Tbs. chopped parsley
2 Tbs. flour thickening
Onion seasoning
Paprika

Slowly boil hen and ham hock together in 3 quarts of water. When done take out chicken, let cool, cut up breast in diced pieces. Remove ham hock from stock. Fry large slice of ham cut in very small pieces. Skim off all fat from stock. Fry onion light brown, pour tomatoes in skillet with onion, cook 15 minutes. Add to stock. Season with salt, pepper. Put tomatoes, diced chicken, finely cut ham in stock, let cook slowly. Add pint chopped oysters, (or same amount of shrimp finely cut), okra, and flour thickening.
　*Excellent served with steamed rice.

HAMBURGER AND CORN PIE

2½ Tbs. bacon fat
¾ lb. fresh ground beef chuck
2 Tbs. chopped onion
¾ tsp. salt
⅛ tsp. pepper
¼ tsp. paprika

2½ Tbs. flour
¾ cup water
4 Tbs. butter
2 cups corn cut from cob
1 Tbs. salt
⅛ tsp. pepper
1 green pepper, medium

Start oven 10 minutes before baking; set to moderately hot (425F). Heat bacon fat in skillet; add ground beef and onion. Stir and cook until meat is separated and gray in color. Add salt, pepper, paprika; then the flour blended with the water smoothly. Cook 2 or 3 minutes and stir constantly until thickened. Heat butter in a saucepan, add corn, salt and pepper; stir constantly and cook 2 or 3 minutes. Pour a little more than half the corn into a well buttered 9 or 10-inch glass pie pan. Place in oven and cook 15 minutes. Remove quickly from oven and add hot hamburger mixture and rest of corn. Lay quarter rings of green pepper around edge. Return to oven; bake another 15 to 20 minutes, or until bottom and top are an appetizing brown. 4 to 5 servings.

* Family reunion favorite. Always brings compliments when served at large gatherings.

Lynda Woodard
Goodlettsville, Tenn.

KISSIN DONT LAST COOKIN DO

DOWN HOME CHILI

3 pounds ground chuck
1 or 2 chopped onions
2 or 3 cloves of chopped garlic
1 tsp. salt
1 tsp. pepper
1 12-oz. can tomato juice

3 Tbs. chili powder or more to
 taste
1½ tsp. cumin
1 15-oz. can kidney beans
3 Tbs. shortening

Melt shortening in Dutch oven or other deep pan; add meat and cook until it browns and separates. Add a little hot water to cover it. In a skillet cook onions and garlic; add to meat. Add salt and pepper. Heat tomato juice and add to meat. Cook this until meat begins to get tender (about 2 hours). Then add chili powder and cumin. Heat kidney beans, then mash well before adding to chili. (This thickens and flavors chili.)

   *If you like whole beans in chili you may add another can of whole beans. Cook 30 minutes longer before serving.

CHILI CON CARNE

2 lbs. round steak
2 cups cooked spagetti or
1 cup cooked rice
¼ cup bacon fat
1 tsp. chili powder

1 tsp. salt
½ can tomatoes
½ can corn
1 onion, chopped
Salt and pepper to taste
3 cups kidney beans

Trim meat, cut in pieces, roll in flour. Heat fat in frying pan, add onions and meat, cook until brown. Add tomatoes, corn mixture, cook until meat is tender. Serve in center of ring mold of hot rice or hot spaghetti.

PASTA IN POT

½ lb. mozzarella cheese, sliced
thin
½ lbs. provolone cheese, sliced
3 cups sour cream
8 oz. uncooked shell macaroni
2 lbs. ground beef-lean

1 can sliced mushrooms
1 lb. can stewed tomatoes
1 clove garlic, minced
2 medium onions, chopped
Vegetable oil

Preheat oven to 350 degrees. Cook ground beef in small amount of vegetable oil in a large deep skillet until brown, stirring often. Drain off fat. Add onions, garlic, spaghetti sauce, tomatoes and undrained mushrooms, mix well. Simmer 20 minutes. Meanwhile, cook macaroni according to package directions, drain and rinse with cold water. Pour half of macaroni into a deep casserole dish, top with half of ground beef and sauce mixture. Spread with half of sour cream. Top with slices of provolone cheese. Repeat with macaroni, remaining ground beef and sauce mixture, remaining sour cream and top with mozzarella cheese. Cover casserole. Bake for 35 to 40 minutes. Remove cover and continue baking until mozzarella melts and browns slightly. Serves 8.

CRAB STUFFED POTATOES

6 baking potatoes, baked
1 6 oz. package frozen crab
   meat, thawed and drained

Milk
1 stick butter
1 cup grated cheddar cheese
Salt and pepper to taste

Cut baked potatoes in half while piping hot. Scoop out as much potato as possible, leaving a shell. Mash potatoes with milk and butter to consistency of mashed potatoes. Add salt and pepper to taste. Mix in crab meat well and fill each potato shell with potato-crab meat mixture. Sprinkle with grated cheese and put under broiler until cheese melts, 2 to 3 minutes. Serve immediately. Serves 12.

SPAGHETTI & HAM BAKE

1 qt. water, salted
Sauce

SAUCE:
¼ cup olive oil
Small onion, chopped
can of tomato paste
Little Salt
Pepper

½ lb. spaghetti

Paprika
Worcestershire sauce
1 can tomato catsup

Break spaghetti into pieces, drop into boiling salted water, cook 12 minutes, place in sieve, let cold water run through the cooked spaghetti. Return to pan to keep hot. Make a sauce of olive oil, small chopped onion, canned tomato paste and heat thoroughly in the oil. Add little salt, pepper, paprika, worcestershire sauce. Then add tomato catsup, finely ground cooked ham. Heat mixture and pour over spaghetti. Sprinkle mixture with grated parmesan cheese and a little paprika before serving.

SOUTHERN FRIED SQUIRREL

1 young squirrel, cut in serving
  pieces
⅛ tsp. pepper

1 tsp. salt
¼ cup flour

In a brown paper bag place flour, salt, and pepper. Drop two pieces of the squirrel into the bag at a time and shake to coat meat. After all pieces of the squirrel have been coated, place in hot cooking oil which is about ½ inch deep in heavy skillet. Brown meat on all sides and then reduce heat under skillet and cook meat for 20 to 30 minutes.

The way to a man's heart... is through his stomach.

SHERIFFS FRICASSEE RABBIT

2 young rabbits, cut into serving
  pieces
1 pint cold water
1 bunch sweet herbs
1 medium onion, minced

Pinch of mace
Half of a nutmeg
Dash of pepper
Half of pound salt pork (cut into
  thin slices)

Soak rabbit pieces in salt water for 30 minutes. Put into a stew pan with the cold water, sweet herbs, onion, mace, nutmeg, pepper, and salt pork. Cover and stew until tender. Remove rabbit pieces and place in a dish to keep warm.

OLD TIMERS RABBIT STEW

1 rabbit cut into serving pieces	2 qts. water
5 small white onions	2 cups diced potatoes
1 cup chopped celery	1½ cups carrots, sliced
2 bay leaves	½ lb. fresh mushrooms
5 tsp. salt	1 tsp. parsley flakes
½ tsp. pepper	½ cup flour
	½ cup water

Place first seven ingredients in a large stew pan with lid. Cover and simmer for 2 hours. Add potatoes, carrots, mushrooms, and parsley flakes, and simmer covered for another 45 minutes or until all is tender. Blend flour and cold water and add to stew. Cook until thickened. Serve.

RABBIT IN BARBECUE SAUCE

1 rabbit (2 or 3 lbs.)	¼ cup lemon juice
3 Tbs. chopped onion	3 Tbs. worcestershire sauce
1 Tbs. salad oil	2 Tbs. brown sugar
1 cup salad oil	½ tsp. salt
1 cup tomato catsup	
Dash of black pepper	
2 Tbs. brown vinegar	

Grease a large pan that has a lid. Place rabbit in greased pan. Sprinkle rabbit well with salt. In a skillet, heat the salad oil and lightly cook onion until glassy looking; add remaining ingredients and simmer for five minutes. Pour sauce over rabbit and cover pan. Bake 425 degrees for 35 to 40 minutes. Serves 6.

CABBAGE AND BEEF ROLLS

1 lb. ground beef
1½ cups corn flake crumbs
⅓ cup chopped onion
1 tsp. Worcestershire sauce
1 tsp. salt

¼ tsp. pepper
1 tsp. paprika
1 can tomato sauce
8 cabbage leaves
¼ cup water

Combine ground beef, corn flake crumbs, onion, worcestershire sauce, salt, pepper, paprika and ½ cup tomato sauce; mix well. Put cabbage leaves in boiling water for 4 minutes, drain. Place equal portion of meat mixture in center of each cabbage leaf; fold ends over, roll up and fasten with toothpick. Combine remaining ½ cup tomato sauce and ¼ cup water, pour over cabbage rolls and simmer, covered 30 minutes. Serves 4.

IRON SKILLET VENISON & BEAN

¼ stick oleo
1 lb. lean venison
2 cups chopped onions
1 tsp. salt
⅛ tsp. black pepper
1 cup tomato catsup

Vinegar or mustard to taste
2 Tbs. brown sugar or dark
   syrup
Dash of celery salt
3—1 lb. cans of pork n beans

Melt oleo in heavy skillet and lightly cook onions and meat until meat is done. Add beans and seasonings. Simmer until well blended or place in casserole in oven for 20 minutes at 350 degrees.

VENISON CHILI

2 lbs. lean ground venison	1 8 oz. can tomato sauce
2 lbs. dry pinto beans	1 16 oz. can tomatoes
1 large onion, chopped	4 Tbs. chili powder
Salt to taste	

Pick over beans and remove any trash and rocks; leave halved beans. Wash beans and place in large utensil and soak overnight. The next morning heat beans in same water and bring to boiling, adding more water if needed. Reduce heat and simmer in covered utensil until beans are almost tender. Brown meat in a skillet and pour off drippings. When beans are almost tender add browned meat and other ingredients to pot of beans. Continue to cook for one hour over low heat until beans are very tender. Serves 14 to 16.

ALL DAY VENISON STEW

2 lbs. venison stew	1 tsp. coarsely ground pepper
2 large potatoes, diced	1 can tomato sauce
4 carrots, diced	3 Tbs. chunky peanut butter
1 cup red table wine	2 Tbs. soy sauce
2 medium onions, chopped	Beef broth to cover
2 bay leaves	1 clove garlic minced
1½ tsp. salt	1 tsp. thyme

Combine all ingredients in a slow cooker. Cook on low for 8 hours and 15 minutes. Serve with hot cornbread.

SMOKY MOUNTAIN RAINBOW TROUT

6 pan-dressed rainbow trout	½ cup flour
¼ cup milk	¼ cup yellow cornmeal
1½ tsp. salt	1 tsp. paprika
Dash of pepper	12 slices breakfast bacon

Combine milk, salt, and pepper. Mix together flour, cornmeal, and paprika. Dip fish in milk mixture and roll in dry ingredients. Fry bacon in a heavy skillet until crisp. Remove bacon and use grease for cooking fish. Fry fish on each side for 5 minutes. Serve at once with crispy bacon.

BUTTER BAKED FISH

½ tsp. salt	½ cup sweet cream butter
¼ tsp. garlic powder	⅔ cup crushed saltine crackers
1 lbs. frozen fillets, Your choice	¼ cup grated cheese
½ tsp. oregano leaves	½ tsp. basil leaves

Preheat oven to 350 degrees. In 9 x 13 inch baking pan, melt butter in oven 5 to 7 minutes. In pan combine cracker crumbs, cheese, basil, oregano, salt and garlic powder. Dip fish fillets in butter and then in crumb mixture. Arrange fish fillets in buttered baking dish. Bake 25 to 30 minutes in center of oven until fish is tender and flakey. Serve immediately. Serves 4.

TENNESSEE FRIED CATFISH

6 small catfish
1 tsp. salt
2 cups self rising cornmeal

¼ tsp. white pepper
Corn oil

If catfish are frozen, thaw them in a bowl of milk. When thawed pat dry and season with salt and pepper to taste. Pour cornmeal into a paper bag and drop in catfish one piece at a time. Shake bag to coat fish. Fry in deep hot fat until golden brown. Drain well and serve hot.

*Serve with tartar sauce and hush puppies.

OPEN HEARTH PERCH

3 lbs. perch
⅓ cup chopped onions
2 tsp. salt

Dash pepper
Dash paprika
3 strips bacon, cut in half

Clean, wash, and dry fish. Cut 12 inch squares of heavy duty aluminum foil. Grease foil, crumble in hand, and spread flat. This will help prevent sticking and will allow for better distribution of steam. Place fish on squares of foil and sprinkle with onion, salt and paprika. Place a slice of bacon on each fish. Fold foil over fish, seal edges by making double folds. Cook on grill for 15 minutes, turning twice. Cut crisscross in foil and fold back. Serve in cooking container or in heated baking dish.

SEAFOOD CASSEROLE

1 cup small cooked shrimp
1 cup crabmeat
1 cup bread crumbs softened
   with 1 cup light cream
1 to 1½ cups mayonnaise
½ tsp. salt

½ tsp. pepper
6 hard boiled eggs
1 Tbs. chopped parsley
¼ tsp. red pepper
1 tsp. grated onion
Extra bread crumbs for topping

Pre heat oven to 350 degrees. Cook shrimp. Drain well. Mix together all ingredients and pour into a 2 quart casserole. Top with bread crumbs and paprika, dot with butter. Bake for 20 minutes.

CRAB-SHRIMP BAKE

1 med. green pepper, chopped
1 medium onion, chopped
1 cup celery, finely chopped
1 can crabmeat, flaked
1 cup cooked cleaned shrimp
½ tsp. salt

Dash Pepper
1 tsp. Worcestershire Sauce
½ cup mayonnaise
½ cup salad dressing
1 cup buttered bread crumbs

Preheat oven to 350 degrees. Drain all ingredients well. Then combine ingredients, except crumbs. Place in individual seashells, in pastry shells or in a 2 quart casserole. Sprinkle with buttered crumbs. Bake about 25 minutes.

TUNA NOODLE CASSEROLE

1 small can tuna, drained
1 can cream of mushroom soup
1 package medium size
   noodles, cooked
1 cup grated cheese

5 Tbs. flour
4 Tbs. margarine
2 cups milk
Salt and pepper to taste

Preheat oven to 350 degrees. Combine flour, margarine, milk, salt and pepper as for white sauce. Add remaining ingredients, except cheese. Place in casserole and top with grated cheese. Bake until cheese melts.

STRIP STEAK

Salt and pepper to taste
1 cup water
1 Tbs. mustard
1 Tbs. brown sugar
2 Tbs. Worcestershire sauce

1 can beef consumme
1 med. onion
2 Tbs. flour
1 can mushrooms, sliced
4 Tbs. butter, melted
1½ lbs. round steak, cut in
   strips

Lightly brown onion and mushrooms in butter for 5 minutes, add steak. Blend flour into mixture, remove from heat. Add consomme, water, mustard, brown sugar, worcestershire sauce, salt and pepper. Cover, simmer on low heat. Heat 30 to 60 minutes or until steak is tender.

   *Serve with rice or noodles—Thicken sauce with flour if desired.

MEXICAN LUNCHEON DISH

1 lb. lean lamb, cut
2 Tbs. shortening
2 medium sized onions
¾ tsp. salt
Hot cooked rice

¼ cup water
1½ cups canned tomatoes
¾ tsp. chili powder
Pepper
Celery Salt

Brown meat in hot shortening with onions. Add tomatoes, seasoning and water. Cover. Cook slowly until meat is tender. Serve hot with hot cooked rice.

MEAT BALLS

1½ lbs. beef, ground
½ lbs. pork, ground
Salt
Pepper

Onion Seasoning
Pinch nutmeg
Pinch ginger

Mix well, form into balls, fry in hot shortening until brown. Put in roaster. Add 1 tablespoon flour to drippings, make gravy, pour over meat. Or use 1 cup cream with flour, and bake 1 hour.

CHOW MEIN MEAT LOAF

1½ lbs. beef
½ lbs. pork
1 can corn
1 can tomato soup
1 egg beaten

1 cup cheese
2 packages noodles
Salt
Pepper
Celery Salt

Add noodles to salted boiling water. Cook 10 minutes. Drain hot water off noodles and rinse with cold water. Drain. Blend all ingredients. Bake in buttered pan in moderate 350 oven for 1 hour.

HUNTERS PRIDE VENISON ROAST

1 venison roast
¼ cup cider vinegar
¼ cup catsup
5 Tbs. flour
1 tsp. dry mustard
2 tsp. salt
Dash Worcestershire
¼ tsp. chili powder

¼ tsp. pepper
2 Tbs. brown sugar
4 strips bacon
1 stick butter
2 cups hot water

Wipe roast with a cloth and trim all fat. Make a mixture of vinegar, catsup, flour, worcestershire sauce, salt, pepper, mustard, chili powder, and brown sugar. Blend until smooth. Rub the meat with this mixture as thoroughly as possible. Then pour the rest over the roast, which has been placed in heavy roaster. Place bacon strips on top of meat and secure with toothpicks. Place small chunks of butter on top of roast and pour water around roast. Place uncovered in a 450 degree oven. Cook until meat is brown. Baste often with drippings. When meat is brown, sprinkle the roast with flour and then wet flour with drippings. As meat becomes well browned, reduce heat to 325 degrees, cover the pan, and continue to cook until meat is very tender. This may take 3 to 4 hours. Baste meat as it cooks and if necessary add more hot water. Serve on warm platter.

CORNED BEEF AND CABBAGE

1 cup rice, cooked
2 cups ground meat
½ tsp. pepper

1 Tbs. salt
Hot water
1 medium sized cabbage

Wash rice thoroughly and cook. Blend with meat, salt and pepper. Form in balls and roll in a leaf of cabbage. Place in a buttered casserole, cover with hot water, cover and bake in a moderate oven about 45 min.

SHRIMP AND CRAB GUMBO

1½ cups okra
1 lb. shrimp
1 can crab meat
1 bay leaf
1 Tbs. parsley
Salt and pepper to taste

3 Tbs. flour
½ cup celery
1 clove garlic
½ cup cooking oil
2 med. onions
2 cups tomatoes

Brown flour in cooking oil. Add celery, onions and garlic and cook about 5 minutes. Add remaining ingredients and 3 pints of hot water. Let simmer for 1½ to 2 hours. Serve over rice.

SHRIMP CREOLE

1 cup onion
½ cup celery
1 clove garlic
3 Tbs. vegetable oil
1 Tbs. flour
1 tsp. salt
1 tsp. sugar

1 Tbs. chili
1 cup water
2 cups canned tomatoes
2 cups frozen peas
1 Tbs. vinegar
2 cups cooked shrimp
3½ cups cooked rice

Cook onions, celery and garlic in oil until golden brown. Add flour, salt, sugar and chili powder, which have been mixed in ½ cup water. Add remaining ½ cup water and simmer, uncovered, for 15 minutes. Add tomatoes, shrimp and vinegar. Add cooked peas last to insure keeping color. Serve over rice.

TUNA PERFECT

1 (10½ oz.) can condensed
 cream of celery, chicken or
 mushroom soup
½ cup milk
1 can tuna, drained & flaked

2 hard boiled eggs, sliced
1 cup cooked peas
1 cup crushed potato chips

Preheat oven to 350 degree. In 1 quart casserole, blend soup and milk. Stir in tuna, eggs, and peas. Top with potato chips. Bake for 30 minutes.

BEEF POT ROAST

5 lbs. beef
¼ head cabbage (small)
2 rutabagas
4 carrots
2 Tbs. shortening

6 potatoes
⅛ tsp. salt
⅛ tsp. pepper
3 small white onions

Five pounds beef. Wipe dry, put into hot pan. Brown meat in little hot shortening. Add hot water, salt, pepper. Cook at least 3 to 3½ hours. Cook cabbage 1 hour, rutabagas 1 hour, carrots 45 minutes, potatoes 30 minutes. Cook vegetables separately, add just before serving. Thicken meat gravy with little flour and water. Let come to boil, strain.

*Serve hot with tomato or horse-radish sauce.

VEAL POT ROAST WITH VEGETABLES

3 to 7 lbs. veal or round steak
Salt
Pepper
Celery Salt
Potatoes

Sifted Flour
Onion Seasoning
Little beef fat
½ cup hot water
Onions
Carrots

Sprinkle meat with salt, pepper, dredge with flour. Tie meat in round loaf, brown in heavy iron pot using beef fat, use low rack under meat to keep from burning. Add water, cover, cook over slow heat until tender, about 3 hours. About 1 hour before meat is done, add vegetables which have been washed, peeled and quartered.

For Gravy: Skim off fat from pot. Add 3 tablespoons flour, mix with rest of drippings, stir over heat until smooth, add seasoning. Serve hot.

RISSOLES FROM LEFTOVER MEAT

1 Tbs. cooked meat
Thin pie crust
Pepper
Celery Salt
Cream sauce

Onion Seasoning
Paprika
Beaten egg
Bread Crumbs

Use cooked chicken, fish, ham, or canned fruit and rice. Roll pie crust very thin, cut in rounds. Add well-seasoned meat with cream sauce or fruit. Moisten edge and fold over dough. Dip into beaten egg, then crumbs. Fry in deep fat. Drain well, serve hot.

CORNED BEEF HASH WITH EGGS

2 cups diced cooked potatoes
1½ cups chopped corned beef
⅓ cup cream
3 Tbs. melted butter

½ tsp. salt
Pepper
6 eggs
Paprika
1 small onion chopped fine

Blend potatoes, beef and onion. Add cream; half of butter; salt and pepper. Blend mixture and place in buttered baking dish. Make 6 inserts in top. Bake 20 minutes in 400 degree oven. Reduce heat to 350 degree add the eggs and cover with teaspoon of cream and dot with butter. Bake until egg is cooked. Add dash paprika.

GREEN BEAN AND GROUND BEEF CASSEROLE

1 lb. lean ground beef
1 lb. can french style green beans
1-12 oz. can tomato sauce
4 oz. noodles cooked and drained
¼ cup chopped onion
2 ribs of celery, chopped

½ cup bell pepper chopped
Salt & pepper to taste
½ Tbs. oleo or oil
½ cup shredded cheese
½ tsp. oregano- optional

Melt oleo in frying pan, electric skillet is best, add meat, onions, celery and peppers and fry while stirring until transparent. Drain off grease. Add drained green beans, tomatoe sauce and let simmer while noodles cook. Drain noodles add to meat mixture and pour into a 9x13 inch baking dish, top with cheese. If cold bake 45 minutes at 350 degrees.

Grace Young
Murfreesboro, Tenn.

BEEF MACARONI CASSEROLE

1 pound ground beef
⅓ cup milk
2 eggs
½ cup ketchup
¼ cup chopped onion
1½ tsps salt
1 (8-ounce) package elbow
  macaroni, cooked

2 tsps. prepared mustard
¼ cup chopped green pepper
½ cup mayonnaise
1 cup grated American cheese
½ cup dry breadcrumbs
2 tbsps. melted butter or
  margarine
6 slices tomato

Mix beef, milk, eggs, ketchup, onion, and salt; set aside. Mix cooked macaroni, mustard, green pepper, and mayonnaise. Spread this mixture in a greased 2 quart baking dish. Spread beef mixture over top. Sprinkle with cheese and top with breadcrumbs and butter. Bake at 325°F. for 20 minutes. Place tomato slices on top and bake 10 minutes longer.

Clara Scott
Goodlettsville, Tenn.

CHESTNUT STUFFING

3½ cups chestnuts, blanch
¼ cup butter
1 tsp. salt
Dash Pepper
Celery Salt

2 cups seedless raisins
½ cup sweet cream
1 cup bread crumbs (dry)
Onion Seasoning

Cook raisins in little water, drain. Cook chestnuts in boiling water until soft. Drain and mash through potato masher. Add remaining ingredients and mix lightly.

CORN BREAD DRESSING

½ cup butter or margarine
5 or 6 cups corn bread, crumbled
1½ qt. (6 cups) soft bread crumbs
½ cup rendered turkey fat
1 cup chopped nutmeats, optional
1 cup diced celery

½ cup chopped onion
½ cup chopped green peppers
2 tsp. salt
½ tsp. pepper
1½ tsp. poultry seasoning
2 beaten eggs
1 to 1½ cups broth from giblets

Cut butter into very small pieces and mix with corn bread and bread crumbs. Heat fat in a heavy skillet, add nutmeats, celery, onion, and green pepper and saute slowly for 5 minutes. Add to corn bread mixture. Add seasonings, mixing thoroughly. Add well-beaten eggs; sprinkle cooled broth over surface stirring lightly until dressing is of desired moistness. Stuff lightly into breast region and body cavity of the bird. Makes enough for 12-lb. turkey.

APPLE STUFFING FOR ROAST GOOSE

4 large cooking apples, peeled
   and cored
1 tsp. salt
1½ cups cold rice

1½ cups dry bread crumbs
⅛ tsp. Pepper
2 Tbs. melted butter

Cook the apples, with just enough water to keep from burning, until tender. Drain. Blend all ingredients and mix thoroughly.

BREAD DRESSING OR STUFFING

2½ cups grated soft bread
   crumbs
1 Tbs. white onion, chopped
¼ cup chopped celery

4 Tbs. butter
½ tsp. salt
½ tsp. poultry seasoning

Cook onion and celery in the butter to a light brown. Cool. Add bread crumbs and seasoning. Mix well. Will make 2 cups. Use for meat or poultry.

BREAD & SAUSAGE DRESSING

8 cups stale bread
1 skillet corn bread
¾ cup turkey or chicken fat
1½ cups chopped onion
1 cup celery

1 lb. sausage
⅓ cup mushroom
¼ tsp. salt and pepper
1 cup stock or more to moisten
1 egg

Cook onion & celery til tender, add sausage, cook. Combine rest of ingredients, put into casserole and bake 350 degrees for 30 minutes. Serves 12.

Ann Horan
Nashville, Tenn.

SAUSAGE 'N CHEESE GRITS

1 package (1 lb.) bulk hot
   sausage
1 cup instant grits
1 tsp. salt
4 cups boiling water

1 stick margarine
1 roll garlic cheese
2 eggs slightly beaten
½ cup milk, approximately

Cook hot sausage in skillet until brown; drain and set aside. Add salt to boiling water and stir in grits. Cook according to package directions. Add 1 stick margarine and the roll of garlic cheese to hot grits. Put beaten eggs into measuring cup and fill with enough milk to make one cup. Add to grit mixture. Crumble sausage into grit mixture and place in buttered 2-quart casserole. Bake at 350 degrees for one hour. Serves 6 to 8.

BREAD STUFFING FOR ROAST TURKEY

1 large loaf stale white bread,
  1½ lbs.
1 cup diced celery
1 Tbs. chopped onion
¼ cup butter or rendered turkey
  fat

2 tsp. poultry seasoning
1½ tsp. salt
⅛ tsp. pepper
¾ cup cooled broth from
  cooking giblets, or milk

Remove crusts from bread and cut in 1-inch dice. Cook celery and onion in butter until soft and yellow. Add bread and seasonings and toss together until well mixed. Cool. Add broth last and again toss until mixed. Stuff lightly into turkey. Makes enough for a 10-lb. bird.

NOTE: Broth may be increased to 1¼ cups and 2 beaten eggs added, if desired. Beat eggs well and add with the cooled broth.

CHESTNUT STUFFING

1 cup shelled chestnuts,
  chopped
10 slices stale bread from 1 lb.
  loaf
½ cup chopped onion
1 cup sliced celery

3 Tbs. margarine or chicken fat
1 tsp. salt
¼ tsp. pepper
1 to 2 tsp. poultry seasoning
¾ cup chicken broth

Prepare chestnuts. Pull bread apart into bite-size pieces, dropping into a 3-quart bowl. Saute onion and celery until transparent. Sift salt, pepper and seasoning over crumbs, toss to mix. Add broth, toss, then add vegetables and chestnuts, mix lightly again. Stuff lightly into chicken or turkey. Sufficient dressing for 4 lb. roasting chicken. Double ingredients for 12 lb. turkey.

VEGETABLES

SOUTHERN STYLE KALE WITH BACON

1 lb. kale
5 cups boiling water
1 tsp. salt
2 to 3 slices bacon

1 onion, size egg, chopped
2 tsp. flour, optional
1 Tbs. vinegar, optional

Wash kale in cold water, at least 4 or 5 times. Break off tough stem ends. Chop coarsely or cut with scissors. Place kale in 3-quart sauce pan, pour in boiling water, add salt, cover, cook 1 hour or until tender. Stir occasionally as greens may mat and stick to bottom. Fry bacon until half cooked, add chopped onion and cook until onion is yellow and soft and bacon is crisp. Cut bacon in ½ inch pieces and add all ingredients in skillet to kale. Cover, cook 5 to 10 minutes longer to blend flavors. If desired, flour may be stirred to a smooth paste with 2 tbsp. water and stirred into kale to thicken liquid slightly. Or instead of water 1 tbsp. vinegr may be added. 4 servings.

NOODLE CASSEROLE

8 ounces ¼ inch noodles,
  cooked
2 cups cottage cheese
1¼ cups sour cream
¼ cup margarine, melted
¼ cup finely chopped onions
1 clove garlic, finely minced
1 can chopped green chilies,
  drained

1 tsp. Worcestershire sauce
Dash of Tabasco
3 Tbs. fresh parsley, chopped
Salt and pepper to taste
Paprika to garnish

Combine cottage cheese, sour cream, margarine, onions, garlic, green chilies, and all seasonings except paprika. Add noodles and turn into buttered 2 quart casserole. Sprinkle with paprika. Cover and bake at 350 degrees for 45 minutes. Serves 8 to 10. This side dish is also delicious served under beef tips or beef stroganoff.

COUNTRY FRIED SQUASH

2 cups yellow squash, finely
  chopped
1 cup onion, finely chopped
1 egg beaten
1 teaspoon salt

1 tsp. pepper
¼ cup plus 1 Tbs. all-purpose
  flour
Vegetable oil

Combine squash, onion, egg, salt and pepper. Stir in flour. Pour enough vegetable oil into a large skillet for the oil to be 1½ inches deep. Heat the oil to a temperature of 320 degrees. Drop the squash mixture by tablespoonfuls into the oil. Cook until browned, turning once. Drain and serve hot. Yields 6 servings.

GREEN AND GOLD SQUASH PIE

1 unbaked 10 inch pastry shell
2 medium zucchini, thinly
  sliced
2 medium yellow squash, thinly
  sliced
½ medium onion, sliced
1 medium tomato, peeled and
  chopped
1 medium green pepper, finely
  chopped

1 large clove garlic, minced
¾ tsp. salt
¼ tsp. pepper
½ tsp. basil
2 Tbs. butter, melted
3 eggs beaten
½ cup whipping cream
¼ cup parmesan cheese

Prick bottom and sides of pastry shell. Bake at 450 degrees for 8 minutes until lightly browned. Set aside to cool. Combine vegetables, garlic, salt, pepper, basil and butter in large skillet. Cook until vegetables are tender. Spoon into pastry shell, spreading evenly. Combine eggs and cream, mixing well. Pour over vegetables. Sprinkle with cheese and bake at 350 degrees for 30 minutes, or until set. Serves 6 to 8.

Beth Scott
Goodlettsville, Tenn.

SQUASH PIE

2 cups squash	½ tsp. cinnamon
3 eggs	½ tsp. ginger
1 cup sugar	Pinch salt
2 cups milk (scalded)	

Add cinnamon and ginger to squash, blend in sugar and well-beaten eggs. Strain mixture and pour into deep pie shell. Bake 10 minutes in 450 degree oven, reduce heat to 350 degrees, bake about 25 minutes.

*Try it . . . you'll be surprised!

DIRTY RICE

2 medium onions, finely chopped	½ cup bacon drippings or oil
1 green pepper, finely chopped	½ cup flour
2 ribs of celery, finely chopped	2 cups water
3 cloves garlic, crushed	Salt and pepper to taste
½ pound chicken giblets finely chopped	Tabasco to taste
1 pound bulk sausage, crumbled	6 green onions tops, chopped
	6 sprigs parsley, chopped
	8 to 10 cups hot cooked rice

Prepare vegetables as directed in food processor or food chopper. Add crushed garlic. Chop chicken giblets in same manner; set aside. Brown sausage in large pot. Remove and set aside. To sausage drippings, add enough bacon drippings or oil to make ½ cup. Add flour and brown, stirring constantly, over medium heat until the roux is very dark brown, about the color of an old penny. Be very careful not to scorch this roux. Immediately add chopped vegetables and stir and cook a few minutes; then add chopped chicken giblets and cook until the pink color is gone. Add water, the sausage and seasonings and simmer two hours or more. Thirty minutes before serving, add onion tops and parsley. Before serving add hot cooked rice and mix well. Serves 16 to 20 people.

*A favorite southern accompaniment to barbecue. Also good with roast beef or turkey.

STUFFED GREEN PEPPERS

4 large green peppers	½ lb. ground chuck
3 tsp. minced onion	8 tsp. fat or salad oil
2 tsp. salt	Dash of pepper
¾ tsp. powdered sage	1¼ tsp. bottle thick meat sauce
1¼ cup canned tomatoes	1 cup cooked rice

Wash peppers, cut a thin slice from stem end, and remove seeds. Cover with boiling salted water and simmer 5 minutes. Drain. Meanwhile cook beef and onion in 4 tsp. fat in a skillet 5 minutes until meat loses red color. Add salt, pepper, sage, meat sauce, rice and tomatoes. Combine thoroughly. Stuff peppers with this mixture and top with bread crumbs which have been combined with the remaining 5 tsp. fat melted. Arrange pepper upright in a greased baking dish and bake in 375 degree oven for 35 to 40 minutes.

TOMATO CASSEROLE

2 Tbs. butter or margarine	½ cup chopped parsley
¼ cup chopped onion	½ cup grated carrots
4 slices day-old bread, cubed	1 tsp. salt
3 large tomatoes, peeled and	⅛ tsp. pepper
diced, 2 lbs.	½ tsp. dry mustard

Start oven 10 minutes before baking; set to moderate (350F)

Melt butter; add onions and bread. Saute until light brown. Save out ½ cup of mixture for the top; combine remainder with all the other ingredients. Turn into a buttered 6-cup casserole and top with the ½ cup bread mixture. Bake 15 to 20 minutes. 4 to 6 servings.

FRIED OKRA

1 package of frozen okra, fresh	Salt to taste
okra or canned okra	Shortening
Cornmeal	

Cut okra into ½ inch slices. Salt lightly. Roll okra in cornmeal, separating each piece and coating well. Heat shortening until hot. Add okra, turning as needed to brown. Drain on paper towels.

OKRA AND TOMATOES

1½ pts. of 3 to 4-inch okra pods
3 Tbs. butter or bacon drippings
2 medium onions, sliced

3 medium tomatoes or 1½ cups cooked tomatoes
Salt & pepper to taste

Choose young tender bright-green okra pods. Pods should be easily pierced with thumbnail. Wash thoroughly, remove stems. Put butter or bacon dripings into skillet, add the sliced onions. Slice the okra ¼-inch thick directly into the skillet on top of the onions. Cover and simmer until onion is soft, or about 5 minutes. Slide okra and onion to one side of skillet (to preserve green color of okra); place the sliced raw or cooked tomatoes in other half of skillet and continue to simmer, covered, until okra is tender. Then fold tomatoes and okra together gently. Season to taste and serve immediately. 5 servings.

Bonnie Sloan
Hendersonville, Tenn.

FRIED GREEN TOMATOES

5 medium green tomatoes, 1½ lbs.
⅓ cup flour
¾ tsp. salt

Few dashes pepper
¼ cup shortening

Select firm tomatoes. Wash, remove the stem end and blossom scars and cut into half-inch, crosswise slices. mix flour, salt and pepper, and dip both sides of tomato slices into the mixture. Heat shortening in a skillet until sizzling hot. Put in the tomatoes and cook rather quickly until browned on underside. Then turn tomatoes carefully, reduce heat and cook until thoroughly hot and soft through center. Remove to a hot platter and serve piping hot, either plain or with a cheese or onion sauce. 4 servings.

FRIED CABBAGE

1½ lbs. green cabbage or 6 cups   ½ tsp. salt
   coarsely shredded   Pepper
2 tsp. bacon fat or butter

Prepare cabbage. Heat fat in a heavy skillet until barely sizzling. Add cabbage, spread out level and sprinkle with salt. Cover, reduce heat and cook gently, shaking skillet occasionally to prevent sticking. After 3 minutes cooking, turn cabbage over with a pancake turner. Replace cover and cook another 2 or 3 minutes or until cabbage is soft but still has a little crispness remaining, is a pale green color and has only suspicion of brown on the bottom. Sprinkle with pepper and turn out into a hot dish and serve piping hot. 4 servings.

NEW CABBAGE WITH TOMATOES

2 Tbs. chopped onion   2 cups canned tomatoes
2 Tbs. bacon fat   2 Tbs. flour
¾ cup boiling water   ¼ cups fine dry bread crumbs
1 tsp. salt   2 Tbs. butter, melted
½ tsp. sugar   3 Tbs. grated parmesan cheese
1 medium head cabbage, 2 lbs.

Sauté onion in fat for 5 minutes. Add the water, salt, sugar, and the cabbage that has been trimmed and cut into thin wedges. Boil vigorously uncovered, for about 8 minutes or until cabbage is tender, turning over once during the cooking. Add tomatoes, reserving some of the juice to combine with flour to make a paste. Add paste to the cabbage mixture, stirring thoroughly, and cook until liquid boils and thickens. Serve immediately topped with buttered crumbs combined with the cheese. 4 servings.

FRESH CORN AND TOMATO CASSEROLE

8 to 12 ears fresh corn
¼ cup butter or bacon drippings
2 cups water

4 slices crisp bacon, crumbled
1 tsp. salt or to taste
2 large tomatoes, peeled and
   sliced

Cut corn from cob as directed for Fried corn. There should be 4 to 5 cups of cut corn. Melt butter or drippings in skillet, add corn, and saute quickly for about 5 minutes. Add water, bacon and salt and pour in buttered casserole. Arrange sliced tomatoes on top. Place in a moderate oven (350F) and bake uncovered about 30 minutes. Serve hot. 5 to 6 servings.

CREAMED CORN WITH GREEN PEPPER

6 ears fresh corn, 2½ cups
2 tsp. butter
¼ cup finely chopped onion
1 tsp. sugar

1 tsp. salt
⅔ cup water
¼ cup chopped green pepper
½ cup milk

Cut corn from cob; be careful not to shave off any bits of cob. Melt butter in a saucepan; add corn, onion, sugar, salt and water. Cover simmer about 6 minutes or until water is almost evaporated and the kernels are tender. Add green pepper and milk; cook just long enough to heat thoroughly. Serve at once. 4 servings.

JAMBALAYA

¾ cup uncooked rice
3 tsp. bacon drippings
1 clove garlic, cut up
2 green peppers, 1½ c. chopped
1 cup chopped onion
1 lb. ground beef
No. 2 can tomatoes, 2½ cups

¼ tsp. paprika
¼ tsp. chili powder
½ tsp. Worcestershire Sauce
1½ tsp. salt
¼ tsp. black pepper
1 small bay leaf
1 tsp. chopped parsley

Follow directions on package for cooking rice. Place bacon drippings in Dutch oven or heavy skillet and cook garlic for 5 minutes. Remove garlic clove and discard. Cook peppers and onions until soft. Push to one side of pan and brown meat. Add remaining ingredients, cover and simmer gently for 30 minutes. Add rice, stir to mix and continue to simmer gently for 15 to 20 minutes. Serve at once. 4 to 6 servings.

HOMINY POTATOES AND ONION SAUTÉ

¼ cup bacon drippings
⅓ cup coarsely chopped dry or
green onions

2 cups diced cooked potatoes
No. 2½ can hominy, drained
1 tsp. salt.

Heat drippings in a heavy skillet and cook onions slowly until transparent but not brown. Add potatoes and hominy, season with salt, and cook over moderate heat, stirring occasionally until vegetables are slightly brown, crusty and thoroughly heated through. 5 servings.

DIXIE OKRA GUMBO

2 Tbs. oil
1 Tbs. flour
½ onion, chopped
2 garlic cloves, chopped
½ green pepper, chopped
2 celery stalks, chopped

½ to 1 pound okra
2 ripe tomatoes
salt and pepper to taste
2 cups boiling water
Rice

Heat oil and stir in flour, lightly brown onion, garlic, green pepper and celery. When onion is clear, add okra, tomatoes, salt and pepper. Stir and add 2 cups boiling water. Cook for 45 minutes and serve over rice.

GREEN ONION CASSEROLE

2 lbs. ground beef
3 tsp. salt
4 tsp. sugar
2 cans tomatoes
2 cans tomatoes sauce
4 cloves garlic, chopped
½ tsp. pepper

1 pkg. (10 oz.) thin egg noodles
8 oz. cream cheese
2 cups sour cream
12 green onions, chopped with tops
2 cups grated cheddar cheese

Combine meat, salt, sugar, pepper, tomatoes, sauce and garlic; simmer 10 minutes. Cook egg noodles, drain. Combine hot noodles with cream cheese. Add sour cream and green onions. In a 4 quart casserole, layer noodles, meat mixture and top with grated cheese. Bake at 325 degrees for 30 minutes. Serves 8 to 10. This casserole can be made ahead of time and frozen.

CHEESE AND SPINACH PIE

½ cup chopped onion
¼ pound mushrooms, sliced
1 small zucchini, sliced
1 green pepper, diced
3 Tbs. oil
1 cup diced cooked ham
1 package frozen chopped
   spinach

1 pound ricotta, drained
1 cup grated Mozzarella cheese
3 eggs, beaten
2 Tbs. olive oil
Nutmeg
Salt and pepper to taste
1 Tbs. dill

Cook onion, mushrooms, zucchini and green pepper in oil until vegetables are tender. Add diced ham and cook for 2 minutes. Thaw and squeeze dry spinach. Combine spinach, ricotta, Mozzarella, eggs, olive oil, and spices. Add vegetables to cheese mixture. Pour into two 8 inch buttered pie plates and bake at 350 degrees for 45 minutes. Serves 8.

CARROT CASSEROLE

2 cups mashed, cooked carrots
1 cup sugar
3 tablespoons all-purpose flour
1 teaspoon baking powder

½ cup melted butter or
   margarine
3 eggs, beaten
Dash of cinnamon

Preheat oven to 400° F. Grease 2-quart casserole dish.
Combine all ingredients in order given. Place in casserole dish. Bake for 15 minutes. Reduce heat to 350° F. Continue baking for an additional 45 minutes. Makes 6 to 8 servings.

DELICIOUS BAKED TOMATOES

6 good-sized, ripe, firm
  tomatoes
1 Tbs. finely chopped onion
½ cup finely chopped
  mushrooms
2 Tbs. bacon fat or margarine

Salt and pepper
½ cup coarse bread crumbs
6 strips lean bacon
6 squares of toast
Parsley

Start oven 10 minutes before baking; set to moderately hot (350F).
Choose even-sized tomatoes shaped to stand level in baking pan.
Wash, but do not peel. Cut out a deep cone from stem ends. Cut core
from removed cone and discard and chop the rest of the cone. Sprinkle salt and pepper into the hollowed out tomato. Heat fat in skillet,
add onion and mushrooms and saute 2 or 3 minutes, then add
chopped tomatoes and bread crumbs. Toss just enough to mix. Add
salt if needed. Heap this mixture into the tomato cups. Cut bacon
strips into halves and cross the two halves over each tomato. Place
tomatoes in shallow baking dish and bake 20 to 35 minutes or until
bacon is crisp and tomatoes are just heated through. Remove
tomatoes to hot toast. Arrange on a hot platter. Garnish with parsley
and serve at once. 4 to 6 servings.

CREAMED PEAS AND NEW POTATOES

1 lb. new potatoes
2 lbs. fresh peas, 1½ cups
  shelled
1 Tbs. finely sliced green onion

1 cup boiling water
1¼ tsp. salt
½ cup evaporated milk
2 Tbs. butter
2 red radishes, optional

Scrape potatoes and if they are larger than a good sized walnut, cut
them in half or quarters. Put the potatoes, shelled peas and onion
into a saucepan, add the boiling water and salt. Cover and cook for 15
to 20 minutes or until vegetables are tender. Add milk and butter and
simmer very slowly until liquid is somewhat thickened. Add the
thinly sliced radishes just before serving. 4 servings.

BAKED POTATOES WITH SALT PORK GRAVY

¼ lb. salt pork	Few drops Worcestershire
⅓ cup flour	sauce, optional
Salt to taste	4 medium-sized potatoes,
3 cups milk	baked
2 Tbs. chopped chives	Paprika

Cut salt pork into quarter-inch cubes. Pour hot water over cubes, let stand 1 minute; then drain well. Pan-fry pork over low heat until brown and crispy. Pour off excess fat, leaving ⅓ cup in the pan. Blend in the flour and salt, add milk gradually, cook and stir until mixture is thickened and smooth. Add chives and Worcestershire sauce. Squeeze potatoes between thick folds of a cloth as soon as they are removed from the oven to crack them open and make them fluffy. Pour the hot salt pork gravy over the potatoes. Sprinkle with paprika and serve immediately. 4 servings.

*A real "taste of the Old South."

SOUTHERN MIXED GREENS

½ pound poke sallet	Grated onion
1 pound mustard greens	Boiling water-3 cups
1 pound turnip greens	Hard-cooked eggs, sliced
1 pound spinach	Vinegar
1 pound smoked hog jowl	Lemon juice

Mix and cook over medium heat for approximately 2 hours or until most of the water is cooked out.

HASHED BROWN POTATOES

⅓ cup hot salt pork fat	⅛ tsp. pepper
2 cups boiled diced potatoes	Pinch of salt

Fry piece salt pork cut into cubes, strain. Take hot fat, add cold boiled diced potatoes, pepper, pinch salt. Mix potatoes thoroughly with fat, cook few minutes stirring constantly, let stand to brown underneath. Fold as an omelet and brown. Serve at once.

CAULIFLOWER CASSEROLE

1 head cauliflower
1¼ teaspoons salt
3 cups water
2 egg yolks
cooking oil

1 cup milk
½ cup all-purpose flour
½ tsp. celery salt
1 Tbs. paprika

Rinse cauliflower. Sprinkle with salt. Place in a deep pan with water. Cover tightly. Steam for 15 minutes or until barely tender. Cool. Lift cauliflower out. Break into flowerets. Beat egg yolks until light. Add milk, flour, celery salt, and paprika. Dip flowerets in batter. Deep fry in oil heated to 390° F. Drain. Serve immediately. Makes 4 to 6 servings.

CHEESEY BAKED POTATOES

4 med. oblong baking potatoes
1 tsp. salt
1 tsp. grated Parmesan cheese

5 tsp. butter, melted
1 tsp. bread crumbs

Heat oven to 425 degrees. Scrub potatoes. Slice each potato part way through crosswise every ¼ to ½ inch. Place on buttered pan. Sprinkle with 2 tsp. of the melted butter, and salt. Bake 30 minutes. Sprinkle bread crumbs on potatoes and other 3 tsp. butter over them. Bake 20 minutes. Sprinkle with Parmesan cheese. Baste with butter from pan. Bake 10 minutes. Makes 4 servings.

POTATO CROQUETTES, BAKED

2 lbs. potatoes
2½ cups water
1 tsp. salt
⅓ cup milk, about
⅓ cup butter or margarine
Pepper

1¼ tsp. grated onion, optional
1 cup fine dry crumbs, buttered
1 egg beaten with 1 Tbs. water

Wash potatoes, pare thinly and if large, cut in half. Add water and salt, cover, boil gently until tender from 20 to 25 minutes. Only a tbsp. or 2 of water should remain on potatoes, no more. Put potatoes through food mill or ricer. Return potatoes to liquid in saucepan. Add butter and most of the milk; beat until light and fluffy, adding rest of milk if needed. Potatoes for croquettes should be quite stiff and hold together well. Stir in pepper and onion. Cool to room temp. Measure ⅓ cup portions onto waxed paper spread with the buttered crumbs. Shape croquettes into cones, roll in crumbs, then in egg mixture and again in crumbs. Grease circles on a cookie sheet or shallow pan for croquettes to stand on. Store in refrigerator. About 20 minutes before serving time, place in oven and bake until golden brown and crusty, about 15 minutes. Serve on hot platter, garnish with parsley. 9 croquettes.

Hint: Potato croquettes bake more satisfactorily than they fry and are more economical in use of shortening. Cold mashed potatoes may be used to make these croquettes.

CANDIED SWEET POTATOES

Sweet potatoes
Brown Sugar
Pepper

Butter
Cream

Wash and scrub potatoes and boil until tender. When cool remove skins. Split potatoes lengthwise, place in baking pan, sprinkle with brown sugar, pieces of butter on each potato, moisten sugar with plenty of cream and add little boiling water in bottom of pan.

*For a distinctive flavor sweeten with honey. Just before serving sprinkle with sliced nuts.

SWEET POTATO CASSEROLE

Casserole:

2 cups cooked and mashed
sweet potatoes
3 eggs, beaten
1½ sticks margarine (¾ cups)

1¼ cups sugar
¼ cup flour
1 large can Pet milk

Combine sugar and flour and add to remaining ingredients. Mix well and pour into 2½-quart baking dish.

Topping:
½ cup coconut
½ cup chopped nuts

½ cup brown sugar
½ cup crushed corn flakes

Combine ingredients thoroughly and sprinkle on top of casserole. Bake at 350 degrees for 25 minutes.

Bonnie Sloan
Hendersonville, Tenn.

SWEET POTATOES WITH APPLES

3 large baking apples
1 cup sugar
1 cup water
¼ cup cream
3 cups mashed sweet potatoes

¼ tsp. salt
Dash cinnamon
Butter
Red Color Mixture

Remove core. Place apples in boiling syrup made of equal quantities of sugar and water, cook slowly until transparent, but not broken. Carefully lift out apples. Continue cooking the syrup until it spins a thread, add a little red color mixture. Beat cream with sweet potatoes, seasoning and butter; fill apple center, place in pan with syrup. Bake. Makes 6 servings.

SWEET POTATO PUDDING

3 medium sized sweet potatoes   1 Tbs. butter
¼ cup cream   Salt
Grated lemon rind   Pepper

Wash, scrub and cook potatoes until tender. Peel, mash, adding a little grated lemon rind, butter, salt and pepper. Add a little brandy to flavor. Add cream, beat well, add a little soft butter. Pour into a buttered baking dish, dot with butter, cover with halves of marshallows. Lightly brown in moderate oven. Or use as filling with cooked red apples.

NEW ORLEANS BOURBON YAM CASSEROLE

5 large sweet potatoes or yams   1 tsp. cinnamon
2 Tbs. oil   ¼ tsp. grated nutmeg
6 Tbs. butter, divided   ⅛ tsp. cloves
⅓ cup Curacao   ¼ tsp. salt
¼ cup bourbon   ⅛ tsp. freshly ground pepper
½ cup sugar

Scrub sweet potatoes or yams. Rub skins with oil; place in shallow dish, and bake at 450 degrees for 30 minutes. Cool slightly; then peel and cut in ¾ inch slices. In saucepan, melt 4 tablespoons of butter; add remaining ingredients and mix thoroughly. Remove from heat. Butter 3 to 4 quart casserole dish and add yam slices in three layers, pouring ⅓ of seasoned butter sauce over each layer. Bake covered, at 350 degrees for 20 minutes. Remove from oven and stir, cutting the yam slices in half. When mixed, smooth and flatten top. Dot surface evenly with remaining two tablespoons butter. Bake uncovered for 20 minutes. Serves 8. A large can (40 ounces) of yams may be substituted for fresh in this dish.

VEGETABLE PUDDING

4 eggs, beaten
3 cups canned cream style corn
2½ cups half and half or milk
1 can green beans, drained
3 cups chopped tomatoes
1 cup chopped onion
2 med. green peppers, chopped
2 cans pimientos

2 cups sliced or chopped ripe
  olives
1 cup sliced mushrooms
½ tsp. Tabasco
1½ tsp. salt
½ tsp. chili powder
½ tsp. paprika
1½ cups yellow corn meal
1 pound bacon, fried crisp and
  crumbled

Combine all ingredients as listed, except crumbled bacon and mix thoroughly. Pour into 5 quart casserole or pan. Bake at 325 degrees for 1- ½ hours or until firm. Garnish with crumbled bacon. Serves 30. Can be refrigerated before or after baking; also freezes well.

OLD TIME DRIED BEANS

½ pound Great Northern beans
Salt and cayenne papper to taste

½ pound Navy beans
piece of boiling bacon

Wash beans. Discard any defects. Add all ingredients to 3 quarts cold water. Cook over medium heat for 3½ hours or until well done. Makes 8 servings.

GREEN BEANS COUNTRY STYLE

3 pounds green string beans
1 onion
Salt and cayenne pepper to taste

2 teaspoons sugar
Small piece of boiling bacon

Wash and snap beans. Place about 2 quarts of water in saucepan. Add all ingredients. Simmer for 2 hours on medium heat. Makes 4 to 6 servings.

B B Q BEANS

2 cans pork and beans
1 cup canned tomatoes, drained
1 cup apple cider
½ cup catsup
½ cup brown sugar
2 Tbs. horseradish, optional

1 Tbs. Worcestershire sauce
1 tsp. seasoned salt
1 tsp. dry mustard
½ tsp. pepper
½ onion, chopped

Mix all ingredients in shallow 3 quart baking pan. Bake uncovered at 350 degrees for 1½ to 2 hours. Serves 10-12 people.

BAKED BEANS WITH BACON

1½ cups dried beans
3 cups water
1 tsp. salt
6 slices pan-broiled bacon

1½ tsp. bacon drippings
1 cup half-inch bread cubes
3 tsp. melted butter
1 tsp. finely chopped parsley

Wash beans thoroughly and soak overnight in cold water. Drain and rinse, then put into saucepan with the 3 cups water and salt. Cover, heat to simmering and simmer until tender, about 15 minutes. Do not drain. Add chopped crisp bacon and melted bacon drippings, and mix well. Turn into a casserole and sprinkle with the bread cubes which have been tossed in the melted butter. Bake, uncovered, in a moderate oven (350F) until crumbs are nicely browned, about 20 minutes. Sprinkle with parsley. Serves 5 to 6.

GLAZED CARROTS

1 bunch carrots
1 quart boiling water
3 Tbs. butter

3 Tbs. brown sugar
Little salt
Paprika

Scrape small whole carrots. Cook in boiling salted water until tender. Drain. Cook sugar, butter and ¼ cup hot water together 5 minutes. Brush over cooked carrots and bake about 20 minutes in 375 degree oven. Baste with syrup.

FRENCH FRIED ONIONS

1 cup flour
Pinch salt
2 eggs

⅔ cup milk
1 Tbs. melted butter

Peel onions under water, slice in bowl of milk, let stand 15 minutes, drain, dry with towel. Beat eggs, add salt, butter, milk and flour to make smooth batter. Fold in onions, drop batter in deep hot shortening. Or dip onions in flour and fry.

FRIED CORN

2 cups tender white corn, cut
   from the cob (5 medium ears)
1 small green pepper, finely
   chopped
1 tsp. paprika

¼ cup light cream
3 Tbs. cooking oil
1 tsp. onion salt
½ tsp. pepper

Combine all ingredients. Spread in heavy skillet. Place over medium heat. Cook until browned on bottom. Reduce heat to very low. Cook until corn is soft. Makes 4 servings.

OVEN HAM & EGG BAKE

1½ cups ground, or finely
  chopped, cooked country
  ham
12 hard-cooked eggs, sliced
1 4-ounce can sliced
  mushrooms

2 10½-ounce cans condensed
  cream of mushroom soup
⅔ cup cracker crumbs

Preat oven to 350° F. Grease 1½-quart casserole dish. Place a layer each of ham, eggs, and mushrooms in casserole dish. Combine soup and milk to make sauce. Pour half of sauce over layers. Repeat layers and sauce. Top with crumbs. Bake about 20 minutes. Makes 8 servings.

STUFFED EGGS

4 hard-cooked eggs
1 Tbs. chopped chives
½ cup mayonnaise

4 tomato cups
1 Tbs. chopped parsley

Shell eggs. Cut in half lengthwise. Remove yolks and mash with a fork. Add chopped chives and enough mayonnaise to make soft paste. Fill whites. Press halves together. Sprinkle tomato cups with salt and pepper. Place an egg in each. Just before serving, top with remaining mayonnaise. Sprinkle with chopped parsley.

MACARONI LOAF

2 cups cooked macaroni
2 cups bread crumbs
2 tsp. minced onion
⅔ cup melted butter
1 can pimento
4 eggs

2 cups grated cheese
⅛ tsp. pepper
1 green pepper
¾ tsp. salt
2 cups milk

Grind onion, green pepper and pimento. Scald milk, pour over crumbs. Add butter and other ingredients, well-beaten egg yolks, fold in beaten whites. Cook in moderate oven 2 hours with pan set in hot water. Serve hot with cream mushroom sauce. Add seasoning.

EGG NOODLE RING

1 package egg noodles
5 egg yolks
5 egg whites
2 Tbs. butter
6 Tbs. cream

¾ tsp. salt
Pepper
½ green pepper, chopped
⅓ red pepper, chopped

Boil noodles in boiling salted water, about 7 minutes. Drain, beat egg yolks, add noodles, butter, cream, seasoning. Fold in stiffly beaten egg whites. Turn into buttered mold, set in pan hot water, bake about 30 minutes. Use creamed fish, chicken or mushrooms in center of mold.

CHILI OMELET

1 Tbs. butter or margarine
3 eggs, beaten
1 Tbs. milk
Dash of pepper

¼ cup chili—no beans
¼ cup American cheese
  shredded
Chopped parsley

Melt butter or margarine in 6-inch fry pan over medium heat. Combine eggs, milk and pepper; pour into fry pan. Reduce heat. As mixture sets, lift slightly with spatula to allow uncooked portion to flow underneath. When mixture is almost set, spoon chili over top; sprinkle with cheese. Fold in half, garnish with parsley. Makes 1 omelet.

SOUTHERN EGG DISH

4 cups chicken stock
2 cups rice
½ cup butter

1½ tsp. salt
6 eggs
Pepper to taste

Wash rice carefully, stir into boiling stock. Cover pan and in about 20 to 25 minutes rice will absorb the liquid. Turn to low heat. Stir well-beaten eggs into mixture add butter, seasoning, serve at once.

CHEESE SCRAMBLED EGGS

6 eggs
¾ cup grated sharp cheese
2 Tbs. milk
1 Tbs. chopped chives

½ tsp. salt
⅛ tsp. pepper
2 Tbs. butter or margarine

Beat eggs slightly in mixing bowl. Stir in cheese, milk, chives, salt, and pepper. Melt butter in skillet over low heat. Add egg mixture. Turn portions of egg mixture with spatula as it begins to thicken. Do not stir and do not overcook. Serve immediately. Makes 6 servings.

LOUISIANA CAJUN EGGS

1 can tomatoes (small)
3 onions, chop fine
3 green peppers, chopped
1 doz. hard cooked eggs
Salt

Paprika
½ cup diced celery
1 Tbs. butter
Pepper
1 tsp. flour

Melt butter, stir in flour, onions, pepper. Stir mixture. Add tomatoes, heat thoroughly. Place 1 dozen hard cooked eggs in buttered baking dish. Cover with hot tomato mixture. Sprinkle with grated cheese. Brown lightly in oven. Add dash paprika.

CORN WITH CHEESE

1 can whole kernel corn
1½ Tbs. butter
4 eggs
1 cup cracker crumbs
Pepper

2 cups milk
½ cup grated cheese
¾ tsp. salt
½ tsp. paprika

Beat eggs, add butter melted over hot water. Add to corn, then seasoning. Add milk and mix well. Add grated cheese. Fill buttered baking
dish half full and cover with one half the crumbs, add remaining corn
mixture, then crumbs and bake in moderate oven until firm about 30
to 40 minutes.

SUNDAY'S EGGS

¼ cup butter
¼ cup minced onion
2 medium-size tomatoes,
  peeled and cubed
6 slices bread, cubed

6 eggs, well beaten
Pepper to taste
¼ cup freshly grated Parmesan
  or Romano cheese
Freshly chopped parsley

Melt butter in heavy skillet. Add onion and tomato cubes. Saute until
onion is soft. Add bread cubes and brown. Add eggs and cook, as you
would scrambled eggs. When eggs are done to taste, add salt and
pepper. Top with cheese. Serve piping hot.

CORN SOUFFLE

1 cup grated sweet corn	3 eggs
2 Tbs. butter	1 Tbs. flour
Salt to taste	1 cup milk
Paprika	

Prepare cream sauce of butter, flour and milk, add to corn, then egg yolks and lastly 3 beaten egg whites. Mix thoroughly, place in buttered dish, bake about 20 minutes and serve at once.

CREAMY HOMINY CASSEROLE

2 cans hominy, drained	½ pint whipping cream
2 cans chopped green chilies, drained	Salt and pepper to taste
	¼ cup margarine
1 carton sour cream	1 cup grated cheese

In a bowl, mix hominy, green chilies, sour cream, whipping cream, salt and pepper. Pour into deep casserole dish, dot with margarine and sprinkle with cheese. Cover and bake at 350 degrees for 30 minutes. Serves 8.

SUNDAY VEGETABLE SOUFFLE

For carrots, spinach or Squash

¼ cup butter	1 full cup vegetables
¼ cup sifted flour	3 eggs
⅓ cup cream	Salt
⅓ cup water	Pepper

Melt butter. Add flour gradually, then cream and vegetable. Add well beaten egg yolks, and fold in stiffly beaten egg whites. Pour into buttered baking dish, place in pan with hot water and bake in slow oven.

CREAM OF TOMATO SOUP

½ pint cream
1 pint milk
1 Tbs. butter
Salt
Pepper

2 quarts canned tomatoes
2 cups soup stock
⅛ tsp. soda
1 tsp. flour
Celery Salt

Put tomatoes and soup stock in pan, add no water, boil for 10 minutes. Strain through colander, add soda, strain through fine sieve. Blend flour and butter, add to milk, add water. In pan heat cream and milk. Combine mixtures, heat. Season. Add whipped cream when serving.

GREEN TOMATO STEW

2 Tbs. flour
1 tsp. salt
Dash of pepper
1¼ lb. chuck round or shoulder
   arm cut into 1½-inch cubes
2 Tbs. shortening
1 cup water

¼ tsp. sugar
1 medium onion, sliced
6 small green tomatoes, 1 lb.
   washed, cored
2 large carrots, sliced, 1 cup

Mix flour, salt and pepper and thoroughly dredge meat. Brown meat slowly with any remaining flour in hot shortening in heavy skillet or Dutch oven. Reduce heat, add ¼ cup water, cover and simmer for 1 hour. Then add remaining water, sugar, onion and the tomatoes cut into quarters. Cover and simmer for 30 minutes. Add carrots and continue to simmer for 15 minutes more. Serve at once. 4 Servings.

ONION SOUP

1 potato
1 onion
1 carrot
2 ribs celery
8 cups water
8 bouillon (beef) cubes
¼ tsp. thyme

1½ tsp. salt
¼ tsp. pepper
1 stick butter (½ cup)
2 Tbs. flour
6 medium onions
Parmesan cheese
Croutons

Boil 1 potato, onion, and carrot with 2 ribs of celery in 8 cups of water for 20 minutes. Remove vegetables and add 8 bouillon cubes, ¼ teaspoon thyme, 1½ teaspoon salt, ¼ teaspoon pepper to taste. Slice 6 medium onions and fry in 1 stick butter until tender and very lightly browned. Blend in 2 tablespoons flour. Add to stock. Simmer ½ hour. Serve in bowls topped with Parmesan cheese and croutons.

PEA SOUP

½ tsp. salt
⅛ tsp. pepper
2 Tbs. butter
Celery Salt
Sprig parsley

3 cups chicken stock
2 cups cooked green peas
1 cup cold water
½ onion
1 cup milk

Set aside one third of peas. Add remainder to water, chicken stock, and seasoning and let simmer for 30 minutes. Press through sieve. Add butter. Let boil for a few minutes then add milk and remaining peas which have been heated. Serve very hot with little whipped cream and paprika.

EGG NOODLE CHICKEN SOUP

2½ qts. water
1 whole broiler, fryer chicken,
  about ¾ lb.
1½ tsp. salt
2 sprigs of parsley
2 chicken bouillon cubes

2 c. sliced celery
1 medium onion, coarsely
  chopped
⅛ tsp. pepper
8 oz. wide egg noodles
¼ c. chopped parsley
2 c. sliced carrots

In Dutch oven, combine water, chicken, salt and parsley sprigs. Heat to boiling. Cover; reduce heat and simmer 1 hour or until chicken is tender. Remove chicken and strain broth. Return broth to pot; add bouillon cubes and heat to boiling. Add carrots, celery, onion and 1 teaspoon salt and pepper. Cover and cook 5 minutes. Gradually add noodles so that soup continues to boil. Cook uncovered, stirring occasionally, until noodles are tender. Meanwhile, cut chicken into bite-size pieces. Discard skin and bones. Add chicken and chopped parsley to soup. Heat 5 minutes. Makes 3 quarts. (A can of corn is a nice substitute if celery isn't handy)

CREAM OF FRESH BROCCOLI SOUP

3 cups fresh broccoli, cut in ½
  inch pieces
1 tsp. salt
½ cup chopped fresh onion
3 Tbs. butter or margarine

3 Tbs. flour
1 cup broccoli liquid
3 cups milk
¾ tsp. salt
¼ tsp. ground black pepper
Paprika

Place broccoli in saucepan in 1-inch boiling salted water. Bring to boiling point and cook uncovered, 5 minutes. Cover and cook 15 minutes or until broccoli is crisp and tender. Drain and reserve 1 cup liquid to use later. Cook onion in butter until limp. Blend in flour. Slowly blend in the cup of broccoli cooking water. Heat milk and add to mixture with broccoli, salt and ground black pepper. Cook until slightly thickened about 5 minutes. Serve hot, garnish with paprika. Yields 2 quarts.

Katherine Coker
Mt. Juliet, Tenn.

MUSHROOM SOUP

4 cups chicken stock
¾ pound mushrooms
1 slice onion
¼ cup butter
⅛ cup flour

¼ cup cream
¼ cup reg. milk
Salt
Pepper
Paprika

Wash, chop mushrooms, add with onion and cook in stock about 20 minutes. Then rub through sieve. Reheat and add thickening, then milk and cream which have been heated in double boiler. Serve very hot with little whipped cream.

NAVY BEAN SOUP

1 cup dried beans
1 quart cold water
½ onion, sliced
1 stalk celery, diced
¼ tsp. salt
2 Tbs. butter

⅛ tsp. celery salt
2 tsp. flour
Grated Cheese
Paprika

Soak beans overnight in cold water, drain. Add 5 cups of cold water, bring to boiling point, cover, simmer 3 hours or until tender. Add more water if needed. Cook onion and celery to light brown in one half of butter, stir in flour and blend well. Stir in strained soup. Cook 3 to 4 minutes. A tablespoon of sherry may be added just before serving. Add cheese and paprika. Serve hot.

TUNA CHOWDER

2 7-ounce cans chunk tuna
3 Tbs. butter
1 large onion, diced
1 12 ounce can whole kernel corn undrained
2 Tbs. tomato paste
1 10½ ounce cans cream of celery soup

2 cups milk
3 or 4 large potatoes peeled & cubed
1 tsp. dry mustard
1 tsp. dill weed
¼ tsp. basil
¼ tsp. fennel
Salt and pepper to taste

Drain tuna and break into pieces in a deep, heavy pot. In skillet heat butter and cook onion until transparent. Put into pot with tuna. Add corn, tomato paste, soup milk, potatoes, mustard, herbs, salt and pepper, all other ingredients and bring to a simmer, stirring several times. Cover and cook 30 minutes or until potatoes are tender.

CORN CHOWDER

¾ cup onion chopped
¾ cup celery cut diagonally in 1 inch pieces
½ stick butter
1¾ cups milk
2 cans cream of chicken soup undiluted

1 20 ounce can Del Monte cream style corn
½ tsp. salt
½ tsp. pepper
½ tsp. sweet basil

Cook onion and celery butter. Add milk, soup, corn, salt, pepper and basil. Heat well. But do not boil. Serves 6.

CLAM CHOWDER

¼ lb. margarine or butter
1-2 medium onions
2 (6 oz.) cans clams, drained and save liquid

3 cans New England clam chowder
1 qt. Half n Half
1 qt. homogenized milk
6 cans cream of potato soup

Melt margarine and cook onions and clams lightly. Then combine all ingredients in large pot. Cook, covered for 3 hours in 300 degree oven.

RICE CASSEROLE

1 cup white rice	½ cup margarine
1 small onion	½ cup chopped green onion
1 can beef broth	1 can mushrooms pieces
1 can sliced water chestnuts	1 cup boiling water w/beef
Salt and pepper to taste	cubes
Tabasco sauce to taste	¼ cup chopped green pepper

Preheat oven to 350 degrees. Melt margarine. Brown rice in margarine and add onions. Cook until onions are wilted. Mix in mushroms, beef broth, water with bouillon cubes, water chestnuts and green pepper. Season with salt, pepper and tabasco sauce. Bake in 1½ quart casserole for 45 minutes uncovered. Stir occasionally.

BAKED STUFFED ONIONS

These may be made the day before, refrigerated, and baked before serving.

6 large onions, peeled	Paprika
3 Tbs. butter or margarine	¼ cup chopped pecans
¼ cup dry bread crumbs	Salt and pepper
	1½ cups grated sharp cheese

TOMATO BAKE

1 qt. canned tomatoes, drained	3 Tbs. butter
1¼ cups toasted bread crumbs	½ cup sugar
	1 tsp. salt

Preheat oven to 300 degrees. Mash tomatoes, mix 1 cup bread crumbs, sugar, salt and butter into tomato pulp. Pour into buttered baking dish and cover with remaining bread crumbs. Bake for 30 minutes. Serves 4.

CORN PUDDING

2 cups corn cut, cream style
1 cup milk
2 Tbs. sugar

6 Tbs. melted butter
2 Tbs. self-rising flour
4 beaten eggs
1 tsp. salt

Preheat oven to 325 degrees. Blend butter, flour, salt and sugar. Add beaten eggs. Stir in corn and then milk. Pour in casserole and bake 40 minutes.

CREAM OF CORN SOUP

2 cups boiling water
2 cups canned corn
    (cream style)
½ cup chopped celery and
    leaves
¼ cup chopped parsley

1 Tbs. chopped onion
2 cups milk
2 Tbs. butter
2 Tbs. flour
1 tsp. salt
¼ tsp. paprika

Add water to corn. Simmer, covered, for 20 minutes with celery, parsley and onion. Melt butter, add flour and when well blended add milk slowly. Strain corn mixture and add to white sauce. Season, heat to boiling point and serve with sprinkling of additional parsley on top of each soup plate. Amount: about 4½ cups.

CREAM OF MUSHROOM SOUP

½ lb. mushrooms
2 cups stock or water
1 small stalk celery
2 carrots
½ onion
Several sprigs parsley

2 Tbs. butter
2 Tbs. flour
2 cups top milk or cream
1¼ tsps. salt
⅛ tsp. paprika
⅛ tsp. nutmeg

Wash mushrooms, trim stems and cover with stock or water. Add celery, parsley, peeled carrots and onion and simmer soup until mushrooms are tender (20 minutes). Drain vegetables, reserving stock, and put through food chopper using finest knife.

Melt butter, add flour and when well blended, add mushroom stock slowly and hot milk or cream. Add ground vegetables and seasoning and serve topped with whipped cream garnished with paprika and parsley. Amount: about 4½ cups.

CORN Á LA KING

2 cups cooked or canned corn
1 green pepper, chopped
1 chopped pimento

1 egg
½ cup milk
1 tsp. salt
Paprika

Mix corn, peppers and milk in double boiler and add beaten egg and seasoning. Cook until thick, stirring occasionally. Serve on hot, buttered toast. Amount: 6 servings.

SCALLOPED APPLES AND ONIONS

6 apples
6 onions
12 slices bacon
½ tsp. salt

½ cup water
¼ cup soft bread crumbs
1 tsp. bacon fat

Peel and cut onions crosswise in ⅛-inch slices. Peel, core and slice apples crosswise to same thickness. Crisp bacon and cut into small pieces. Arrange apples, onions and bacon in alternate layers in greased baking dish and sprinkle apples and onions with salt. Add water and sprinkle top with bread crumbs which have been tossed in 1 tbsp. melted bacon fat. Cover and bake in moderate 350° oven about 35 minutes, uncovering baking dish during last 15 minutes to brown top. Amount: 6 servings.

CABBAGE AND APPLE CASSEROLE

1 small head green cabbage
1 small head red cabbage
1 cup green pepper, minced

3 cups diced apples
½ cup brown sugar
Juice of one lemon
½ cup butter
Salt, pepper and nutmeg

Grind red and green cabbage separately. Season red cabbage with salt and pepper, place in greased casserole and dot with butter. Add sugar, lemon juice and nutmeg to apples and place on top of cabbage. Mix green cabbage with green pepper, season, place over apples, dot with butter. Cover with buttered bread crumbs and bake in moderate 375° oven about 25 minutes. Amount 6 or 8 servings.

SPAGHETTI LOAF

4 cups cooked spaghetti
1½ cups milk
2 Tbs. butter
1½ Tbs. flour
½ tsp. salt

⅛ tsp. pepper
⅛ tsp. paprika
1 pimento, chopped
3 eggs
1 cup grated cheese

Melt the butter, stir in the flour, seasoning, slowly stir in milk. let come to boil, stir in cheese, cooked spaghetti, pimento. Stir in beaten eggs. Press into a greased loaf pan. Place pan in hot water, bake in moderate oven, 350 degrees about 55 minutes.

SWEET AND SOUR GREEN BEANS

4 cups fresh green beans
⅓ cup cider vinegar
2 small onions, chopped
2 tsp. flour
⅛ tsp. pepper

½ cup water
4 slices bacon
3 Tbs. sugar
¼ tsp. salt

Preheat oven to 350 degrees. Cut beans in pieces. Cook in boiling, salted water until crisp and tender and drain. Plunge into ice water. Drain and set aside. In large skillet, cook bacon until crisp. Drain and crumble. Drain off all but 2 tablespoons of drippings. Lightly brown onion in drippings until tender. Stir in flour; cook and stir until bubbly. Stir in water, vinegar and sugar. Heat to boiling and continue to cook until slightly thickened. Add beans, tossing lightly. Sprinkle with salt, pepper and bacon. Cook until bubbly. Serves 4.

CHICKEN CHEESE CASSEROLE

3 Tbs. butter or margarine
3 Tbs. all-purpose flour
2 cups milk
½ cup grated, sharp cheese
2 Tbs. chopped pimiento

½ cup grated Swiss cheese
1 tsp. Worcestershire sauce
1 cup chopped, cooked chicken

Melt butter in saucepan. Blend in flour. Cook until bubbly. Add milk.
Cook and stir until sauce is thick and smooth. Remove from heat.
Stir in cheeses. Stir until melted. Add remaining ingredients. Heat
thoroughly. Serve over "Cornmeal Pancakes." Makes 4 servings.

CREAMED POTATO BAKE

8 to 10 med. potatoes
1 package cream cheese

1 cup sour cream
Garlic powder to taste

Pre heat oven to 350 degrees. Peel potatoes, boil in water until tender.
Drain. Beat potatoes, adding cream cheese and sour cream. If too
stiff, add some milk. Add garlic powder to taste. Put in buttered
casserole, brush with melted butter and sprinkle with paprika.
Brown for 30 minutes.

MUSTARD GREENS

2 lbs. mustard greens
6 cups boiling water
¼ lb. salt pork

½ tsp. salt
⅛ tsp. sugar
½ pod red pepper

Use a sharp knife to strip leaves from stems and to trim off damaged portions. Wash several times in warm water. Shake off excess water; place in kettle, cover with boiling water and slowly heat to boiling. Dice pork very fine; pan-fry until crisp and light brown. Skim off about 2 tbsp. of the clear fat, then turn pork, remaining fat and residue into greens. Add salt, sugar and pepper and cook covered for 1¼ hours, turning heat very low during last half of cooking period. Turn over occasionally while cooking. Serve with the pot liquor. 4 servings.

MUSTARD GREENS AND SPINACH WITH BACON

2 lbs. fresh, tender mustard
    greens
¼ lb. bacon
1 quart boiling water

½ tsp. salt
Black pepper to suit taste
½ lb. spinach

Wash mustard greens very thoroughly, trimming off roots and tough stems. Trim and wash spinach. Put mustard greens into kettle with bacon, add water and cover and boil gently for 45 minutes. Add salt and pepper, and put spinach into kettle, pressing down well. Again cover and cook until spinach is tender, from 10 to 15 minutes. More water may be added as needed, but amount of pot liquor should be just right to serve with greens when they are done. Serve pipping hot. 4 servings.

CORN CHOWDER

2 cups canned corn
1 small onion, chopped fine
1 pint diced potatoes, raw
2 Tbs. butter
Celery Salt

¼ tsp. salt
2 pints milk, scald
1 cup boiling water
Pepper

Cook onion in one half of butter to light brown, drain. Boil potatoes until tender, drain. Blend all ingredients, add seasoning to taste. If a thicker soup is desired, blend 2 tablespoons of flour with little cold milk, and stir into soup 10 minutes before serving.

GREEN BEAN CASSEROLE

2 pkg. frozen french style green beans
1 can cream of mushroom soup
¼ tsp. celery salt
¼ tsp. soy sauce
1 can french fried onions

Cook beans in 1 cup boiling water, do not add salt. Bring to boil and break up beans with fork. Cover and boil 3 minutes or until beans lose their raw taste but still green and quite crisp. Drain beans, reserving ¼ cup of the liquid. In a 1½ qt. casserole, combine the beans with mushroom soup, celery salt, soy sauce and ½ of the onions. Add the ½ cup reserved liquid. Arrange the remaining onions over the top. Bake at 350 degrees until very hot and onion rings are crisp and brown 20 to 30 minutes. Makes 6 servings.

BAKED HUBBARD SQUASH

Cut squash into pieces, remove seeds and strings. Place pieces in dripping pan in moderate 375° oven for 1 hour. Cover generously with butter and sprinkle with brown sugar. Cook for 1 hour longer, basting frequently, adding butter, if necessary.

Cooked squash may be scalloped with drained, crushed pineapple, dotted with butter and covered with bread crumbs. Bake until top is brown. Squash may be baked whole, in a moderately hot 375° oven.

ACORN SQUASH

Cut into halves, take out seeds. Boil in salted water, or spread inside and out with butter, season and bake until tender in moderate 375° oven. It is then ready to be served, or it may be filled with creamed food (ham, fish, spinach, etc.) or hash.

BROCCOLI RING

2 lbs. broccoli
½ lb. American cheese
3 eggs

2 cups thick cream sauce
1 tsp. salt
Pepper

Boil broccoli until tender and cut into small pieces. Cut cheese into cubes and add to cream sauce, then stir in beaten egg yolks. Add broccoli and then fold in beaten egg whites. Bake about 40 minutes in moderate 325° oven in buttered ring set in pan of water. Turn out of ring and serve. Amount: 6 servings.

HARVARD BEETS

3 cups cooked sliced beets	½ tsp. salt
½ cup sugar	½ cup mild vinegar or
1 Tbs. cornstarch	6 Tbs. vinegar and 4 Tbs. cream

Cook and stir last 4 ingredients. When clear add beets and place pan, covered, over hot water for ½ hour. Just before serving, heat beets again and add 2 tbsps. butter. Amount: 6 servings.

FRIED OKRA

1 pound fresh okra or one 10-ounce package frozen whole okra	Cooking oil
	½ cup all-purpose flour
	½ cup corn meal
1 Tbs. paprika	1 tsp. salt

Wash okra, remove stems. Combine flour, meal, salt, and paprika in heavy paper bag. Add okra. Shake to coat okra. Fry in oil heated to 375° F. until brown. Drain and serve at once. Makes 6 servings.

HOPPING JOHN

1 cup dry black-eyed peas
8 cups water
6 slices bacon
¾ cup chopped onion

1 clove garlic, minced
1 cup regular rice
2 tsps. salt
¼ tsp. pepper

Rinse the black-eyed peas. In a large saucepan combine the peas and water, bring to a boil, then boil for 2 minutes. Remove from heat and let stand 1 hour. Drain, reserving 6 cups of the cooking liquid.

In a heavy 3-quart saucepan, cook the bacon, onion, and garlic until the bacon is crisp and the onion is tender but not brown. Remove bacon; drain on paper towels; crumble and set aside.

Stir the black-eyed peas, raw rice, salt, pepper, and the reserved cooking liquid into mixture in saucepan. Bring to a boil; cover and reduce heat. Simmer 1 hour, stirring occasionally. Stir in crumbled bacon. Turn into a serving bowl. Serve immediately.
Makes 8 servings.

HAM HOCKS AND BLACK-EYED PEAS

3 cups dry black-eyed peas
12 cups water
3 pounds smoked ham hocks
1¼ cups chopped onion
1 cup chopped celery

1 tsp. salt
⅛ tsp. cayenne pepper
1 bay leaf
1 (10-ounce) package frozen cut
  okra

Rinse peas. In a 6-quart dutch oven, combine water and peas. Bring to a boil and simmer 2 minutes. Remove from heat; cover and let stand 1 hour. (Or, combine water and peas; soak overnight.) Do not drain. Stir in hocks, onion, celery, salt, cayenne pepper, and bay leaf. Bring to a boil. Cover; simmer until hocks are tender and beans are done, about 1½ hours. Stir in okra; cook until tender, from 10 to 15 minutes. Discard bay leaf. Season to taste.
Makes 6 servings.

COUNTRY SUNSHINE BRUNCH

1 8¾-ounce package hash
 brown potatoes
½ cup chopped onion
2 Tbs. chopped parsley
¼ cup butter or margarine
½ cup all-purpose flour

1 tsp. salt
¼ tsp. pepper
1½ cups milk
1 cup sour cream
1½ pounds Canadian bacon
8 eggs

Preheat oven to 350° F. Grease a 9- x 13-inch baking dish. Prepare potatoes according to directions. Stir in onion and parsley. Place in prepared baking dish. Melt butter in a saucepan. Blend in flour, salt, and pepper. Add milk. Cook over low heat, stirring constantly until thick. Blend in sour cream. Pour over potatoes. Arrange bacon in overlapping row down center of dish. Bake for 45 minutes. Remove from oven. Make 4 indentations in each side of bacon. Slip egg into indentation. Season with salt and pepper. Bake 15 to 20 minutes, or until eggs are set. Makes 8 servings.

LYNDA'S STUFFED PEPPERS

6 medium green peppers
1 pound pork sausage meat
¼ tsp. pepper
⅔ cup tomato juice

½ pound ground veal
1 tsp. salt
1 cup uncooked oats (quick or
 old-fashioned)

Preheat oven to 350° F. Cut ¼-inch slice from top of each green pepper. Remove seeds. Cook green peppers in enough boiling water to cover for about 5 minutes. Drain. Mix remaining ingredients and stuff peppers and bake for 1 hour.

Lynda Woodard
Goodlettsville, Tenn.

Salads

SALMON SALAD

1 can pink salmon
1½ cups cooked macaroni
½ cup chopped pimiento

½ cup chopped sweet pickles
½ cup mayonnaise
Salt and pepper to taste

Flake the salmon. Cook macaroni according to package directions. Drain. Combine all ingredients; chill. Yield: 6 servings.

Clara Scott
Nashville, Tenn.

TOMATO ASPIC SALAD

1 can tomatoes (No. 2½)
1 small onion minced
1 bay leaf
4 ribs of celery with leaves

1 tsp. salt
½ tsp. paprika
1 tsp. sugar
2 Tbs. mild vinegar or lemon juice

Boil ingredients for 20 minutes. Strain. Soak 2 tbsps. gelatin in ½ cup cold water. Dissolve it in hot tomato juice. Add water to make 4 cups liquid. Chill aspic until set. Olives diced, celery, green peppers, carrots minced, or diced meat, or fish may be added to the aspic when it is about to set.
Note. Four cups tomato juice, seasoned, may be substituted for water and tomato stock. Amount: 8 servings.

TOMATO ASPIC RING

Prepare Tomato Aspic. Pour into wet ring mold. Chill until firm, unmold onto lettuce. Fill center with cottage cheese, sliced cucumbers, or fish salad, chicken salad, etc.

COLD MIXED VEGETABLE SALAD

1 pkg. frozen mixed vetegables
½ c. each of celery, onion and
   green pepper
1½ Tbs. chopped pimento

½ c. vinegar
1 Tbs. mustard
1 Tbs. flour
¾ c. sugar

Cook mixed vegetables, drain. Mix celery, onion, pepper and pimento; Set aside.
Combine and cook remaining ingredients until thick. Combine all ingredients and refrigerate for 1 day. Serves 6.

MACARONI AND VEGETABLE SALAD

2 c. spiral or shell macaroni
1½ c. cubed cheese
2 c. bite size broccoli

1 c. halved cherry tomatoes
1 c. cucumber slices
¾ c. Italian dressing

Combine all ingredients. Toss with salad dressing. Chill several hours or over night. Toss before serving. 10 servings.

CUCUMBER SALAD

Peel three average size cucumbers. Take fork and run down sides to add scalloped affect. Put into bowl, salt each layer, pour small amount of vinegar over top, add a small onion cut up very fine. Put ice cubes on top then cover with dish. Refrigerate for approximately two to three hours. Remove, drain well, best to take paper towel and dry off all moisture then add chopped dill (juice will do) and blend ½ pint sour cream. Keep cool until serving.

TACO SALAD

1 lb. hamburger	¾ c. water
1 env. taco seasoning	1½ c. taco chips
½ cup sour cream	½ c. taco sauce
1 avocado	1 small onion, chopped
Dash lemon juice	1 medium tomato, chopped
8 oz. cream cheese	1 head lettuce (in bite size
1 bag shredded cheddar cheese	pieces)

Brown meat and drain. Add taco seasoning and water and cook 15 minutes. Place lettuce on serving plates. Top with onion, tomato, and cheese. Crumble chips on top. Pour hamburger and juice over top. Pour avocado mixture over meat and top with taco sauce. Garnish with halved black olives. Serves 6.

TUNA SALAD

2 cans tuna	⅓ c. mayonnaise (real)
1 c. macaroni (cooked)	2 Tbs. milk
4 eggs (hard boiled)	2 tsp. sugar
¼ c. relish (sweet)	

Mix tuna, macaroni and eggs. Mix relish, mayonnaise, milk and sugar to make sauce. May need to adjust mayonnaise or milk slightly for creamy texture. Pour sauce over tuna. Mix and serve. Serves 5 to 6, good size portions.

POTATO SALAD

8 medium potatoes, cooked and diced
1 onion, chopped
2 hard boiled eggs, chopped
1-2 tsp. celery seed

1-8 ounce bottle Italian dressing
1-8 ounce carton sour cream
½ tsp. salt
⅛ tsp. pepper

Combine all ingredients and chill overnight.

CABBAGE SLAW

1 4 oz. can crushed pineapple
1 medium head cabbage, shredded
½ cup mayonnaise

2 cups miniature marshmallows
1 small jar Maraschino cherries, chopped

Drain pineapple, reserving ¼ cup juice. Combine pineapple, cabbage, mayonnaise and reserved juice. Mix in chopped cherries. Chill at least 1 hour. Yield: 6 to 8 servings.

DRESSING FOR CABBAGE SALAD

½ cup sugar
¼ cup flour
¼ cup vinegar
2 egg yolks

¼ cup butter
1½ cups boiling water
Salt and pepper to taste

Mix flour, sugar, vinegar and egg yolks, add salt, pepper and butter. Mix well. Add boiling water.

Henrietta Davis
Smyrna, Tenn.

LIME GELATIN SALAD

Combine in a sauce pan;

1 cup boiling water
1 pkg. lime jello
½ tsp. plain gelatain

Stir until the gelatin is dissolved, then set aside to cool

To cooled gelatin mixture add:

1 scant cup mayonnaise
1 cup small curd cottage cheese
3 tsp. horseradish

Beat with rotary egg beater until well mixed, then add:

1 cup #2 pineapples, drained
1 cup chopped pecans
Dash salt

Put into a pan or individual molds and put in refrigerator until set.
Serves 6.

TWENTY FOUR HOUR SLAW

12 cups shredded cabbage	1 tsp. salt
2 large red onions, thinly sliced and separated into rings	1 tsp. celery seed
	1 tsp. dry mustard
2 large green peppers, thinly sliced, optional	1 tsp. dill weed
	¼ tsp. white pepper
1 cup sugar	½ cup salad oil
1 cup white vinegar	

Alternate cabbage, onion and green pepper in glass bowl, ending with
onion rings. Combine remaining ingredients except oil, and bring to
a mixture. Do not stir. Cover and refrigerate 24 hours or longer before
serving. Serves 12.

SLIM WALDORF CHICKEN SALAD

1 person

4 oz. chilled cubed chicken-
 cooked
¼ c. diced celery
½ small apple-cubed
6 large seedless grapes- green-
 cut in half

2 Tbs. plain yogurt
1½ tsp. mayonnaise
½ packet instant chicken broth
1 tsp. sunflower seeds

Combine first four ingredients. In a small bowl combine yogurt, mayonnaise and broth mix. Mix well. Pour over salad and toss. Sprinkle with seeds.

 * Just as good as the fattening kind. For larger amounts multiply all ingredients by the amount of servings you want.

OLD-FASHIONED CHICKEN SALAD

2 cups stewed chicken
¼ cup french dressing
1 cup thin-sliced celery
½ cup mayonnaise, chilled

1 to 2 Tbs. capers or sweet
 pickle, optional
Crisp lettuce or romaine
2 hard-cooked eggs

Chicken for salad should always be moist. It should be stored well-covered or in its own cooking liquid until ready to use so it will not dry out. Remove skin and fat and cut chicken neatly into cubes. Measure cubes firmly packed in a cup, turn into a flat bowl and sprinkle on the French dressing so that all the pieces are well-coated with dressing. Cover tightly and place in refrigerator to marinate for 2 or 3 hours. Just before serving time, drain off any excess French dressing, add the celery and the mayonnaise and capers and toss just enough to mix well. Arrange crisp greens on salad plates. Heap a half-cup of the salad mixture on each plate. If desired, a chilled slice of pineapple may be placed on lettuce first, and the salad heaped on this. Garnish salad with a few capers or thin slices of choice pickles and slices of egg. Serve immediately with additional mayonnaise, if desired. 5 servings.

RICE SALAD

2 cups cooked rice
2 Tbs. oil
1 Tbs. vinegar
1 package frozen English peas,
  cooked

¼ cup chopped onion
1 cup chopped celery
¾ tsp. curry powder
¾ cup mayonnaise

Marinate rice, oil, and vinegar overnight. Combine peas, onions, and celery, and add to marinated rice. Stir curry powder into mayonnaise. Mix with rice mixture being careful not to crush the peas. Serves 4 to 6.

CRANBERRY CHERRY SALAD

1 can white cherries, halved and
  pitted
1 cup reserved cherry juice
1 small package cherry gelatin
¼ cup chopped pecans

1 can whole cranberry sauce
2 Tbs. lemon juice
3 ounces cream cheese,
  chopped in small pieces

Heat cherry juice to boiling. Add gelatin and stir until dissolved. Blend in cranberry sauce and lemon juice. Chill until partly set. Fold in cherries. Cream cheese and pecans. Pour into mold, Chill.

BING SHERRY SALAD

1 can pitted bing cherries,
  drained
1½ cups sherry
1 cup sugar

2 cups orange juice
3 Tbs. unflavored gelatin
¾ cup chopped pecans
Whipped topping or mayonnaise
  to garnish

Mix cherry juice with 1½ cups of the orange juice, sherry, and sugar; bring to a boil. Soak gelatin in remaining ½ cup orange juice. Dissolve in hot fruit syrup. Chill mixture until partially set; pour into a mold or a 9 inch square pan. Stir in cherries and nuts and distribute evenly. When congealed, top with whipped topping or mayonnaise. Serves 12.

SPINACH SALAD

6 slices bacon, cooked and
  crumbled
1 Tbs. bacon drippings
4 Tbs. olive oil
3 Tbs. red wine vinegar
1 pound fresh spinach

2 hard cooked eggs, sliced
1 small onion, cut into rings
1 cup fresh mushrooms, sliced
Salt and pepper to taste

In a small jar or bowl, combine bacon drippings, olive oil and vinegar. Mix well and set aside. Place spinach, eggs, onion, mushrooms and bacon in a small bowl. Season with salt and pepper. Sprinkle with dressing and toss.

SPINACH AND MANDARIN ORANGE SALAD

1½ lbs. fresh spinach, cut in
  bite size pieces
1 can mandarin oranges,
  drained

10 bacon slices, cooked and
  crumbled
1 can pineapple chunks,
  drained

Combine all ingredients and toss with honey and mustard dressing or any fruit salad dressing.

DINNER SALAD

¾ cup chopped bacon cracklins
2 tsp. lemon juice
1 tsp. salt
4 tsp. green pepper, chopped
2 tsp. parsley

½ tsp. mustard
½ cup mayonnaise
2 cups shredded cabbage
4 tsp. chopped onion

Place chopped bacon in pan and fry to golden color. Add lemon juice, salt and mustard. Stir well and mix with mayonnaise. Toss finely chopped vegetables lightly together with mixed dressing. Serve in a large bowl.

CRANBERRY SALAD

1 lb. bright red cranberries
Sugar to taste
1 cup oranges, cut small
¼ cup nuts

1 pint water
1 cup sliced bananas
1 cup diced pineapple

Cook the cranberries with the water. When tender, rub through sieve and add sugar to taste. When ready to serve add the other ingredients, which must be prepared when wanted or the bananas will be soft. It does not congeal, nor is it supposed to.

SPAGHETTI SALAD

¾ cup mayonnaise
2 cloves garlic, crushed
¼ cup chopped onion
½ teaspoon cumin seeds, crushed
Salt to taste
¼ cup diced celery

½ cup green olives, chopped
1 can tomatoes and green chilies, drained and chopped
1 pkg. spaghetti, cooked and rinsed.

Mix mayonnaise, garlic, onion, cumin seeds, salt and tomatoes. Add a little juice if too thick. Toss with spaghetti, celery, and olives until well coated. Serves 8 to 10.

STRAWBERRY SALAD

2 pkg. strawberry jello
1 pkg. frozen strawberries
1 mashed banana
1 can crushed pineapple

1 cup hot water
2 cups cold water
1 pkg. sour cream

Dissolve jello. Pour half ingredients into dish and let congeal. Spread 1 pkg. sour cream then add remaining ingredients. Chill thoroughly.

FRUIT SALAD

1 cantaloupe
¼ pineapple diced
4 celery ribs, thinly sliced
Artificial sweetner to taste
   (liquid)
Few drops vanilla extract

Trim rind from cantaloupe and dice. Combine with pineapple and celery. Add sweetner and vanilla. Chill. Serves 3.

STRAWBERRY AND NUT FRUIT SALAD

2 small packages strawberry
   gelatin
1 cup boiling water
2 packages frozen sliced
   strawberries thawed, reserve
   juice
1 can crushed pineapple,
   drained

3 medium bananas, mashed
1 cup coarsely chopped walnuts
1 pint sour cream

Combine gelatin with boiling water, stirring until dissolved. Fold in strawberries, pineapple, bananas and nuts. Pour one half of the strawberry mixture into an oblong baking dish. Refrigerate until firm. About 1½ hours later, evenly spread top with sour cream. Gently spoon on remainder of strawberry mixture. Cut into squares and serve on a bed of lettuce.

JELLO SALAD

⅓ cup sugar
1 envelope Knox unflavored
  gelatin
½ cup cold water
1 pkg. Philadelphia cream
  cheese

1 can crushed pineapple
1 large box Dream Whip
1 pkg. pecans

Dissolve sugar in the pineapple, bring to a boil. Dissolve one envelope of unflavored gelatin in ½ cup cold water and add to pineapple. Pour in oblong dish or pan. Put in refrigerator to set. Dissolve 2 boxes strawberry jello in 3 cups hot water. Let set until mushy or whip with a spoon. Whip one box dream whip according to directions. Then add one pkg. Philadelphia cream cheese to Dream Whip. Whip until smooth. Spread over set pineapple. Chop nuts and sprinkle over top. Then spread jello over top. Put in refrigerator to set.

HOLLY-WREATH HOLIDAY SALAD

2 small boxes or one large box lime-flavored gelatin
1 pint sour cream
1 No. 2 can crushed pineaple
1 medium jar (8 oz.) of maraschino cherries

Mix gelatin with one cup boiling water. Beat with mixer or egg beater until frothy. Fold in sour ceam. Mix well. Add cherries and pineapple. Pour in 1½ or 2 quart mold and chill until firm.

   *This colorful congealed salad is seasonal, scrumptious and so easy to make.

MACARONI SALAD

1 eight oz. pkg. elbow macaroni
½ cup fine chopped onion
½ cup fine chopped celery
¼ cup chopped sweet pickle
1 cup tomatoes (fresh), half the tomato and then quarter (you may substitute boiled eggs.)
1 dash salt
½ cup salad dressing or mayonnaise

Boil macaroni until tender (not mushy) with dash of salt. Drain water, add onions and celery with hot macaroni. Cool then add other ingredients. Serves approximately 8.

VEGETABLE SALAD

1 can French cut beans, drained
1 can small peas, drained
4 pieces celery, diced fine
1 green pepper, diced fine
1 onion, diced fine
1½ cups sugar
½ cup salad oil
1 tsp. salt

Pour liquid over all ingredients and refrigerate. Drain before serving. Can be made several days ahead.

145

SOUTHERN VEGETABLE CRUNCH SALAD

2 cups broccoli flowerets
2 cups cauliflowerets
1 cup sliced celery
1 cup cherry tomatoes, halved
1 cup sliced zucchini

¾ cup sliced green onions
½ cup ripe olives, sliced
¼ cup sliced carrots
1 cup Wishbone dressing
1 jar bacon bits

In large bowl, combine all ingredients except bacon. Cover all marinate in refrigerator, turning occasionally, 4 hours or overnight. Just before serving, toss with bacon. Serves 8.

HAM & RICE SALAD

1 8 oz. carton sour cream
½ cup mayonnaise
1 package Hidden Valley Ranch
  Dressing Mix
2 cups cooked and cubed ham
2 cups parboiled rice, cooked
  and cooled
2 raw carrots, grated

1 cup cooked English peas,
  drained
½ cup finely chopped celery
½ cup finely chopped green
  pepper
¼ cup sliced mushrooms
¼ tsp. garlic salt
½ tsp. salt
⅛ tsp. pepper

Mix sour cream, mayonnaise and salad dressing mix. Combine remaining ingredients in large bowl and fold in sour cream dressing. Chill. Yield: 8 to 10 servings.

COKE SALAD

1 can pitted, dark, sweet cherries
1 can crushed pineapple
1 pkg. grape gelatin
1 pkg. strawberry gelatin
1 pkg. 8 oz. cream cheese
1 cup coca-cola
1 cup chopped nuts

Pour juice of pineapple and cherries into pan and boil. Add gelatin and allow to melt. Chill until slightly thick; add softened cream cheese, nuts, pineapple and cherries. Pour coke into mixture and gel in refrigerator. Serves 10 to 12.

ORANGE PINEAPPLE SALAD

1 pkg. orange-pineapple jello
1 small can crushed pineapple
1 can small orange slices
1 cup marshmallows
1 small package cream cheese

Drain fruit and measure to make one cup, add water if necessary. Bring liquid to a boil and add marshmallows and cream cheese. Cook mixture over low heat until marshmallows and cheese are melted. Combine mixture with jello, stir until jello is dissolved. Add 1 cup cold water and fruit. Stir well. Place in refrigerator until molded.

SOUTHERN STYLE SWEET-SOUR COLESLAW

2 qts. moderately finely grated
  cabbage
¼ cup finely grated onion
2 med. carrots, peeled and
  grated fine
2 Tbs. minced sweet green
  pepper

½ cup relishtype sandwich
  spread
½ cup sour cream
2 Tbs. vinegar
1 tsp. salt
⅛ tsp. pepper

Place all ingredients in a large bowl and toss thoroughly to mix. Cover and chill 2-3 hours. Stir well and serve. Makes 6 to 8 servings.

EGG SALAD

12 hard cooked eggs, chilled,
  peeled and chopped
1 Tbs. minced onion
¼ cup minced celery
1 Tbs. parsley

1 tsp. salt
⅛ tsp. pepper
¼-⅓ cup mayonnaise or salad
  dressing
3-4 Tbs. milk

Mix all ingredients together, adding just enough mayonnaise and milk to give salad a good consistency. Cover and chill several hours. Stir well and use as a main course salad in lettuce cups or hollowed out tomatoes, or as a sandwich spread. Makes enough for 4 salads.

KIDNEY BEAN SALAD

1 No. 2 can kidney beans (2¼ cups)
¾ cup chopped sweet pickle
2 hard-cooked eggs, sliced

½ cup sliced celery
¾ cup mayonnaise or cooked salad dressing, or
½ cup cream and ¼ cup pickle vinegar

Combine ingredients in order given, chill thoroughly. Serve on lettuce.

DANISH FRUIT AND VEGETABLE SALAD

Yield: 4 servings
2 carrots
2 large unpeeled apples
2 stalks celery
Lettuce
Salt and pepper

½ can mandarin oranges, drained
½ cup plain yogurt
½ cup chopped pineapple
½ tsp. grated orange peel

Prepare and slice or dice all vegetables and fruits where needed. Mix with yogurt and orange peel, season and serve on a bed of lettuce.

SALMAGUNDI SALAD

1 cup boiled potatoes, diced
2 cups cooked meat, diced
½ cup cooked peas

2 pimientos, chopped
½ cup celery, diced
2 sweet pickles, finely diced
½ cup mayonnaise

Toss ingredients together lightly. Meat may be ham, tongue, pork, veal, beef, or combination. Salt to suit taste. Arrange on lettuce. Garnish with additional mayonnaise and sections of hard-cooked egg, if desired.

PARTY SALAD

2 oranges
2 bananas
4 slices canned pineapple
4 halves canned peaches
¼ cup raisins or green grapes

1 cup quartered marshmallows
½ cup mayonnaise
1 cup whipped cream (Use ½
    for garnish)
2 Tbs. sugar
Maraschino cherries (optional)

Peel oranges and bananas, cut fruit in pieces and mix together. Add raisins or green grapes and marshmallows, cut in quarters with damp scissors. Whip cream with sugar. Add half the whipped cream to mayonnaise and fold into salad mixture. Let stand several hours in refrigerator or cold place before serving. Will keep well if made day before using. Top each serving with spoonful of whipped cream and maraschino cherry, if desired.

For Frozen Fruit Salad, omit marshmallows, add ½ cup juice from canned fruit and freeze in mechanical refrigerator or mold, packed in ice and salt.

CARDINAL SALAD

1 pkg. lemon gelatin
1 cup hot water
¾ cup beet juice
3 Tbs. vinegar
½ tsp. salt

2 tsps. lemon juice or grated
    onion
1 Tbs. horseradish
¾ cup celery, diced
1 cup cooked beets, diced

Dissolve gelatin in hot water. Add beet juice, vinegar, salt, onion juice, and horseradish. Chill. When slightly thickened, fold in celery and beets. Turn into mold. Chill until firm. Unmold on crisp lettuce. Garnish with mayonnaise. Amount: 8 servings.

GOLDEN GLOW SALAD

1 pkg. orange gelatin
1 cup hot water
1 cup canned pineapple juice
1 Tbs. vinegar

½ tsp. salt
1 cup canned pineapple, diced
  and drained
1 cup grated raw carrot

Dissolve gelatin in hot water. Add pineapple juice, vinegar and salt. Chill. When slightly thickened, add pineapple and carrot. Turn into individual molds. Chill until firm. Unmold on crisp lettuce. Garnish with mayonnaise. Amount: 8 servings.

PEACH CUP SALAD

12 halves canned or fresh ripe
  peaches, peeled
½ cup diced celery

¼ cup choped nuts
¼ cup seeded raisins
2 or 3 Tbs. apple butter

On bed of lettuce arrange two peach halves for each serving. Fill centers with mixture made by combining celery, nuts, raisins and apple butter. Garnish with mayonnaise, or half mayonnaise and whipped cream.

PINEAPPLE-STRAWBERRY SALAD

1 pt. strawberries
½ Tbs. lemon juice
¾ cup diced pineapple (sweeten
  if fresh)

⅓ cup mayonnaise
⅓ cup whipped cream

Sprinkle berries with lemon juice and sugar. Add well-drained pineapple. Arrnge on lettuce and top with dressing of mayonnaise and whipped cream. Sprinkle with chopped nut meats, if desired. Amount: 6 servings.

WHITE SAUCE, OR CREAM SAUCE

2 Tbs. butter
1½ Tbs. flour
¼ tsp. salt

⅛ tsp. paprika
1 cup of milk

Melt butter and add flour. Stir until ingredients are smooth, add seasoning and gradually the milk. Use a wire whisk to stir sauce and boil it for 2 minutes. This will make a thin sauce. For a heavier sauce, increase flour to 2 or 3 tbsps. and use an equal amount of butter. Cream may be substituted for milk. Nutmeg, lemon juice, etc., may be added for flavor. Amount: about 1 cup sauce.
Variations:
1. Use part cream and part vegetable or meat stock instead of milk.
2. When sauce is cooked (either with milk or stock) remove from fire, beat in 1 or 2 egg yolks. Return sauce to fire and stir over low heat for 1 or 2 minutes to permit egg to cook, but do not let sauce boil again. Season egg sauce with 2 tbsp. of lemon juice.
3. Minced onion, celery or green pepper may be added to sauce, also chopped hard-cooked eggs, minced olives or pickles, tarragon or parsley.
4. Sauce may be seasoned with prepared or dry mustard, curry powder, Worcestershire sauce, soy sauce, horseradish, sherry or white wine, etc. Do not cook sauce after sherry or wine is added.

ONION BUTTER

Serve over potatoes, green beans, carrots, green peas, fish, or spread on bread.

⅓ cup melted butter or
    margarine
1 tsp. minced onion

Dash of cayenne pepper
1 tsp. lemon juice
⅛ tsp. herb seasonings

Combine all ingredients. Mix well, Cover and let stand about 30 minutes for flavors to blend. May be refrigerated and reheated if desired. Chill for a spread. Makes about ⅓ cup.

CREAMED SALAD DRESSING

(For Fruit Salads)

½ tsp. dry mustard
½ tsp. salt
⅛ tsp. paprika

2 egg yolks
¼ cup vinegar
¼ cup butter
⅓ cup whipped cream

Add sifted dry ingredients to beaten egg yolks, add vinegar and butter. Cook in double boiler, stir until smooth and creamy. Remove from heat when cool add stiffly beaten egg whites, beat over hot water. Chill. Before using, add cream and paprika.

RAISIN SAUCE

½ cup raisins
2 cups water
1¼ Tbs. cornstarch
⅛ tsp. salt

⅛ tsp. pepper
1 tsp. dry mustard
⅓ cup brown sugar
¼ cup vinegar or cider

Add raisins to water and simmer 10 minutes. Combine cornstarch, mustard, salt, pepper, and brown sugar; add vinegar and blend well. Add cornstarch mixture to raisins and water; cook about 3 minutes longer. Amount: About 2 cups.

CHEESE SAUCE

Soft cheese may be melted in double boiler and thinned with a little milk, or grated cheese may be added to white sauce and stirred over low heat until melted. Use ¾ cup or less diced or grated cheese. Season sauce with red pepper and mustard (optional).

HOLLANDAISE SAUCE

¾ cup butter
2 Tbs. lemon juice
3 egg yolks, beaten
Few grains salt

⅛ tsp. Paprika

Melt one third of butter in top of double boiler, stir in lemon juice and beaten egg yolks. Place over hot water, cook slowly, beat constantly using wire whisk. Add one half of remaining butter, beat, add rest of butter. Beat until mixture thickens. Remove from water. Add seasoning. If sauce should separate, add hot water by teaspoon and use rotary beater.

SAUCE FOR VEGETABLES

2 egg yolks
1½ tsp. butter
1 tsp. vinegar

⅓ pint cream
1 Tbs. lemon juice
Pepper

Add melted butter to beaten yolks and cream. Cook in double boiler until mixture begins to thicken. Remove from heat, add vinegar and lemon juice, beat.

CREAM SAUCE

2 Tbs. butter
1½ Tbs. flour

1 cup cream
¼ tsp. salt
Paprika

Melt butter, stir in flour and seasoning. Slowly stir in cream, bring to boiling point, boil 2 minutes. Paprika. ¼ tsp. dry mustard may be blended with flour.

TOMATO SAUCE

2 cups or more canned
   tomatoes, or fresh tomatoes
   stewed
1 slice of onion
2 ribs of celery with leaves
   (optional)
Parsley (optional)
1 carrot (optional)

½ green pepper (optional)
3 Tbs. butter
3 Tbs. flour
¼ tsp. salt
⅛ tsp. pepper
¼ tsp. sugar

Cook vegetables for 15 minutes. Strain and season. Melt butter, add flour and when smooth, add strained stock gradually. Stir sauce until smooth and thick. If vegetables other than tomatoes are cut in small pieces, tied in a bag and cooked with tomatoes, they may be taken from bag and replaced in sauce just before it is removed from fire.

BROWN SAUCE

2 Tbs. butter
½ slice onion
2 Tbs. flour

1 cup brown stock
salt
⅛ tsp. paprika or pepper

One cup boiling water and 1 beef cube may be substituted for stock. Melt butter and brown onion in it. Remove onion. Add flour and seasoning and permit them to brown. Add stock gradually, bring sauce to the boiling point and boil for 2 minutes. This sauce is good for left-over meat dishes. Chopped mushrooms, pickles or olives may be added. Amount: 1 cup.

POPPY SEED DRESSING

¾ cup sugar
1 tsp. dry mustard
1 tsp. salt
⅓ cup cider vinegar

1 Tbs. onion juice
1 cup cooking oil
1½ Tbs. poppy seed

Combine sugar, mustard, salt, vinegar, and onion juice in medium bowl. Using mixer or rotary beater, gradually beat in oil until mixture is thick and smooth. Fold in poppy seed. Store in refrigerator until ready to use. Makes about 2 cups.

DRESSING FOR HEAD LETTUCE

1 cup cooking oil
½ cup orange juice
2 Tbs. lemon juice
1 tsp. salt
8 stuffed green olives, finely
  chopped

½ tsp. paprika
2 tsp. onion juice
2 tsp. Worcestershire sauce
½ tsp. dry mustard
2 hard-cooked eggs, chopped

Combine all ingredients. Mix well. Chill. Shake vigorously before serving. Makes about 2 cups dressing.

Canned Goods

PICKLED PEACHES

6 lbs. sugar
3 cups 5% cider vinegar
2½ cups water
1 tsp. whole cloves

1 tsp. cassia buds
2 four inch sticks cinnamon
10 lbs. choice flavorful
   freestone peaches

Choose fully ripe well-developed peaches without bruises or soft spots. Put ⅓ of the sugar, vinegar and water into a 3 or 4-quart preserving kettle and heat to simmering, stirring occasionally until sugar dissolves. Add ⅓ the spices. Have ready enough boiling water to dip ⅙ of peaches in just long enough to cause skins to slip. Be careful not to leave peaches in long enough to soften the flesh and make it impossible to skin peaches smoothly. Drop skinned peaches into syrup; simmer until tender, about 6 minutes. Dip out peaches with slotted spoon into two jars. This fills jars only half full. Cover jars, let stand on back of stove. Now add another sixth of prepared peaches to syrup and again cook until tender. Finish filling the two jars with fruit and add syrup to fill up to ¼-inch of jar top. The amount of syrup should just fill the jars. Seal immediately with either glass lids or metal lids lined with enamel. Proceed in same manner with remaining peaches. Add any pickling syrup left from one batch to next. Cool pickles. Store in cool place. 6 quarts.

*The way to a man's heart...
is through his stomach.*

HOT PICKLED BEETS

Beets
2 Tbs. sugar
3 Tbs. vinegar

Paprika
Butter
Little Flour
4 Tbs. cream

Boil and peel beets, cut in pieces, add salt, sugar, vinegar and paprika, blend with butter, add little flour. Simmer. Serve hot.

TOMATO PRESERVES

1 lb. yellow tomatoes
1 lb. sugar

2 ounces ginger
2 lemons

Pour boiling water over tomatoes. Remove skin, add sugar, let stand overnight. In morning pour off syrup, boil syrup until quite thick, skim. Add tomatoes, ginger, cut in small pieces and lemon sliced very thin. Boil until tomatoes are clear.

YELLOW TOMATO PRESERVES

3 quarts yellow pear tomatoes,
   4¾ lbs
5½ cups sugar

2 pieces crushed ginger root,
   each 1-inch long
8 lemons, sliced paper thin

Wash tomatoes, hold in boiling water ½ minute or until the skin loosens easily. Cool and slip off skins. Place in bowl in alternate layers with sugar and let stand overnight or at least 4 hours. Turn the tomatoes gently once in the juice which has formed. Drain off juice, about 3½ cups and boil until the syrup gives the jelly test. Simmer lemon slices in one cup of water for 5 minutes or until soft. Add lemon slices and water, ginger root and tomatoes to syrup and simmer until tomatoes are transparent at least 15 minutes. Pour into hot sterilized jars. Seal. Makes 3½ pints.

MILLION DOLLAR PICKLES

4 qt. sliced cucumbers
8 to 10 onions, small sliced

2 green peppers, remove seeds,
  cut
1 cup salt

Place in stone jar, cover with water. Let stand overnight. In the morning drain. Then prepare syrup given below.

SYRUP:

1 qt. vinegar cider
4 cups sugar
1 tsp. celery seed

1 tsp. turmeric powder
2 Tbs. white mustard seed
Mixed spices

Blend ingredients, let mixture come to boil and add the cucumbers. Cook until tender, about 20 minutes. Pack at once in hot sterilized jars. Add 1 to 2 red peppers if you wish, remove the seeds.

MUSTARD PICKLES

2 qts. cucumbers, small
1 qt. white onions, small
4 green peppers

2 heads cauliflower
1 qt. green tomatoes
4 stalks celery

DRESSING:

½ cup dry mustard
½ cup flour
2 level tsp. turmeric powder
1 cup water

1½ cups sugar
¼ tsp. paprika
3 cups cider vinegar

Soak vegetables in brine made of 1 cup salt to 3 quarts water and cover. Let stand 24 hours. Drain vegetables. Add a fresh brine, cook vegetables until tender, but not soft. Drain. Blend mixture for dressing, cook in pan 30 minutes. Add to vegetables, bring to boil. Seal hot.

WATERMELON PICKLES

7 lbs. prepared watermelon rind	1 cup water
2¼ quarts water	1 Tbs. whole cloves
⅓ cup salt	1 stick cinnamon
6½ cups sugar	2 tsp. cassia buds
2 cups vinegar	1 lemon, sliced paper thin

Prepare rind by cutting into 1½-inch strips. Slice away pink flesh and pare off green rind. Now cut strips neatly into diamonds, squares or triangles. Add salt to water, stir to dissolve, pour over the rind placed in an enamelware or glass bowl. Brine should barely cover rind. Cover bowl and let stand overnight. Next morning rinse in 3 or 4 changes of cold water. Drain, turn into 4-quart aluminum or enamelware preserving kettle. Barely cover rind with cold water, cover kettle, heat to boiling, reduce heat and simmer until rind is tender when pricked with a fork, from 40 to 60 minutes, time depending on thickness of rind. Drain in a colander. Make syrup in same kettle by heating 5½ cups of sugar, vinegar and 1 cup water to boiling; add drained hot rind, heat to boiling, reduce heat, and simmer uncovered about 1 hour until rind begins to appear transparent. Add spices last 10 minutes of cooking. Remove from heat, cover and let stand overnight. Drain off syrup, add lemon slices and remaining cup sugar. Reheat to boiling, and again pour syrup over rind. Cover, let stand again overnight. Drain off syrup, heat to boiling. Pour over rind now packed in hot sterilized jars. Seal with glass or enamel-lined lids. Process 10 minutes in boiling water bath. Chill before serving, or reheat in syrup for delicious hot relish. 6 pints.

TOMATO PICKLE

1 gallon chopped ripe tomatoes
1 quart chopped onions
1 gallon chopped cabbage
2 red sweet peppers or bell
  pepper
3 tsp. tumeric

1 can pimientos
1 cup salt
6 cups sugar
½ gallon vinegar
3 tsp. ginger
3 tsp. powdered mustard
1 bag pickling spices

Sprinkle salt over vegetables and mix well; let stand 3 to 4 hours. Drain thoroughly. Press to remove liquid. Place in a large saucepan; add sugar, vinegar, ginger, mustard, tumeric and bag of pickling spices. Cook for 30 minutes. Process in boiling water bath for 10 minutes. Start counting processing time as soon as the jars are in the water.

CHILLED SWEET AND SOUR RED ONIONS

1 pound red onions
1 Tbs. soy sauce
2 Tbs. wine vinegar
2 Tbs. sugar

2 Tbs. oil
1 large clove garlic, mashed
¼ tsp. salt

Peel and cut each onion into 1 inch wide wedges. Separate the layers. Combine soy sauce, wine vinegar, and sugar in a small bowl and stir until sugar dissolves. Heat wok until hot. Add the oil and swirl and heat for 30 seconds. Toss in garlic and press into the oil. Toss in the onions and stir rapidly in turning motion for about 40 seconds, until they glisten with oil. Sprinkle in the salt and stir briskly. Splash in the sauce and as it sizzles, stir a few times. Let cool and serve.

SWEET PICKLE RELISH

4 c. chopped cucumbers	3½ c. sugar
2 c. chopped onions	2 c. cider vinegar
1 chopped green pepper	1 Tbs. celery seed
1 chopped sweet red pepper	1 Tbs. mustard seed
	¼ c. canning salt

Combine cucumbers, onions, green and red peppers in a large bowl; sprinkle with salt and cover with cold water. Let stand 2 hours. Prepare home canning jars and lids according to manufacturer's instructions. Drain vegetables thoroughly; press out liquid. Combine sugar, vinegar, celery seed and mustard seed in a large saucepot, bring to a boil. Add drained vegeables. Simmer 10 minutes. Carefully pack hot relish into hot jars, leaving ¼ inch head space. Adjust cap. Process 10 minutes in boiling water bath canner.

Teresa Meyer
Antioch, Tenn.

PEAR RELISH

1 peck hard pears	1 Tbs. uniodized salt
6 large onions	5 cups vinegar
6 red sweet peppers	1 Tbs. ground allspice
6 green sweet peppers	1 Tbs. mustard seed
6 hot red peppers	1 Tbs. celery seed
3 cups sugar	

Wash, peel, and core pears. Remove seeds and stems from red, green, and hot peppers. Put through food grinder or chop fine in food processor fitted with steel blade the pears, onions, red, green, and hot peppers. In a large enamel or stainless pot, mix ground vegetables with sugar, salt, vinegar, allspice, mustard seed, and celery seed. Let stand at least 8 hours or overnight. Bring to a boil and cook, stirring occasionally, for about 10 minutes. Pack in hot sterilized jars leaving ¼ inch head space. Seal. Process in boiling water bath (212 degrees F.) for 20 minutes. Makes 10-12 pints.

PICKLED YELLOW SQUASH

8 cups yellow squash	2 cups white vinegar
2 cups onions	3 cups sugar
4 bell peppers	2 tsp. mustard seed
¼-½ cup uniodized salt	2 tsp. celery seed

Cut squash, onions, peppers into circles and mix with salt. Place plate on top to cover and weight it down for 1 hour. (Salt makes squash release liquid.) Drain in colander (do not rinse) and pat dry with paper towel. Mix in large kettle the vinegar, sugar, mustard seed, and celery seed. Boil and add squash, onions, and bell pepper. Then pour into sterile jars and seal. Process in water bath canner (212 degrees F.) for 10 minutes. Yield: 8 pints.

SQUASH PICKLES

½ tsp. dry mustard	2 cups vinegar
2 tsp. celery seed	3 green peppers
2 tsp. mustard seed	2 cups sliced onions
2½ cups sugar	8 cups sliced squash

Layer squash, onions and green peppers. Sprinkle with salt and let stand one hour. Drain off excess liquid. Heat other ingredients and pour over vegetables. Bring to a boil. Spoon into sterilized jars. Cool. Chill at least 24 hours before serving.

PICKLED CUCUMBERS

¼ cup water
¾ cup white vinegar
⅓ cup sugar
¼ cup finely chopped parsley

¾ tsp. salt
⅛ tsp. pepper
4 medium cucumbers, pared
   and sliced

Early in day or day before, combine water with vinegar, sugar, parsley, salt and pepper. Add cucumbers and toss well. Refrigerate at least 3 hours covered. Serves 10.

KOSHER DILL PICKLES

20 to 25 small cucumbers
½ teaspoon powdered alum
1 clove garlic
2 Tbs. dill seed or 1 head and
   stalk fresh dill

1 red pepper
1 quart cider vinegar
1 cup salt, not iodized
3 quarts water

Wash cucumbers well; soak in cold water overnight. Next day, pack in hot, sterilized jars. To each quart jar add the above amount alum, garlic, red pepper, dill seed or head with piece of the stalk of dill. Combine vinegar, salt, and water; boil; pour over cucumbers. Process in boiling water bath for 15 minutes. Start counting the processing time as soon as the jars are put in the water. Let rest several weeks. Place in refrigerator to crisp. Yield 6 to 8 quarts.

FARM HOUSE CORN RELISH

5 or 6 fresh ears sweet corn
1½ cups chopped green
  peppers, 3 peppers
¾ cup chopped sweet red
  pepper, 1 small
1 cup pared chopped ripe
  cucumber
½ cup diced celery
1 cup chopped onion

3 cups diced red tomatoes, free
  of seeds
1½ cups vinegar
1 cup sugar
2½ Tbs. salt
1 tsp. white mustard seed
¾ tsp. turmeric
1 tsp. celery seed
¼ tsp. dry mustard

Wash and drain all vegetables. Cut corn from cob, scraping it to get all milk from kernels—there should be 1 quart. Combine all vegetables except tomatoes; turn into a colander to drain well. Then add tomatoes and remaining ingredients. Heat just to boiling, reduce heat and simmer 30 minutes or until vegetables are just tender. Pour at once into hot sterilized jars. Seal with glass or enamel-lined lids. Makes 4 pints.

GREEN TOMATO RELISH

5 cups green tomatoes
4 cups sugar
5 cups vinegar
3 cups chopped cabbage
2 cups chopped celery
Celery salt

1 cup chopped onions
1 red pepper
1 green pepper
½ cup salt
Pepper
Mixed spices

Prepare and blend all ingredients. Boil over slow heat 2 hours. Seal in sterilized jars.

GARDEN RELISH

1 med. head cauliflower cut in pieces	1 3 ounce jar pitted green olives
2 carrots, peeled and cut in strips	¾ cup wine vinegar
2 stalks celery, cut in pieces	½ cup olive or salad oil
1 green pepper, cut in strips	2 Tbs. sugar
1 4 ounce jar pimientos	1 tsp. salt
	½ tsp. dried oregano leaves
	¼ tsp. pepper

In a large skillet combine ingredients with ¼ cup water. Stirring ocassionally, bring to a boil, reduce heat and simmer, covered, 5 minutes. Cool; then refrigerate at least 24 hours. Drain well before serving. This may be used as an appetizer, a relish, or on a bed of lettuce as an antipasto.

MOUNTAIN CHUTNEY

8 good sized green tomatoes	1 lb. raisins
8 medium onions	1 c. sugar
8 tart apples	1 pt. cider vinegar
6 green peppers	3 Tbs. salt

Chop tomatoes, onions, apples, and peppers. Grind raisins. Mix and cook until apples are tender (about one hour). Seal in jars.

OLD FASHIONED CHOW CHOW

2 quarts green tomatoes,
chopped
4 quarts cabbage, shredded
6 green peppers, chopped
6 onions, chopped
1 bunch celery, chopped

2 quarts apple cider vinegar
4 Tbs. salt
1 tsp. turmeric
2 ounces mustard seed
4 cups sugar

Combine all ingredients and cook on high heat until boiling. Cut heat to simmer and cook 1 hour. Pour in hot, sterilized jars, and seal.

CRANBERRY AND NUT RELISH

1 lb. whole fresh cranberries
2½ c. sugar
1 c. marmalade

1 c. walnut pieces
juice of 1 lemon

Combine cranberries and sugar in deep baking dish. Cover with lid or foil. Bake 1 hour, stirring twice. Spread walnuts in shallow pan in same oven and toast last 12 minutes of cooking. Remove nuts and cranberries. Stir in marmalade immediately. Mix well. Add lemon juice and nuts. Stir again. Makes 1 quart.

CINNAMON CUCUMBER RINGS

Use 24 big cucumbers—
2 gallon jug or crock

Peel and remove seeds, cut into ¼ rings. Cover with 2 cups lime, 8- ½ quarts water. Let set 24 hours. Drain, rinse in clear water 2 or 3 times. Cover with clear water. Let set overnight. Drain, put in pan, cover with 1 cup vinegar, 1 Tablespoon alum, 1 small bottle red food coloring, enough water to cover. Simmer 2 hours. Drain and throw away liquid. In another pan mix 2 cup water, 2 cup vinegar, 6 cinnamon sticks, 10 cup sugar, 1- 6 oz. pkg. red-hots. Mix and boil with rings 5 minutes. Let set overnight. Pour off syrup and save. Add 1 cup sugar, 1 cup vinegar, boil 5 minutes. Pour over rings. Let set overnight. Do this 3 nights. Pour off syrup and heat it. Put rings into sterilized jars. Pour in hot syrup and seal. Chill before serving.

Nell McClung
Murfreesboro, Tenn.

FAST DILL PICKLES

24 med. cucumbers
3 cups cider vinegar
3 cups water
6 Tbs. pickling salt

2 or 3 large bunch dill
6 cloves garlic
2 tsp. mustard seed

Wash cucumbers, combine vinegar, water, salt, bring to boil. In each sterile quart jar, place a generous portion of dill, 1 clove garlic, ½ teaspoon mustard seed, pack cucumbers in jars. Add vinegar mixture, leave ½ inch space at top of jar.

Nell McClung
Murfreesboro, Tenn.

CARROT PICKLES

1 gallon small carrots (approximately 8 pounds)	1 Tbs. ground allspice
	2 sticks cinnamon
1 cup sugar	2 cups water
1½ tsp. salt	4 cups white, distilled vinegar

Wash, peel, or scrape carrots. Wash again. Cover with boiling water. Cook until tender. Combine sugar, salt, spices, water, and vinegar. Simmer for 15 minutes. Drain carrots. Pack into hot, pint jars (approximately 10). Pour boiling liquid over carrots. Top and seal. Process pint jars for 3 minutes in boiling water. Makes 10 pints.

TOMATO & ONION SWEET PICKLES

1 peck green tomatoes, sliced	4 Tbs. dry mustard
10 onions, sliced	2 Tbs. allspice
¾ cup salt	2 Tbs. cinnamon
5 qt. cider vinegar	1 Tbs. ginger
2 lbs. light brown sugar	

Add salt to peeled and cut tomatoes, let stand overnight. Drain well. Cook tomatoes and onions in 1 qt. vinegar and 2 qts. water. Let come to boil then cook slowly 20 minutes. Drain. Blend dry mustard and sugar, add vinegar to make a smooth paste, add rest of vinegar, cook entire mixture about 15 minutes. Tie spices in small bags and place in jars with pickles.

BREAD AND BUTTER PICKLES
Green Tomato or cucumber

3 lbs. green tomatoes—10 med.
  (or 3 lbs. cucumbers)
⅓ cup cooking salt
5 cups cold water
½ lb. onion, 3 med.
2 cups vinegar
Few dashes red pepper

1⅔ cup sugar
1 tsp. celery seed
2 tsp. prepared mustard
1 tsp. ginger
¼ tsp. turmeric
⅛ tsp. mace

Choose smooth, even-sized tomatoes that have acquired the whitish color which appears just before ripening, or use fresh crisp green cucumbers. Wash. Remove stem-end and blossom scar neatly from tomatoes, then cut into ¼-inch crosswise slices. Put into an enamelware or glass bowl. Sprinkle with the salt and add water. Cover and let stand 24 hours. Turn into a colander and drain 10 to 15 minutes. Now put into a preserving kettle, add onions, peeled and sliced ⅛-inch thick, then vinegar, sugar and spices. Heat to boiling, simmer only 3 or 4 minutes. Pack into hot sterilized jars with glass or enamel-lined lids. Seal. 3 pints.

SWEET STICK PICKLES

Pickling cucumbers
3¾ cups vinegar
3 Tbs. uniodized salt
4½ tsp. turmeric

3 cups sugar
4½ tsp. celery seed
¾ tsp. mustard seed

Use fresh, firm medium cucumbers. Wash and cut lenghwise into quarters. Pour boiling water over them and let stand overnight. Next morning, pack solidly into sterilized jars. Mix in an enameled, stainless, or glass kettle the salt, turmeric, sugar, celery seed, and mustard seed. Boil for 5 minutes. Pour hot mixture over cucumbers. Seal while hot. Process in a water bath canner (212 degrees F.) for 5 minutes. Makes 6 pints.

ICICLE STICKS

7 pounds large ripe (yellow) cucumbers
2½ cups builder's lime
2 gallons water
4 ounces alum
2 gallons water
2 quarts clear, distilled vinegar

1 quart water
1 Tbs. salt
2 Tbs. mixed whole pickling spices
5 pounds sugar (10 cups)
Red or green food coloring (optional)

First day: Begin the process at 7:00 p.m. Use 7 pounds of very large cucumbers that have been peeled, seeded, and cut into sticks not longer than the jars you plan to use. Soak cucumbers in lime water for 24 hours. Use 2½ cups lime in 2 gallons of water.

Second day: At 7:00 p.m., take cucumbers out of lime water. Wash in clear water several times. Soak in alum water for 12 hours. Use 4 ounces of alum in 2 gallons of water.

Third day: At 7:00 a.m., remove cucumbers from the alum water. Wash thoroughly!! Soak in clear water for 6 hours. Make a syrup of vinegar, water, salt, pickling spices (tied in a cloth bag), and sugar. Bring syrup to a boil and pour over well-drained cucumbers. Let stand 4 hours. Bring to a boil and cook until pickles are transparent or clear, about 30 minutes. Remove spices. Add as much red or green food coloring as you wish.1 (I usually use red, since I use for gifts done up in red gingham as described under 14-Day Pickles.) Pack into pint jars and process in water bath canner (212 degrees F.) for 10 minutes.

PICKLED SNAP BEANS

6 c. vinegar
1 c. water
½ c. salt
1 qt. tender green beans

2 pods hot pepper
2 buttons garlic
1 Tbs. dill seed

Place snapped tender green beans, pepper, garlic and dill seed in pint jars. Heat ingredients and pour over beans. Pour off. *Repeat* heating solution and pour over second time. Seal.

RED CINNAMON PICKLES

7 pounds large yellow
  cucumbers
1 cup lime
3 cups white vinegar, divided
1 (2-ounce) bottle red food
  color

1 Tbs. alum
6½ cups sugar
8 sticks cinnamon
1 large package red cinnamon
  candies

Peel and seed cucumbers. Soak 24 hours in 1 cup lime to 1 gallon water. Drain, rinse, and soak in ice water for 3 hours. Mix 1 cup vinegar, food color and alum with enough water to cover cucumbers. Pour mixture over cucumbers in pot and simmer 2 hours. Pour off liquid. In another pot, boil 2 cups vinegar, 2 cups water, sugar, cinnamon sticks and candy until candy melts. Pour over cucumbers. Let stand 24 hours. Pour off liquid into another pot and bring to boiling again. Meanwhile, pack cucumbers in warm jars. Pour syrup over cucumbers in jars and seal. Process in water bath canner (212 degrees F.) for 10 minutes.

SWEET PICKLE SLICES

6 pts. cucumbers (24 medium)
3¾ c. vinegar
4 c. sugar
3 Tbs. pickling salt

4 tsp. celery seed
4 tsp. tumeric
¾ tsp. mustard seed

Wash cucumbers and cut into sticks or slices. Place in crock and cover with boiling water. Let stand 12 to 14 hours. Drain and pack into clean jars. Combine vinegar, sugar, salt, celery seed, tumeric and mustard seed; boil mixture for 5 minutes. Pour boiling hot mixture over cucumbers in jars; adjust lids. Process in boiling water bath for 5 minutes. Yield: 6 pints.
  *This recipe can be made without sealing and processing and stored in the refrigerator for up to 1 year.

CANTALOUPE PICKLES

2 lbs. prepared cantaloupe
2 c. vinegar
2 c. corn syrup
4 tsp. cloves, whole

2 c. sugar
8 sticks cinnamon
1 Tbs. mustard seed

Cut melon in oblong strips. Trim all the seeds and rind off. soak melon in salt water (4 T. salt to 1 qt. water) overnight. Drain, and cook in clear water until tender. Place spices in a bag. Bring syrup and spices to a boil. Add melon and cook slowly until melon is clear. Pack into hot, sterilized jars and seal. Yield: 3 to 4 pints.

FRUIT PICKLES
Pickled Peaches or Pears

12 lbs. peeled fruit
1 qt. vinegar
6 lbs. sugar

1 Tbs. cloves
1 piece ginger root
4 or 5 sticks cinnamon

Make a syrup of vinegar and sugar and add spices, in bag to prevent darkening. Drop a few of the peaches or pears into this boiling syrup at a time. Cook until fruit can be readily pierced with a straw, let stand in covered kettle over night. Next day pack into clean jars, covering fruit to within ½ inch of top with the syrup. Process in water bath at simmering temperature (180° F.) for 20 minutes. Or fruit may again be brought to boil, packed into jars, and covered with boiling syrup to be sealed at once.

GARLIC PICKLE

1 gallon whole sour pickles
5 pounds sugar
1 (2-ounce) box peppercorns

1 (2½ ounce) box mustard seed
8 cloves garlic

Drain pickles and then slice them about ¼ inch thick. In the gallon jar, layer pickles, sugar, peppercorns, mustard seed, and garlic until all is used up. Pack the pickles down so they all will fit with the lid on. Turn jar over each day until all the sugar has melted. Then let sit in jar for 1-2 weeks. You can put in smaller containers which make great Christmas gifts.

GARLIC DILL PICKLES

Pickling cucumbers (not more
  than 5 to 6 inches long)
½ gallon white vinegar
½ gallon water
1 cup uniodized salt

1 tsp. alum
8 flowers of dill
8 cloves garlic
8 pods of red pepper (optional)

Place cucumbers in clean container with very hot water. They should be hot through and through; add more hot water if necessary. Bring to a boil the vinegar, water, salt, and alum. In each of 8 quart jars, put a dill flower, a clove of garlic, and a pod of pepper. Fill jars with hot cucumbers and pour boiling liquid over them. Seal. Process in a water bath canner for 5 minutes (212 degrees). Makes 8 quarts.

PICKLED OKRA

6 cloves garlic
6 tsp. celery seed
6 small hot red peppers
6 tsp. dill seed
3 pounds small okra

½ cup canning salt
1 cup sugar
1 quart water
1 quart white vinegar

Divide garlic, celery seed, red peppers and dill seed evenly among 6 pint jars. Pack washed okra in jars. Combine salt, sugar, water and vinegar, and bring to a boil. Fill jars and seal. Process in hot water rack for 15 minutes.

DILLED OKRA

3 pts. tender okra with stem
3 garlic cloves
3 hot peppers
3 heads dill

1 c. vinegar
3 c. water
2 Tbs. pickling salt

Pack whole tender okra in sterlized pint jars. In the center of each, place 1 garlic clove and 1 hot pepper and 1 head of dill. Bring vinegar, water and salt to a boil. Pour over okra and seal. Yield: 3 pints.

PICKLED EGGS

24 cloves
6 eggs, hard cooked
2 c. vinegar

¼ tsp. salt
½ tsp. pepper
½ tsp. ground mustard

Shell eggs and stick 4 cloves into each egg. Heat vinegar. When boiling, add the spices which have been mixed with a little cold vinegar. Place eggs in a sterilized glass jar. Pour vinegar over eggs. Cover and let stand 2 weeks before serving. Yield: 6 eggs.

CUCUMBER RELISH

1 qt. cucumbers
1 qt. onions
1 qt. cabbage
3 red peppers
1 qt. vinegar
4 cups light brown sugar

½ cup flour
3 tsp. celery seed
3 Tbs. dry mustard
3 tsp. turmeric
Salt to taste
Mixed Spices

Peel and chop first four ingredients. Mix thoroughly. Add remaining ingredients. Boil slowly for 15 minutes. Pack in sterilized pint jars while hot.

TOMATO CONSERVE

6 lbs. ripe tomatoes
1 pint vinegar
2 Tbs. cinnamon
3 lbs. sugar

½ Tbs. nutmeg
½ Tbs. cloves
½ Tbs. pepper
2 tsp. salt

Cook slowly until mixture begins to thicken, then add 1 lb. raisins and let come to a boil quickly. Pour into jars and seal.

SEVEN MINUTE STRAWBERRY PRESERVES

3 pints strawberries
⅓ cup sugar

3 Tbs. lemon juice
2½ cups sugar

Use only perfect, firm, ripe brilliant red strawberries. Wash. Hull and leave whole. Place in a 3-quart saucepan. Sift the ⅓ cup sugar over berries, add lemon juice and let stand overnight. Next morning, add the 2½ cups sugar. Heat to boiling; then boil 7 minutes, starting to count time when boiling starts. Shake pan occasionally during cooking. Pour into hot sterilized jars and seal. Makes about 1½ pints.

SPICED PEACH JAM

4 cups peaches
¼ cup lemon juice
7½ cups sugar
1 pouch Certo

2 tsp. cinnamon
1 tsp. powdered cloves
½ tsp. allspice

Peal and pit ripe peaches. Chop or mash. Put fruit in a large pan and add sugar. Mix well. Over high heat bring to a full boil and boil hard one minute. Stir constantly. Remove from heat. Immediately stir in certo. Skim off foam with metal spoon. Stir and skim for five minutes. Add spices and mix well. Put into sterilized jars and cover at once with ⅛ inch hot paraffin.

PEPPER RELISH

12 sweet red bell peppers	12 green bell peppers
3 pods hot pepper	9 medium onions
1 C. sugar	3 Tbs. mixed spices
1 Tbs. salt	2 C. vinegar

Chop peppers and onions. Cover with boiling water and let stand 5 minutes. Drain. Cover again with boiling water. Let stand 10 minutes. Drain. Add sugar, seasoning and vinegar. Cook 15 minutes. Pack into hot jars and seal at once; preferably ½ pt. jar.

SPICED FIGS

2 quarts boiling water	2 Tbs. broken cinnamon sticks
3 quarts ripe figs	2 Tbs. whole cloves
6 cups sugar	1 cup water
1 cup vinegar	

Cover figs with 2 quarts boiling water, let stand 5 minutes and drain. Mix 1 cup water with vinegar and sugar in a large saucepan and add spices in a bag; bring to a boil and add figs. Boil 10 minutes and let stand until next day. Second day, boil 10 minutes and third day boil 10 minutes. Remove spice bag. Pour into hot jars and process in a boiling water bath for 20 minutes. Makes 6 pints.

PEPPER JELLY

½ cup green and red hot peppers, finely chopped	6½ cups sugar
¾-1 cup bell pepper, finely chopped	1½ cups apple cider vinegar
	1 (6-ounce) bottle Certo
	Food color, if desired

In a large saucepan, bring peppers, sugar, and vinegar to a *hard* rolling boil. Remove pan from heat and cool for 5 minutes. Add Certo and food color. Pour into sterilized jars. (usually add all green, but at Christmas-time halve the mixture with red and green.) Makes about 12 baby food jars, or 4-5 half-pint jelly jars.

PICKLED PEACHES

5 qts. peaches, whole
1 Tbs. whole cloves
2 c. water
1 tsp. salt

3 c. honey
3 c. vinegar
2 sticks cinnamon

Scald peaches, remove skins and insert 3 or 4 whole cloves into each peach. Heat next 4 ingedients to boiling. Place a few clove studded peaches in the boiling syrup, add cinnamon and cook until peaches are tender and slightly transparent. Pack in sterile jars, cover with boiling syrup and seal. Yield: 8 pints.

BRANDIED PEACHES

9 lbs. peaches (yellow cling
   stones)
9 lbs. sugar
1 qt. water

2 sticks cinnamon
2 Tbs. whole cloves (heads
   removed)
3 pts. brandy

Select large clingstone peaches. Peel and weigh fruit. Boil sugar and water with spices tied in a bag until clear. Drop in peaches a few at a time and cook until tender but not soft. They must remain whole. Repeat until all peaches have been cooked. Place fruit on platter to drain. When syrup has cooled, add brandy and stir well. Place peaches in sterile jars and cover with syrup. Makes about 4 quarts.

PRESERVED BRANDIED FRUIT

10½ cups sugar
3 quarts water
½ cup orange liqueur (can
   substitute peach or any other
   you prefer)
¼ cup brandy
Crest of 3 lemons, grated
3 fresh peaches, halved and
   peeled

3 fresh nectarines, halved and
   peeled
3 fresh plums, whole but prick
   in 3 or 4 places with a skewer
3 fresh Bartlett pears, halved
   and peeled (or unpeeled, as
   you prefer)
3 small clusters seedless green
   grapes

Combine sugar and water in a large heavy kettle or Dutch oven. Stir over medium heat until sugar is dissolved and mixture comes to a full rolling boil. Boil for 5 minutes more, remove from heat. Stir in liqueur, brandy, and lemon. Arrange fruit in hot sterilized quart jars and pour hot syrup over fruit. Screw lids on jars but not too tightly. Place in hot water bath and process for 25 minutes (212 degrees F.). Count processing time when water begins to boil. Remove from water bath, tighten lids and cool away from drafts. Makes 3 quarts.

PEAR PRESERVES

1½ cups sugar
3 cups water
6 medium hard-ripe pears,
   cored, pared, and cut in
   halves or quarters (about 2
   pounds before preparing)

1½ cups sugar
1 lemon, thinly sliced

Combine 1½ cups sugar and water; cook rapidly 2 minutes. Add pears and boil gently for 15 minutes. Add remaining 1½ cups sugar and lemon, stirring until sugar dissolves. Cook rapidly until fruit is clear, about 25 minutes. Cover and let stand 12 to 24 hours in a cool place. Pack fruit into hot canning jars, leaving ¼ inch head space. Cook syrup 3 to 5 minutes, or longer if too thin. Pour boiling liquid over fruit, leaving ¼ inch head space. Adjust lids. Process half-pints 20 minutes at 190 degrees F. in simmering hot-water bath.

PEAR HONEY

1 pound ground pears (1½ cups)   1 tsp. lemon juice
¼ cup canned crushed   1½ cups sugar
  pineapple

Wash, peel, and core fruit. Put pears through a food chooper or food processor, using coarse blade. Mix pears, pineapple, lemon juice, and sugar; heat mixture, stirring thoroughly until sugar is dissolved. Boil mixture until it is thick and clear. Pack in hot canning jars. Adjust lids. Process in a boiling water bath canner (212 degrees F.)— pints and quarts, for 10 minutes.

FIG PRESERVES

1 gallon figs   2 lemons, sliced
1 cup baking soda   8 cups sugar (or 4 cups sugar
Boiling water   and 1 quart honey or corn
                       syrup)

Select only perfect figs which are ripe but not soft. They may be peeled or not, according to taste. If not peeled, sprinkle baking soda over figs, cover in boiling water, let stand 5 minutes, and drain. Place figs and sugar in alternate layers in an enamel or aluminum boiler. Let stand overnight. Next morning, lift the figs out of the syrup which formed during the night. Bring syrup to boil. Drop figs into boiling syrup a few at a time. Add lemons and cook until figs are tender, transparent, and amber colored (about 1-1½ hours). Pack while hot into hot canning jars. Adjust lids. Process in boiling water bath canner (212 degrees F.) for 10 minutes.

SPICED GRAPE JAM

9 lbs. blue grapes
6 lbs. sugar
1 tbsp. whole cloves

1 Tbs. broken stick cinnamon
1 Tbs. whole allspice
3 cups vinegar

Stem grapes and separate pulp from skins. Bring pulp to boiling point, cover and let simmer until soft enough for seeds to separate. Press through sieve to remove seeds and add pulp to skins. Add sugar, spices, tied in cheesecloth bag, and vinegar. Boil until thick enough to jell and seal in sterilized jars.

ORANGE MARMALADE

Sugar
6 oranges
3 lemons
1 C. lemon juice

Wash fruit and slice. Remove seeds. Cover with cold water and let stand overnight. Next morning put on stove and boil for 45 minutes. Take off and cool overnight. Next morning measure pulp and then add 1½ times as much sugar as pulp. Boil 45 minutes. Before revoming from heat, add 1 C. lemon juice. Delicious.

Helen Clark
St. Petersburg, Fla.

BURGUNDY WINE JELLY

2 cups burgundy wine
3 cups sugar

½ bottle liquid pectin

Combine wine and sugar in top of a double boiler and blend well. Heat over boiling water, stirring constantly until sugar is dissolved, about 5 minutes. Remove from heat and add pectin. Stir until well blended. Let stand a few minutes and skim off foam with a metal spoon. Pour into hot sterilized jars and seal with melted paraffin. Makes 5 6-ounce jars.

APRICOT CONSERVE

2 pounds pitted dried apricots
2 lemons, unpeeled, coarsely
   chopped and seeded

6 cups sugar
⅓ cup brandy or cognac
1 cup toasted, chopped walnuts

Rinse apricots thoroughly. Allow to soak overnight in bowl with water to cover. Drain thoroughly, reserving juice. Combine apricots and lemons in food processor or blender and chop finely—do not puree. Add enough water to reserved juice to make 4 cups liquid. Blend liquid with apricot-lemon mixture in large saucepan. Cook uncovered, over medium heat, stirring frequently, until mixture is thick and glazed, about 1 to 1¼ hours. Remove from heat and stir in brandy or cognac. Stir in toasted, chopped walnuts. Spoon into 8 sterilized half-pint jars. Process in boiling water bath 5 minutes. Makes 4 pints or 8 half-pints.

OLD TIME GREEN TOMATO MINCEMEAT

2 lbs. green tomatoes
3 lbs. tart cooking apples
1½ lbs. seedless raisins
3¾ cups light brown sugar, pkd.
3½ tsp. salt
¾ cup vinegar

¼ lb. finely chopped suet
1½ tsp. cinnamon
1 tsp. nutmeg
1 tsp. cloves
3 Tbs. lemon juice
1 tsp. grated lemon rind

Choose tomatoes that are whitish just before ripening. Wash well, remove core and blossom scar, cut into quarters and put into a chopping bowl. Chop medium fine, or if more convenient put through food chopper, using coarse blade. Turn tomatoes into a colander, press out the juice and discard. Turn tomatoes into a 5-quart kettle, add 1 cup of water, heat just to boiling, then drain off water. Again add 1 cup water, heat to boiling and again drain. Now add 1 cup of water, the apples pared thinly, quartered, cored and chopped fine, or put through the food chopper. Then add raisins, sugar, salt, vinegar and suet, mix thoroughly and cook slowly until tomatoes and apples are transparent in appearance, or about 45 minutes. Stir often to prevent scorching. Add the spices, lemon juice and rind the last five minutes of cooking. Pack in hot sterile jars. Tap jar as it is filled to exclude air bubbles. Seal with glass or enamel-lined lids. 2½ quarts.

  * This "Farm Style" mincemeat tastes a lot like the commercial product you find in the stores but every one agrees it is a lot better than the "store boughten" version.

APPLE BUTTER

20 lbs. apples
2 qts. sweet cider
4 to 5 cups sugar
½ tsp. salt

1 Tbs. fresh ground cinnamon
  and
½ tsp. ground anise, or
  preferably
3 large sticks cinnamon and 1
  tsp. anise seeds

The best time for making Apple Butter is in Sept. or Oct. when the tart fall varieties still have a lively flavor and are firm, crisp and juicy. Jonathans, Northern Sprys, Baldwins or Rhode Island Greenings are the best. Pare apples thinly, core and slice; there should be about 11 quarts of sliced apples. Add cider and cook to a sauce; if a fine-textured butter is desired, rub through a food mill. Turn sauce into a large flat pan; an ordinary enamel-ware pan is very satisfactory. Place in a moderately slow oven (325F) and cook about 1 hour or until sauce is reduced about half; stir occasionally. Add sugar and salt, stir thoroughly. Cook about 1½ hours longer until butter is thick and a rich reddish amber color. If ground spices are used, stir them in when butter is removed from the oven; if whole cinnamon and anise seeds, tie them in a loose cheesecloth bag and add them about 30 minutes before the butter is done. Mixture should be stirred frequently after sugar is added to prevent sticking. When done, remove bag of spices and turn hot butter into hot sterilized jars. Seal. Makes about 3 quarts.

PLUM CONSERVE

5 lbs. blue plums	1 lb. raisins, chopped
2 oranges	½ lb. walnuts
1 lemon	3 lbs. sugar

Wash, peel plums and remove stones. Chop orange with peel, add grated rind and juice of lemon. Add raisins and walnuts. Mix thoroughly and boil until quite thick. Seal in pint jars.

DAMSON PLUM CONSERVE

2 lbs. Damson plums	¼ cup water
½ cup raisins, chopped	3½ cups sugar
⅔ cup walnuts	

Wash plums 2 or 3 times in lukewarm water and drain; cut in halves, discard pits. There should be 1 quart pitted plums, pressed down. Wash raisins, drain; place on cutting board, and with a knife, chop through a few times. Cover walnuts with briskly boiling water; let stand 2 minutes, then drain. Break nuts in medium pieces and remove loose skin which peels over easily. Skinned nuts are more tender and delicate in flavor. Combine plums, water and sugar in a 4-quart perserving kettle. Heat to boiling, stirring constantly with a wooden spoon, cook 10 minutes or until mixture barely gives jelly test. Add raisins, cook 2 or 3 minutes, then add nuts and cook 2 minutes longer. Pour immediately into hot sterilized glasses to within ¼-inch from top. Then pour melted paraffin over conserve. Cool and cover with lids. Makes about six 8-ounce glasses.

Bread

POTATO ROLLS

4 cups plain flour
¼ cup sugar
3 eggs
1 tsp. salt
1 large white potato (boiled and mashed well)
1 cup potato juice (drained from potatoes after cooked)
2 yeast cakes (dissolved in potato juice)

Mix ingredients and form into rolls; place in a greased pan and cook at 350 degrees until brown.

Dot Casteel
Madison, Tenn.

QUICK YEAST BREAD

6¼ cups all-purpose flour
2 reg. cakes compressed or 2
    pkgs. dry granulated yeast
¼ cup lukewarm water
2 Tbs. sugar

1 cup milk, scalded
2 tsp. salt
1 cup water
1 Tbs. melted shortening

Sift flour and measure. Crumble compressed or dry granular yeast into the lukewarm water, stir in 1 tsp. of the sugar; let soften 10 minutes. Put hot milk into 4-quart mixing bowl, stir in remaining sugar and salt and the 1 cup water. Cool to lukewarm. Now stir in yeast, then beat in 3 cups of the flour until smooth, then the shortening. Add all but 2 tbsp. of remaining flour, mixing thoroughly. Turn dough onto board of pastry cloth sprinkled with remaining flour, cover with bowl and let rest 10 minutes. Knead until smooth and elastic, about 10 minutes. Cut dough in half, round up portions, cover with bowl, let rest 10 minutes. Shape into loaves. Place in 9 x 5 x 3-inch greased pans. Grease top lightly, cover and let rise in warm place until double, about 1 hour. Bake in a moderately hot oven (400F) 30 to 35 minutes. Remove from pans to cake racks to cool uncovered and out of draft. 2 loaves.

HOMEMADE BISCUITS

5 cups flour
2 cups buttermilk
¾ cup shortening
1 tsp. soda
1½ tsp. salt

3 tsp. baking powder
2 Tbs. warm water
2 Tbs. sugar
1 envelope dry yeast

Sift together dry ingredients. Dissolve yeast in warm water and add to buttermilk. Cut shortening into flour mixture. Add liquid and work lightly. Roll and cut like any biscuit. Let stand about 2 hours. Preheat oven to 400 degrees and bake biscuits for 15 minutes.

Note: Dough will keep in refrigerator for several days. Use as you need it.

MRS. FOSTER'S BISCUITS

Plain flour
2 cups buttermilk
1 heaping tsp. soda

3 heaping tsp. baking powder
1 cup cold lard

Add enough flour to make dough a light consistency. Dough should not be stiff.

*Make sure you use cold lard, not shortening, and buttermilk, then it will be a cinch to earn a reputation as the world's best biscuit maker.

Pearlie Scott
Goodlettsville, Tenn.

OATMEAL BREAD

5 cups all-purpose flour
2½ cups rolled oats
⅓ cup molasses
2 tsp. salt
2 Tbs. shortening
1¼ cups boiling water

1 reg. cake compressed or 1
  pkg. dry gran. yeast
¼ cup lukewarm water
1 tsp. sugar
1 cup milk, scalded

Sift flour and measure. Measure next 4 ingredients into 4-quart mixing bowl. Pour boiling water over mixture, stir well; let stand 1 hour. Soften yeast in lukewarm water with sugar, let stand 10 minutes. Combine yeast and lukewarm milk and stir into oatmeal mixture. Beat in about ½ the flour, then add all but ¼ cup of remaining flour and mix to a stiff dough. Turn out on board or pastry cloth sprinkled with remaining flour. Cover dough with bowl; let rest 10 minutes, then knead until smooth and elastic about 10 minutes. Place in the washed, greased bowl, turn once to bring greased side up. Cover. Let rise in a warm place until double, about 2 hours. Turn out on lightly floured board, cut in half, quickly round up and cover with bowls; let rest 10 minutes. Shape into loaves. Place in 9x5x3-inch greased loaf pans. Cover and let rise in warm place until double, about 1 hour. Bake in a moderate oven (375F) 40 to 45 minutes. Remove from pans to cake rack to cool. Two 2-lb. loaves.

BUTTERMILK DOUGHNUTS

3½ cups all-purpose flour
4 tsp. baking powder
½ tsp. salt
¼ tsp. nutmeg
1 tsp. soda
    Shortening for frying

2 eggs
1 cup sugar
½ tsp. vanilla
1 cup buttermilk
2 Tbs. melted butter

Sift flour, measure and resift 3 times with baking powder, salt, nutmeg and soda. Beat eggs, add sugar and vanilla and beat well for about 2 minutes. Stir in buttermilk and butter, then the flour mixture until dough is smooth. This dough is too soft to handle immediately, but first must be chilled in refrigerator for two or three hours. Rub flour into pastry cloth for rolling. Remove one-fourth of the chilled dough from refrigerator. Roll out quickly to a little more than ¼ inch in thickness. Cut with doughnut cutter. Remove trimmings carefully and pile on top of each other. Re-roll these, using as little flour as possible. Lift doughnuts carefully into frying basket. Lower into hot fat (360F). Turn as soon as browned on lower side and fry until brown on other side. Remove doughnuts with a fork or skewer and drain on absorbent paper.

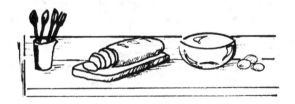

SPEEDY DOUGHNUTS

1½ cups sifted flour
2 tsp. baking powder
½ tsp. salt
⅓ cup sugar

1 egg beaten
½ cup milk
1 tsp. vanilla
1 tsp. melted butter

Sift flour once, measure and resift with salt, baking powder and sugar. Beat egg, add milk and vanilla. Blend into dry ingredients. Stir in melted cooled butter. Fry in deep hot fat. Dust with powdered sugar or roll in sugar and cinnamon. Drop off teaspoon into hot fat.

STICKY ROLLS

ROLLS:
¾ cup milk
¼ cup sugar
1 tsp. salt
¼ cup butter, softened
2 packages yeast
½ cup warm water
1 egg, beaten
3¼ cups flour

TOPPING:
¾ cup butter
1 cup brown sugar, packed
2 Tbs. sugar
1 tsp. cinnamon
1 Tbs. light corn syrup
1 Tbs. hot water
¾ cup chopped pecans

Scald milk. Combine milk and sugar, salt, add butter; stirring until butter is melted. Dissolve yeast in warm water; stir in egg; add to milk mixture. Add 2 cups flour and beat until smooth. Gradually mix in remaining flour to make a stiff batter. Cover; let rise until light and doubled in size.

Combine all topping ingredients in saucepan. Heat over low heat until well combined. Place 1 scant tablespoon topping mixture into well-greased muffin cups.

Stir down yeast batter and drop by tablespoon into prepared muffin cups. Cut completely through with scissors. Cover and let rise in warm place until light and doubled in size. Bake at 375 degrees for 10-15 minutes until golden brown. Let cool 1 minute in muffin pans before inverting onto wire racks covered with waxed paper.

   *Note: Place muffin pans on foil or cookie sheets in case topping spills over. Yields 2 to 2½ dozen rolls.

BROWN SUGAR REFRIGERATOR ROLLS

½ cup brown sugar
1 tsp. cinnamon

½ cup chopped walnuts

Prepare dough as for Ice Box Rolls.

Roll dough one fourth inch thick on floured board. Spread with soft butter, then mixture made of brown sugar, cinnamon and chopped walnuts. Roll as for chocolate roll, cut dough in 1 inch pieces. Place cut side down in buttered muffin pans, sprinkle with brown sugar. Cover, let rise until double the size, about 2 hours, bake in 425 degree hot oven 15 to 20 minutes.

PANCAKES

1½ cups flour	1 tsp. salt
2½ Tbs. sugar	1 egg beaten
3½ heaping tsp. baking powder	1½ cups milk
⅓ cups margarine, melted	

Mix dry ingredients thoroughly, add egg and milk, using only enough milk to make a thick or heavy pourable batter. Then add margarine. Yields 20 3-inch pancakes.

BUCKWHEAT CAKES-RAISED

1 qt. lukewarm water	½ ounce compressed yeast
1 tsp. salt	2 Tbs. molasses
3¼ cups buckwheat flour	1 tsp. sugar
½ cup bread flour, sifted	

Crumble yeast in 1 cup warm water, add sugar. Stir mixture with remaining warm water into flour, salt and buckwheat until a thin batter. Let rise overnight. Next morning, add molasses, bake on hot griddle. Save 1 cup of batter to use in place of fresh yeast. After two mornings add ½ tsp. of baking soda dissolved in 2 tablespoons boiling water. Beat mixture well. Continue this process each day. After three weeks, make fresh sponge.

GRANDMA'S WHITE BREAD

6 cups sifted bread flour
1 to 2 cakes yeast
2 cups milk, scald

2 level tsp. salt
6 level tsp. sugar
4 Tbs. shortening

Crumble yeast cake, dissolve in small amount of lukewarm milk. Add rest of lukewarm milk, salt and sugar. Mix well and add all of flour. When partially mixed add shortening, melted. Mix well with hands. Keep side of bowl clean. Turn out on lightly floured board and knead until dough is smooth, elastic, and bubbly at surface. Cover. Let stand in warm place 2 to 4 hours or double in bulk. Knead down, let stand 45 minutes. Knead again, let stand 15 minutes. Divide dough for loaves if more than 1 loaf is being made. Put in well-greased loaf pans. Brush top with melted butter. Allow to rise 1 to 2 hours until light and about double in bulk. Temperature 400 degrees for first 20 minutes, then reduce heat to 350 degrees or moderately hot oven. Bake another 40 minutes until well browned and shrunk from pan.

*Milk is preferred to water. Will make 2 loaves or 1 pound each or 1 pound loaf and 1 dozen rolls.

CHEERIE CHERRY BREAD

1 c. sugar
2 eggs, beaten
1½ c. flour
1½ tsp. baking powder
¼ tsp. salt

¾ c. nut meats, chopped
1 6-ounce glass red maraschino
    cherries, quartered
Juice from cherries

1. Beat sugar and eggs together.
2. Sift flour. Measure. Sift with baking powder and salt.
3. Add nuts and cherries. Alternately add flour and cherry juice
   Use part green cherries for a Christmas bread.
4. Bake for 1 hour at 350° in 1-lb. loaf pan.

BUCKWHEAT GRIDDLE CAKES

1 cup sifted flour
1 cup buckwheat flour
3 tsp. baking powder
¾ tsp. salt

3 Tbs. sugar
2 eggs, beaten
1½ cups milk
3 Tbs. butter, melted

Beat eggs, add milk, stir in sifted dry ingredients. Add shortening. Blend well. Bake in ungreased hot griddle. Serve with hot syrup and butter.

BOSTON BROWN BREAD

1 cup yellow corn meal
1 cup rye flour
1 cup graham flour
2 tsp. baking soda

1 tsp. salt
2 cups sour milk
¾ cup molasses
1 cup chopped raisins

Mix dry ingredients together and slowly mix in milk and molasses, mixed together, and raisins.
Pour batter into buttered mold. Fill full. Steam for 3½ hours, over boiling water. In smaller molds, such as baking powder cans, batter will steam in 1½ to 2 hours.

GRIDDLE CAKES

2 cups sifted flour
1½ cups sweet milk
¾ tsp. salt, sifted with flour
3 eggs, yolk and white beaten
    separately

1 Tbs. granulated sugar
3 tsp. baking powder
1 tsp. vanilla
Little Salt

Sift flour, baking powder, salt and sugar together. Beat yolks of eggs, add flour mixture alternately with milk. Just before baking add butter and fold in stiffly beaten egg whites. Use hot griddle. For thick cakes, use 1 to 1⅓ cups milk.

CHEESE POPOVERS

2 eggs
1 cup milk
1 cup sifted flour

¼ tsp. salt
¼ cup grated sharp cheddar
   cheese

Beat eggs slightly; add milk. Then add flour and salt; beat vigorously 2 minutes. Pour batter into very hot greased custard cups, filling two thirds full. Sprinkle with cheese. Bake in hot oven, 425 degrees about 40 minutes. Serve at once. Makes 6.

CHEESE STRAWS

½ tsp. salt
¼ tsp. paprika
1 egg
2 Tbs. milk
Red Pepper

1 cup grated American cheese
1 cup sifted flour
1 tsp. baking powder

Mix cheese, flour, baking powder, and seasoning. Add well beaten eggs, enough milk to make stiff dough. Roll about one eighth inch thick on floured board, cut into strips four to five inches long and one fourth inch wide. Bake about 10 minutes in hot oven.

GRANNYS BANANA NUT BREAD

½ cup butter, no substitute
¾ cup honey
¼ cup molasses
2 eggs
1 cup mashed bananas
2¼ cups whole wheat flour
½ tsp. soda

1 tsp. baking powder
½ tsp. salt
⅔ cup milk
1 tsp. vanilla
1 cup coarsely chopped pecans

Cream butter, honey, and molasses; add eggs and mix well. Stir in bananas. Sift dry ingredients together and add to creamed mixture alternating with milk. Beat only until smooth. Add vanilla and nuts. Pour into well buttered loaf pan. Bake at 350 derees for 60 to 80 minutes or until done. Yields 1 loaf.

BANANA BREAD

1¾ cups all-purpose flour
2 tsp. baking powder
¼ tsp. soda
¾ tsp. salt

⅓ cup shortening
⅔ cup sugar
2 eggs
1 cup mashed ripe banana, 2 or
3

Grease an 8 x 4 x 2½ inch loaf pan well. Sift flour, measure and resift 3 times with baking powder, soda, and salt. Cream shortening and sugar in a 3 quart mixing bowl until smooth and fluffy. Add eggs one at a time and beat well after each addition. Stir in freshly mashed bananas. Add flour in 4 portions and beat until smooth after each. Turn into prepared pan and bake in moderate oven (350F), 50 minutes or until a cake tester inserted into bread comes out clean. Remove to cake rack to cool before slicing. 1 loaf.

WAFFLES

3 eggs beaten separately
2 cups flour
½ cup melted butter

2 cups milk
3 heaping tsp. baking powder
1 tsp. salt

Beat egg yolks, add milk and flour alternately, baking powder and salt added to flour. Add beaten whites last. Heat waffle irons until very hot before cooking waffles.

HAM WAFFLES

2 cups sifted flour
1 tsp. baking soda
½ tsp. salt
1 Tbs. sugar
1 cup chopped ham

2 cups buttermilk
¼ cup melted shortening
2 egg yolks, well beaten
2 egg whites, stiffly beaten

Sift flour once, measure, add baking soda, salt and sugar, and sift again. Combine milk, shortening and egg yolks. Add to flour mixture stirring only enough to blend. Add ham. Fold in egg whites. Bake on hot waffle iron. Serve with butter and syrup. Makes six waffles.

SOUTHERN WAFFLES

1 cup boiling water
1 cup yellow corn meal
2 cups sifted flour
1 tsp. baking soda
1 tsp. salt

1 Tbs. sugar
2 cups sour milk
¼ cup shortening, melted
2 egg yolks, well beaten
2 egg whites, stiffly beaten

Pour boiling water over corn meal. Sift flour once, measure, add baking soda, salt and sugar and sift again. Combine milk, shortening and egg yolks. Add slowly to corn meal. Add flour, stirring only enough to blend. Fold in egg whites. Bake on hot waffle iron. Serve with butter and syrup. Makes 8 waffles.

ORANGE BREAD

5 Tbs. butter
½ cup sugar
1 egg
3 Tbs. orange rind, chopped
½ cup milk

½ cup orange juice
2 cups sifted flour
4 tsp. baking powder
½ tsp. salt

Cream butter, slowly add sugar, mix thoroughly. Add orange rind chopped fine, well-beaten egg. Add orange juice and milk alternately with flour, baking powder and salt which have been sifted together. Mix thoroughly, let stand 30 minutes, bake in moderate oven about 1 hour at 350 degrees.

Peggy Warren
Smyrna, Tenn.

CURRANT BUNS

2 cups sifted flour
½ tsp. baking soda
½ tsp. salt
1 Tbs. sugar
4 Tbs. shortening

¾ cup sour milk or buttermilk
¼ cup sugar
½ tsp. cinnamon
¼ cup finely cut raisins or
    currants

Sift flour once, measure, add baking soda, salt and sugar and sift again. Cut in shortening. Add enough milk to make a stiff dough. Turn onto floured board. Knead slightly. Roll into a rectangle ¼ inch thick. Spread with soft butter. Sprinkle with sugar, cinnamon and currants or raisins. Roll as a jelly roll. Cut in slices ¾ inch thick. Place cut side down on baking sheet. Bake in hot oven 475 degrees for 20 minutes. Makes 12 buns.

APRICOT NUT BREAD

1½ cups cooked dried apricots
2 Tbs. butter
½ cup sugar
2 eggs
1 cup milk

2½ cups flour sifted
4 tsp. baking powder
1 tsp. salt

Mix as for any bread dough. Fold in apricots and ½ cup chopped nuts.
Bake in greased loaf tins about 55 minutes in oven of 350 degrees.

NUT BREAD

3 cups flour
1 Tbs. butter
1 tsp. salt
1 cup sweet milk

2 eggs beaten
2 tsp. baking powder
1 cup sugar
1 cut nuts chopped fine

Mix all ingredients together in mixing bowl. Let stand in warm place
for 30 minutes before cooking. Bake in moderate oven about 30
minutes. Makes two small loaves.

RAISIN BREAD

3 cups flour
3 tsp. baking powder
1 egg beaten
½ pkg. raisins

1 tsp. salt
2 tsp. butter
1½ tsp. sugar
1½ cups milk

Sift and mix flour, salt, baking powder and sugar. Work in the beaten
egg and butter, adding milk last. Stir in raisins, turn into greased loaf
pan and bake about 50 minutes at 350 degrees.

MAMMYS' CRACKLIN' CORN BREAD

1 cup yellow corn meal
½ cup all-purpose flour
1½ tsp. baking powder
1 egg
½ cup pea-size cracklings

1 tsp. salt
2 tsp. sugar
1 cup buttermilk
¼ tsp. soda
1 Tbs. bacon fat

Heat a heavy 10-inch skillet with oven-proof handle in oven 5 to 10 minutes. While skillet heats, spoon corn meal lightly into measuring cup. Sift flour, measure and resift 3 times with corn meal and next 4 ingredients, the last time into mixing bowl. Add buttermilk, egg and cracklings, beat hard until well mixed. Remove skillet from oven, add bacon fat and tilt back-and-forth to coat inside. Pour batter into hot skillet. Bake in hot oven (450F) 25 to 30 minutes. Serve very hot.

MEMPHIS CORN FRITTERS

1 cup all-purpose flour
1 tsp. baking powder
½ tsp. salt
2 Tbs. sugar
1 egg
⅓ cup milk

1 Tbs. melted shortening
12 oz. can drained whole kernel
  corn or 1⅔ cups fresh-cut
  corn
shortening for frying

Sift flour, measure and resift with next 3 ingredients. Beat egg, add milk and shortening, then flour mixture and beat until just smooth. Fold in drained corn. Let stand 5 to 10 minutes while heating shortening. Fry at 360F. Serve hot with fried chicken, roast ham or pork, or with syrup. 20 fritters.

BREAD STICKS

¾ cup boiling water
2 Tbs. shortening
2 tsp. sugar
1 tsp. salt
¼ cup warm water

1 package active dry yeast
3½ cups sifted flour
2 egg whites, beaten to soft
   peaks
1-2 Tbs. milk

Mix boiling water, shortening, sugar and salt and cool to lukewarm. Pour warm water into a warm mixing bowl, sprinkle in yeast, and stir to dissolve. Add cooled mixture and 1½ cups flour and beat well. Mix in egg whites, then remaining flour. Knead on a lightly floured board until elastic, about 8 minutes. Shape into a ball, place in a greased bowl turning to grease all over. Cover and let rise in a warm, draftfree place until doubled in bulk, about 1 hour. Punch dough down, knead lightly 1-2 minutes, and divide in half. Roll out 1 portion into a rectangle about 15″ long, 8″ wide, and ⅓″ thick, keeping edges as straight as possible. Cut into strips 8 ″ long and ½″ wide and roll lightly with floured palms, just enough to round cut edges. Place sticks ½″ apart on greased baking sheets, repeat with remaining dough. Cover and let rise until doubled in bulk, about ½ hour. Meanwhile, preheat oven to 400 degree. Brush sticks with milk and bake with a shallow baking pan, half full of water set on rack underneath, 12-15 minutes until lightly browned. Cool on wire racks and store airtight. About 5 dozen.

SOUTHERN CORN BREAD

1½ cups white corn meal
¾ tsp. soda
1 tsp. salt

1⅓ cups buttermilk
2 eggs, separated
¼ cup melted shortening

Heat a 10-inch heavy skillet in oven 5 to 10 minutes. Spoon corn meal lightly into measuring cup, then level off. Sift with soda and salt 3 times, the last time into mixing bowl. Add buttermilk to well-beaten egg yolks and add to corn meal mixture, beat well. Add hot melted shortening and again beat well. Fold in stiffly beaten egg whites. Turn immediately into the greased hot skillet. Bake in hot oven (475) 20 to 25 minutes. Serve very hot with butter.

HUSH PUPPIES

1¾ cups white corn meal
⅓ cup all-purpose flour
3 tsp. baking powder
1 tsp. salt
Shortening for frying

2 Tbs. chopped onion
1 egg
½ cup plus 1 Tbs. buttermilk
½ cup tomato juice

Fluff up corn meal by stirring with spoon. To measure, spoon meal into cup, level off. Sift flour, measure, add it with baking powder and salt to meal. Stir thoroughly to mix. Add onion, more or less. Beat egg, stir in buttermilk and tomato juice. Turn liquid into dry ingredients and beat until well blended. Mixture should be a drop batter. Have enough shortening melted in frying kettle or deep skillet to make it 2½ inches deep. Heat to 380F. To drop batter into hot fat, dip tsp. first into hot fat, then into batter. Fry 6 to 8 hush puppies at a time. Fry to rich brown on underside, flip over with fork. When brown and done all way through, lift out with fork onto paper towel to drain. Cover with sheet of paper towel until all batter is fried. Serve very hot.

4 to 5 servings.

DEPRESSION CORN MEAL MUSH

3 cups yellow corn meal

2 quarts boiling water with salt
   to taste

Slowly add meal to boiling water, stirring constantly until well blended. Stir mixture few minutes. Cover, cool in double boiler 2 to 4 hours. Pour into oblong pan, when cold slice. Fry slowly with little shorting and butter, serve with hot maple syrup.

CORN MEAL MUFFINS

1 cup corn meal
1 cup slifted flour
4 tsp. baking powder
⅔ tsp. salt

2 Tbs. sugar
2 eggs
1 cup milk
4 Tbs. melted butter

Mix flour, corn meal, salt, baking powder, add milk, beaten eggs, butter. Use well-greased gem pans and bake in hot oven, 425 degrees about 20 minutes.

CORN MEAL GRIDDLE CAKES

¾ cup corn meal
2 Tbs. molasses
1¼ cups flour, sifted
2 Tbs. butter

1 tsp. salt
1¼ cups sweet milk
3 tsp. baking powder
2 eggs

Mix corn meal, molasses and salt. Beat eggs and add. Add milk and sifted dry ingredients. Add butter. Bake slowly on hot greased griddle. For thick cakes, use 1 to 1⅓ cups meal.

SALLY LUNN

½ cup shortening
½ cup sugar
3 eggs
2 cups sifted flour

3 tsps. baking powder
½ tsp. salt
1 cup milk

Cream shortening, add sugar gradually, beat well. Sift together flour, baking powder and salt and add alternately with milk to first mixture. Bake in greased pan in hot 425° oven, about 20 minutes. Break into 12 squares. Serve hot.

DIXIE SPOON BREAD

1 cup corn meal
2 cups sweet milk
2 eggs, yolks, whites beaten
¼ cup melted butter

2 tsp. sugar
2½ tsp. baking powder
1 tsp. salt

To boiling milk, add salt, slowly add corn meal stirring constantly. Cook to soft mush. Cool. Add egg yolks, butter, baking powder. Fold in beaten egg whites. Bake in buttered baking dish about 30 minutes in 375 degree oven. Serve hot in baking dish.

CHEESE BREAD

½ cup butter (1 stick)
8 oz. cheddar cheese
2 Tbs. milk

1 egg white
1 loaf french bread

Melt butter and cheese (chipped or grated), add milk and stir. Remove from heat and fold in beaten egg white. Cut French bread in half length wise. Then cut in 1½" pieces. Dip pieces of bread in mixture, put on greased cookie sheet and let stand several hours. Bake in 300 degree oven till brown and bubbley.

*Very good with spaghetti and a salad.

SULTANA SCONE

4 cups sifted flour
1 tsp. baking soda
2 tsp. cream of tartar
1 tsp. salt
1 cup milk

6 Tbs. sugar
½ cup shortening
½ cup raisins
1 egg well beaten

Sift flour once, measure, add baking soda, cream of tartar, salt and sugar and sift again. Cut in shortening. Add raisins. Combine egg and milk. Add to flour mixture, stirring quickly to form a stiff dough. Turn onto floured board. Knead slightly. Divide in two parts. Roll into circles 7 inches in diameter. Cut dough almost through crosswise with a sharp, floured knife. Brush with slightly beaten egg, leaving cuts untouched. Bake in hot oven 475 degrees for 20 minutes.

SHUBERT TEA BREAD

2 cups sifted flour
½ cup sugar
½ tsp. salt
½ cup butter
½ tsp. baking soda

¼ tsp. nutmeg
¼ tsp. cinnamon
¼ tsp. ginger
1 egg well beaten
⅔ cup sour milk

Sift flour once, measure, add sugar and salt and sift again. Cut in butter until mixture resembles coarse crumbs. Reserve 1 cup crumbs. To remainder add baking soda and spices. Mix well. Combine egg and sour milk; add and stir only until blended. Sprinkle half of crumbs in bottom of shallow, greased pan. Turn batter on them and sprinkle remaining crumbs on top of batter. Bake in moderate oven 20 to 25 minutes. Serve warm.

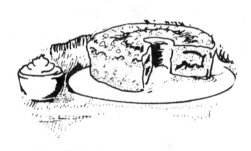

PUMPKIN BREAD

Cream together: 3 cups sugar
                 1 cup
                 margarine

ADD: 3 eggs, beat well, add 1 can pumpkin. Sift together and add to first mixture 3 cups flour, 1 tsp. soda, ¼ tsp. salt, ½ tsp. baking powder, 1 tsp. cinnamon, 1 tsp. cloves, 1 tsp. nutmeg and 1 tsp. vanilla. Bake in 2 large or 4 small loaf pans at 350 degrees; 30 minutes for large and 45 minutes for small pans.

OLD TIMERS ROLLS

½ cup lukewarm water
1 tsp. sugar
1 package dry yeast
2 cups milk
½ cup sugar

1 tsp. salt
½ cup shortening
1 egg
6 to 6½ cups flour, sifted
½ cup shortening, melted

Put yeast and 1 teaspoon sugar in water and let dissolve. This will also serve to prove the yeast. If it does not foam in the water, pour it out and start over. Scald the milk and allow it to cool to room temperature. Cream ½ sugar, salt and ½ cup shortening. Beat in egg, then add milk and yeast. Add flour, ½ cup at a time and mix. This mixture should be sticky and if too much flour is added the rolls will not be light. Let dough rise in bowl until double in size. Punch down; cover with a thin layer of salad oil and place in refrigerator. Refrigerate at least overnight, but not more than 2 days. On floured surface, knead dough slightly; place in ungreased pan. Let rise until doubled. Bake at 400 degrees for 10 minutes or until golden brown. These may be baked until slightly brown and then frozen.

PARKER HOUSE ROLLS

1 to 2 cakes yeast
3 Tbs. sugar
2 cups milk, scald then cool

6 Tbs. butter or shortening
3 pints flour, sifted for soft
   dough
2 tsp. salt

Dissolve yeast and sugar in warm milk. Add shortening and one half of flour. Blend mixture thoroughly. Cover, keep in warm place, let raise 1 hour. Add remaining flour sifted with salt. Knead thoroughly. Put in greased bowl, cover, let rise 45 minutes until double its bulk. Roll 1 inch in thickness. Brush with melted butter, cut with 2-inch cutter, crease through center with dull blade of knife, fold over. Place in well greased shallow pans one inch apart. Brush with melted butter. Cover, let rise, 1 to 2 hours in warm place. Bake 20 minutes in hot oven, 400 degrees.

PRUNE NUT BREAD

¼ c. shortening
¾ c. sugar
2 eggs, beaten
½ tsp. cinnamon
½ tsp. nutmeg
½ tsp. allspice
1¼ c. flour
½ tsp. salt

1 tsp. baking powder
¼ tsp. soda
¼ c. buttermilk
¼ c. cream
½ tsp. vanilla
½ c. chopped nuts
½ c. chopped, cooked prunes

Cream thoroughly shortening and sugar. add beaten eggs and beat well. Sift all dry ingredients together. Add to sugar mixture alternately with the milk, cream and vanilla, which have been stirred together. Then stir in nuts and prunes. Pour in greased 5"x9" loaf pan and bake in 350° F. oven for 50 to 60 minutes.

PRUNE BREAD

¼ cup shortening
½ cup sugar
1 egg
¾ cup prune pulp
¼ cup prune juice
1 cup sour or buttermilk

1½ cups sifted flour
½ tsp. salt
1 tsp. baking soda
1½ cups whole wheat flour
1 cup broken nut meats

Cream shortening with sugar, beat in egg and add unsweetened cooked prune pulp and juice; or if pulp from sweetened prunes is used, omit sugar. Sift dry ingredients together and add alternately with milk to creamed mixture.
Blend batter with a few swift strokes and fold in nut meats. Place bread in 2 small or 1 large greased loaf pan. Bake in moderate 350° oven for about 55 minutes to 1¼ hours. Let cool in pan.

DEEP SOUTH GINGER MUFFINS

¾ cup butter
½ cup sugar
2 eggs
⅛ tsp. cinnamon
1 tsp. ginger
⅛ tsp. allspice

½ cup buttermilk
1 tsp. soda
½ cup dark molasses
½ cup chopped nuts
½ cup raisins
2 cups flour

Mix ingredients in order given. Put into well greased muffin tins or cup cake liners. Bake at 400 degrees about 10 minutes. Yields 24.

BLUEBERRY MUFFINS

2 cups unsifted flour
3 tsp. baking powder
1 tsp. salt
1 tsp. to 4 tsp. sugar

1 egg
1½ cups milk
⅓ cup vegetable oil
½ cup well drained blueberries

Place flour, baking powder, salt and sugar in bowl; stir together. In separate bowl, beat egg then add milk and oil. Add liquid ingredients to dry ingredients all at once. Stir only until flour is dampened. Batter will be lumpy. Add blueberries and stir sparingly. Spoon batter into greased floured muffin tins. Bake in 425 degree oven 15 to 18 minutes. Makes 12 large muffins.

TWIN MOUNTAIN MUFFINS

2 cups all-purpose flour	¼ cup sugar
3 tsp. baking powder	1 egg, beaten
½ tsp. salt	1 cup milk
¼ cup butter or shortening	

Grease muffin pans with 18 small cups. Start oven 10 minutes before baking; set to moderate heat (375F). Sift flour, measure and resift 3 times with baking powder and salt. Cream soft butter, add sugar gradually and blend thoroughly. Add egg and beat until fluffy. Add flour mixture alternately with milk in 3 portions, beginning and ending with flour and beating well after each addition. Spoon batter into prepared pans, filling ⅔ full. Place in heated oven and bake 18 to 20 minutes or until delicately browned. Serve hot.

NOTE: ¾ cup washed drained berries or other fruit may be folded into this batter for a rich, cake-like muffin.

SIX WEEK MUFFINS

1 quart Buttermilk	4 cups flour
4 eggs	2 cups chopped dates, raisins or
2 cups sugar	both
1 cup shortening	4 cups All Bran
2 cups boiling water	2 cups 40% Bran
5 tsp. baking soda	1 tsp. salt

Add soda to boiling water; cool. Cream shortening and sugar; add eggs and soda mixture, add remaining ingredients; mix well. Store covered in the refrigerator. Do not stir again. Spoon into muffin tins. Bake at 375 degrees for 25 minutes. Keeps up to six weeks.

THANKSGIVING CRANBERRY MUFFINS

1 cup raw cranberries, chopped
½ cup sugar
2 cups flour
¾ tsp. baking soda

¼ tsp. salt
¼ cup sugar
1 egg, beaten
¾ cups buttermilk
¼ cup shortening, melted

Let cranberries stand overnight in ½ cup sugar. Combine dry ingredients. Add liquid ingredients all at once. Stir until moistened. Add cranberries and stir. Fill greased muffin pans two-thirds full. Bake in a 400 degree oven for 20 minutes. Yields 18 muffins.

ROLLED OAT MUFFINS

1 cup milk
1 cup quick rolled oats
2 tsp. shortening
1 cup all purpose flour
3 tsp. baking powder

1 tsp. salt
⅓ cup moist brown sugar pkd.
½ cup moist raisins
1 egg, well beaten

Grease well muffin pans w/ 12 medium cups. Heat milk to scalding over hot water; stir in oats and shortening and cool. Meanwhile, sift flour, measure, resift three times with baking powder and salt, the last time into mixing bowl. Add brown sugar and raisins and mix well. When oat mixture is lukewarm, add egg and stir quickly into dry ingredients until just mixed but not smooth. Spoon quickly into prepared pans, filling ⅔ full. Bake in moderately hot oven (425) 18 to 20 minutes. Serve hot.

BRAN MUFFINS

1 cup whole bran
¾ cup milk
1 cup all-purpose flour
2½ tsp. baking powder

½ tsp. salt
2 tsp. butter
¼ cup sugar
1 egg, beaten

Grease well muffin pans with 12 medium cups. Add bran to milk and let stand 10 to 15 minutes. Sift flour, measure and resift 3 times with baking powder and salt. Cream butter in a 3 quart mixing bowl, blend in sugar, add egg and beat until fluffy. Stir in bran and milk. Then add flour mixture, stirring until flour is just dampened. Fill prepared pans ⅔ full. Bake in a moderately hot oven (400) 25 to 30 minutes or until muffins are done and nicely browned. Serve piping hot with butter.

BANANA MUFFINS

1½ cup all-purpose flour
1¼ tsp. baking powder
½ tsp. soda
1 tsp. salt
3 Tbs. sugar
2 small eggs

2 medium bananas, ½ lb.
¼ tsp. grated lemon rind, pkd.
1 tsp. lemon juice
3 Tbs. buttermilk
3 Tbs. shortening

Grease muffin pans with 8 to 10 medium muffin cups. Start oven 10 minutes before baking; set to moderately hot (400F). Sift flour, measure, resift 3 times with next 4 ingredients, the last time into a 3-quart mixing bowl. Beat eggs, add sliced bananas and crush with silver fork to size of small peas. Add lemon rind, juice and buttermilk, then stir in shortening. Add liquid all at once to dry ingredients; stir quickly and vigorously until flour is just dampened, but no more. Stirring should take about 20 seconds. Spoon into prepared pans. Place in heated oven and bake about 30 minutes or until well browned. Serve hot.

POTATO DUMPLINGS

For meat stews, roast pork or Sauerkraut

1 lb. potatoes, 3 to 4 medium
1 egg
½ cup all-purpose flour
Dash of nutmeg

¾ tsp. salt
¼ tsp. baking powder
2 Tbs. melted butter

Pare potatoes, add enough water to cover, then cover pan and boil until done. Drain well, rice potatoes into a 2-qt. mixing bowl and cool slightly. Drop egg into potatoes, beat well and add next 4 ingredients which have been sifted together. Beat thoroughly. Shape into roll about 1-inch in diameter and cut into 1-inch lengths. Drop pieces into boiling salted water, stirring gently for a minute to keep them from sticking to bottom of pan. Dumplings will then rise to top. Cook uncovered 8 to 10 minutes. Drain dumplings and pour butter over them to keep from sticking together. Serve immediately with meat stew or roast with gravy. Or cook dumplings on top of sauerkraut in a covered pan. Serve with the kraut. 4 servings.

DROP DUMPLINGS

For poultry or meat stews

1½ cup all purpose flour
3½ tsp. baking powder
Chopped parsley

½ tsp. salt
¾ cup milk

Sift flour, measure, resift 3 times with baking powder and salt, the 3rd time into mixing bowl. Add milk all at once and stir rapidly with a fork until well blended. If desired, stir in about 1 tsp. finely chopped parsley. There must be at least 3 cups of boiling liquid to have enough gravy left after cooking dumplings. Drop batter by tsp. on top of stew chicken, beef or lamb stew. Dipping spoon into the hot broth each time before dipping into batter prevents batter from sticking to spoon. As soon as dumplings are all in, cover and boil moderately fast for 12 minutes without uncovering. Then remove all dumplings to a hot platter, arranging them around the outside and the stew in the center. 5 servings.

BAKED APPLE OR PEACH DUMPLINGS

1 recipe rich baking powder
   biscuit
Fruit

Cinnamon or Nutmeg
Butter
Sugar

Roll baking powder biscuit dough ¼ inch thick. Cut in 4 inch squares. Place fruit, pared, cored, or pitted in center of square. Add sugar, butter, cinnamon or nutmeg. Draw four corners of dough together, press edge closely. Prick with fork. Bake to medium brown in 350 degree oven about 35 minutes. Serve hot with cream or pudding sauce.

YEAST BISCUITS

5¼ cups flour
5 tsp. baking powder
1 tsp. salt
1 tsp. baking soda
5 Tbs. warm water

1 cup shortening (veg. rather
   than butter)
2 cups buttermilk
1 package dry yeast

Combine dry ingredients; sift. Add and cut in shortening. Add buttermilk and the yeast which has been dissolved in the warm water. Knead, roll out and cut into desired shapes. Place on greased pan; bake in a preheated 450 degree oven for 10-12 minutes.

*These are very good and may be keep in refrigerator for days.

LOUISIANA RICE PANCAKES

1 cup cooked rice, warm	2 tsp. baking powder
1 tsp. butter	$\frac{1}{16}$ tsp. baking soda
$\frac{2}{3}$ cup milk	1 Tbs. syrup
2 egg yolks	2 egg whites, beaten stiff
$\frac{1}{3}$ cup thick sour cream	
$\frac{1}{3}$ tsp. salt	
1$\frac{1}{4}$ cups sifted flour	

Blend all the ingredients in the order given. Drop by spoon on a hot griddle, brown and serve on a hot plate.

BANANA FRITTERS

6 large ripe bananas	Flour
1 egg	Bread Crumbs

Peel bananas and cut in pieces, roll in well beaten egg and flour then in bread crumbs. Fry in hot shortening until golden brown.

MOUNTAIN POPOVERS

2 cups sifted flour	2 cups milk
$\frac{1}{2}$ tsp. salt	2 Tbs. melted butter
3 eggs	

Sift flour and salt into bowl. Drop eggs in dish, with fork break eggs enough to mix with milk. Pour all together, beat until bubbles form on batter. Pour into hot greased pans, bake 40 minutes in hot oven, decreasing heat after they have popped. Serve immediately.

215

SIX-WEEK BRAN MUFFINS
Yield: 5-6 dozen

2 cups boiling water
2 cups 100% Bran Cereal
5 cups whole wheat flour
5 tsp. soda

1 tsp. salt
1 cup shortening or margarine
3 cups sugar
4 eggs
4 cup All Bran cereal
1 qt. buttermilk

Mix water and Bran. Let stand. Sift together flour, soda and salt. Cream shortening and sugar. To this, add eggs, one at a time beating after each addition; add All Bran and buttermilk. Combine and mix all 3 mixes only until moistened. Put into greased muffin tins. Bake 15-20 minutes at 350°. The batter may be covered, refrigerated and baked as needed. It will keep 6 weeks.

PEARLS BEST ROLLS

½ cup luke warm water
¼ cup sugar
½ cup Crisco Oil
Dash of salt

1 egg
3 cups plain flour
1 package yeast

Dissolve yeast in ½ cup water. Mix together sugar, salt, crisco oil, add egg. Add flour ½ cup boiling water and yeast mixture. Stir together to make a stiff dough. Leave in pan and refrigerate, for 1 or 2 hours. Take out and let stand. Let rise 1 to 2 hours before baking.

Annie Pearl Matthews

MY BEST HOME MADE BREAD

1 cup margarine	2 pks. dry yeast
1 cup boiling water	1 cup warm water
1 tsp. salt	2 eggs beaten
¾ cup sugar	6½ to 7 cups flour-Gold Metal best

Combine margarine, boiling water in large bowl, stirring until margarine is melted. Stir in salt, and sugar. Let cool to lukewarm. Dissolve yeast in very warm water 105 to 115 degrees. Add to shortening, mix. Add eggs. Mix well. Gradually add ½ the flour to make a soft dough. Turn dough out onto a lightly floured board. Knead until smooth and elastic about 8 to 10 minutes. Add the remaining flour. Place dough in greased bowl, cover let rest in warm place until double in bulk, about 1 hour. Punch down, divide in half, shape into loaf. Place seam side down into greased loaf pans. Cover let rise, till double in bulk about 1 hour. Bake at 300 degrees for 1 hour. Yield 2 loaves.

Nell McClung
Murfreesboro, Tenn.

NELLS STRAWBERRY BREAD

3 cups self-rising flour	1¼ cup oil
2 cups sugar	4 eggs
1¼ cups nuts	1 tsp. cinnamon
2 cups crushed strawberries	

Mix all ingredients together and bake at 350 degrees for 60 minutes. Makes 2 loaves

Nell McClung
Murfreesboro, Tenn.

MAMMYS SWEET POTATO BISCUITS

2 cups sifted, all-purpose flour
2 tsp. baking powder
1 tsp. salt
2 Tbs. light-brown sugar
¾ cup buttermilk

½ cup melted butter or
  margarine
¾ cup mashed, cooked sweet
  potatoes
½ tsp. baking soda

Preheat oven to 400° F. Sift together flour, baking powder, and salt. Combine brown sugar, melted butter, and sweet potatoes in small bowl. Beat until fluffy. Stir soda into buttermilk. Combine all ingredients. Stir only until moist. Turn out on floured board or cloth. Knead slightly. Roll out and cut into biscuits. Bake on ungreased baking sheet for about 20 minutes or until done. Makes about 18 biscuits.

BANANA NUT LOAF

⅓ cup shortening
⅔ cup sugar
2 eggs, slightly beaten
3 tablespoons buttermilk

½ cup chopped nuts
2 cups sifted, self-rising flour
¼ tsp. baking soda
1 cup mashed, ripe bananas
  (about 3)

Preheat oven to 350°F. Grease a large loaf pan. Cream shortening. Add sugar. Stir in eggs and buttermilk. Combine flour and soda. Stir into mixture. Add bananas and nuts. Pour into prepared pan. Bake 50 to 60 minutes or until done. Makes 1 loaf.

Desserts

APPLE SAUCE CAKE

2 cups sifted flour	½ cup butter or shortening
1 tsp. baking soda	1 cup sugar
¼ tsp. salt	1 egg unbeaten
¼ tsp. cloves	1 cup raisins, cut
½ tsp. nutmeg	1 cup nuts
1 tsp. cinnamon	1 cup thick apple sauce

Sift flour once, measure, add baking soda, salt and spices and sift together three times. Work butter with spoon until creamy. Add sugar gradually, beating after each addition until light and fluffy. Add egg; beat well. Add nuts and raisins. Add flour alternately with apple sauce, a small amount at a time, beating until smooth after each addition. Turn into greased loaf pan. Bake in a moderate oven 350 degrees for one hour and 15 minutes.

ANGEL FOOD CAKE

1 cup cake flour, sifted 6 times	⅛ tsp. salt
1½ cups granulated sugar sifted 6 times	1 tsp. cream of tartar
	1 tsp. vanilla
2 cups egg whites (room temperature)	½ tsp. almond extract

Sift cake flour 6 times, lift sifter to incorporate air. Beat eggs after adding salt, use wire beater. When foamy, add cream of tartar. Preheat oven to 350 degrees. Beat eggs stiff. Slowly fold in sugar, 3 tablespoons at a time, fold gently. Add vanilla. With sifter, add little flour at a time, fold lightly. Add 2 tablespoons cold water. Rinse cake tin with cold water, drain well. Add mixture, bake 50 to 55 minutes in 350 degree oven. Invert cake tin 1 to 2 hours until cold.

   *For a small Angel Food Cake, reduce above receipe one half. Use a 9-inch ungreased tube cake tin, bake 35 minutes in a 350 degree oven.

RICE PUDDING IN MOLD

1 cup rice
2 cups boiling water
1 cup milk
Pinch salt
½ cup sugar

½ pint whipped cream
1 tsp. vanilla
¾ cup shredded coconut

Slowly stir rice in boiling water, later add milk, cook in double boiler until done. Drain, when cool, put through ricer. Add sugar, flavoring fold in whipped cream. Turn into mold, let stand several hours or overnight.

MAPLE SAUCE:

½ cups maple syrup

¼ tsp. vanilla

Cook until slightly thickened, add 2 tablespoons butter, vanilla. Beat until smooth, serve with rice pudding.

POOR MANS BREAD PUDDING

2 cups dry bread crumbs
½ cup granulated sugar
1 pint milk
Few grains salt

4 eggs
¼ tsp. cinnamon
½ tsp. vanilla
4 Tbs. butter

Soak bread crumbs in milk. Add sugar and butter, beaten eggs, salt, flavoring. Place in buttered baking dish, add little chopped lemon, chopped raisins and dates. Bake about 40 minutes in 350 degree oven.

STEAMED BREAD PUDDING

1 qt. bread crumbs
1 cup molasses
1 cup flour, sifted
1 tsp. soda

1 cup raisins
1 tsp. cinnamon
1 heaping Tbs. butter
1 tsp. vanilla

Blend all ingredients, pour into buttered mold, cover, steam 2½ hours. Serve with whipped cream or vanilla sauce. 1 cup seeded raisins may be added, or 1 cup orange marmalade, or 1 cup chopped dates and 1 cup coconut.

CARAMEL PUDDING

1 cup brown sugar
½ cup butter
2 cups milk
⅓ cup cornstarch

1 tsp. vanilla
¾ cup shredded coconut

Melt sugar, butter over hot water, add hot milk. Blend in cornstarch which has been dissolved in little milk. Cook in pan. Remove from heat. Cool. Add shredded coconut and vanilla.

CINNAMON-APPLE JELLY

1 quart bottle apple juice
1 package Sure jel
4½ cups sugar

2 Tbs. cinnamon candies

Combine apple juice and Sure Jel in large saucepan. Bring mixture to a rolling boil over moderate heat (250 degrees.) Add sugar and cinnamon candies and cook, stirring constantly, until sugar and candies are melted. Bring to a boil and cook two minutes, stirring occasionally. Remove from heat, let mixture settle a few seconds and then skim off foam with metal spoon. Pour into hot sterilized jars and seal with paraffin. Makes seven half-pint jars.

VINEGAR PIE

Pastry for 9-inch single crust

1 cup seedless raisins, chopped
  or cut
¼ cup soft butter
2 cups sugar
½ tsp. cinnamon
½ tsp. allspice

¼ tsp. cloves
4 eggs, separated
2½ to 3 Tbs. 5% cider vinegar
dash of salt

Adjust rack 4 to 5 inches above bottom of oven. Start oven 10 minutes before baking, set to moderately hot (425F).
Make pastry. Roll out and line 9-inch pie pan, fitting well into angles. Trim off with scissors ½-inch from pan rim, turn overhang under so fold is even with trim, then flute. Do not prick pastry. Wash raisins, drain and chop or snip each into 2 or 3 pieces with scissors. Cream butter and sugar thoroughly. Add spices and blend well. Beat in yolks with rotary beater until smooth and creamy. Add vinegar and again beat until smooth. Remove beater and wash. Stir in raisins with wooden spoon. Beat egg whites with dash of salt until stiff, then slide onto sugar mixture. Cut and fold in lightly but thoroughly. Turn into pastry-lined pan. Bake 15 minutes, then reduce heat to slow (300F) and bake 20 minutes longer until top is nicely browned and center of filling is jelly-like. Remove to cake rack to cool 2 or 3 hours before cutting. 6 servings.

CARROT PUDDING

½ cup butter
1 cup sugar creamed together
1 cup grated carrots
1 cup grated potatoes
1¼ cups flour
1 tsp. soda

¼ tsp. cinnamon; allspice
Little salt
1 cup raisins, cut
1 cup dates and figs, chopped
½ cup chopped walnuts
1 tsp. vanilla

Cream butter, beat in sugar. Blend all ingredients in the order given. Pour into well buttered mold. Place oiled waxed paper over pudding then lid. Steam 3 hours. Serve hot with ginger or pudding sauce.

BANANA PUDDING

6 Tbs. sugar	Vanilla wafers
3 bananas	1 cup water
1 tsp. vanilla	1 cup evaporated milk
3 eggs, separated	1 cup sugar
	⅓ cup flour

Preheat oven to 350 degrees. Combine 1 cup sugar and flour in top of double boiler. Add milk and water and stir. Pour over rapidly boiling water and stir occasionally. When slightly thick, beat 3 egg yolks in cup and add ½ cup of custard to yolks. Return to boiler and cook until medium thick. Put a layer of vanilla wafers and a layer of sliced bananas in baking dish. Pour ½ of mixture over them. Repeat with wafers, bananas and remaining mixture. Beat egg whites until stiff. Gradually add 6 tablespoons of sugar. Beat well. Put egg white mixture on top of pudding and wafers with bananas and bake in oven until lightly brown.

STEAMED FRUIT PUDDING

2 eggs	¼ tsp. salt
4 tsp. melted butter	1 tsp. grated lemon rind
½ cup brown sugar	1 Tbs. vanilla
½ cup chopped figs	1 cup flour, sift before
½ cup chopped dates	measuring
½ cup chopped walnuts	½ tsp. soda dissolved in hot
	water
	add last, ¼ cup milk

Cream butter and sugar. Add well-beaten egg and chopped fruit. Fruit should be mixed with small amount of flour to prevent settling to bottom of mixture. Fill well buttered mold two thirds full. Cover with waxed paper and steam 1½ hours. Use hard sauce for topping.

FRESH BLACKBERRY PIE

Pastry for 9-inch double crust
5 cups blackberries, washed
　and drained
½ to ⅔ cup sugar, depending on
　ripeness of berries
Dash of salt

1½ to 2½ Tbs. flour, depending
　on juiciness of berries
1 Tbs. butter

Adjust rack 4 to 5 inches above bottom of oven. Start oven 10 minutes before baking; set to hot (450F).

Make pastry; roll out ½ of it and line a 9-inch pie pan, fitting well into angles, trim off even with rim of pan. Roll out remaining pastry for top crust; cut design in center for wide-open steam vents. Prepare berries. Blend sugar, salt and flour; sprinkle 3 Tbs. of mixture over bottom of lined pan. Turn in berries, spreading out compactly level; sprinkle rest of sugar mixture over them. Dot with butter. Moisten edge of lower pastry; then lay on top pastry. Press gently around edge to seal. Trim off top pastry with scissors ½ inch beyond pan rim. Fold overhang under bottom pastry so fold is even with rim of pan. Again press gently to seal, then crimp edge with tines of fork. Bake 12 to 15 minutes or until pastry begins to brown, then reduce heat to moderately slow (325F) and bake 20 to 25 minutes longer, or until pastry is nicely browned and juice bubbles up through vents. Remove to cake rack to cool. 2 to 3 hours. Serve lukewarm. 5 to 6 servings.

CHOCOLATE PIE

¾ cups sugar
2 heaping Tbs. flour
3 eggs, separated
1 cup milk
3 Tbs. cocoa or 1 square
　unsweetened chocolate

⅛ tsp. vanilla
1 Tbs. butter
1 baked 8 inch pie shell

Mix sugar, flour, egg yolks, milk and chocolate in top of double boiler. Cook until thick. Using electric mixer, beat in vanilla and butter. Pour into baked crust. Top with meringue made by beating egg whites with an additional 6 tablespoons of sugar. Brown in 325 degree oven. Serves 8.

CHESS PIE

Pastry for 9-inch single crust

1 cup butter or margarine room temperature	¼ tsp. salt
2 cups granulated sugar	4 egg yolks, beaten
2 tsp. vanilla	1 cup evaporated milk
½ cup all-purpose flour	

Adjust rack 5 or 6 inches above bottom of oven. Start oven 10 minutes before baking; set to hot(450F)

Make pastry and line 9-inch pie pan, fitting well into angles. Trim pastry off with scissors ½ inch beyond pan rim, then fold overhand under even with pan rim; crimp with fork, leaving edge flat. Cream butter with wooden spoon, gradually adding sugar and cream well. Stir in vanilla, then flour and salt, and beat until well blended. Stir in egg yolks, then the milk gradually. Turn into pastry-lined pan. Bake 10 minutes, then reduce heat to moderately slow (325F) and bake 25 to 30 minutes longer. Remove to cake rack to cool. Custard should be slightly soft in center when pie is removed from oven; it becomes firm as it cools. After cooling, pie may be placed in refrigerator. Fortunately this pie is just as delicious chilled as it is lukewarm and crust retains crispness remarkably well. So serve warm or cold. 7 or 8 servings.

* A favorite of the South. Rich, high in calories—But worth it.

BANANA CREAM PIE

9-inch pastry shell
⅓ cup all-purpose flour
½ cup sugar
¼ tsp. salt
2 cups milk
3 small egg yolks
1 Tbs. firm butter

½ tsp. vanilla
2 large ripe bananas
1 tsp. powdered sugar
½ cup whipping cream
1 tsp. sugar
⅛ tsp vanilla

Bake and cool pastry shell. Blend flour, sugar and salt in heavy saucepan. Slowly stir in 1 cup of the milk until smooth; add rest of milk and cook and stir over direct heat until mixture boils and thickens, for 5 or 6 minutes. Remove from heat. Quickly stir about ½ cup of hot mixture into well-beaten yolks, pour back into saucepan and cook and stir 2 minutes longer. Remove from heat and stir in butter and vanilla. Cook about 5 minutes, then pour half the mixture into pastry-lined pan, spreading well up sides of shell. Peel and slice bananas and arrange over filling; sprinkle with powdered sugar. Spread rest of filling over bananas. Cool. Whip cream until stiff but still smooth, adding the 1 tsp. sugar and flavoring with last few turns. Spread smoothly over filling and mark criss-cross with tines of fork about an inch apart. Serve immediately, or place in refrigerator for not more than an hour or two. 6 servings.

To make an 8-inch pie: Use an 8-inch pastry shell; ¼ cup flour, 6 Tbs. sugar, ⅛ tsp. salt, 1½ cups milk, 2 egg yolks, 2 tsp. butter, ½ tsp. vanilla, 2 medium bananas, 1 tsp. powdered sugar, ⅓ cup whipping cream, ⅛ tsp. vanilla, 1 tsp. sugar.

Hint: Whipping the cream and folding into the cooled filling before spreading in the pie makes an extra rich, delicious pie.

BLUEBERRY PIE

3 cups fresh blueberries, wash
   carefully
¾ cup sugar
1 Tbs. butter

2 Tbs. flour
½ tsp. cinnamon
⅛ tsp. salt

Sift flour and sugar together, add berries and mix well. Pour into pastry lined pie tin, moisten edge of dough with water, cover with top crust making opening for steam to escape. Press pastry well over edge and trim. NOTE: If canned berries are used, measure scant ½ cup sugar and 2 tablespoons flour.

NUT TORTE

4 egg yolks
1 cup granulated sugar
⅓ cup cracker crumbs
⅓ cup walnuts
1 cup chopped dates

1 tsp. baking powder
1 tsp. vanilla
4 egg whites, beaten stiff
½ cup shredded coconut
Pinch of salt

Mix all ingredients, beaten egg whites last. Bake in 325 degree oven about 30 minutes, serve with whipped cream. 1 cup figs, cut fine may be added.

BUTTERMILK PIE

¼ cup flour
½ cup butter, melted
½ cup buttermilk
1½ cups sugar

½ tsp. vanilla
3 eggs
1 unbaked 9 inch pie shell

Mix all ingredients together thoroughly and pour into pie shell. Bake at 350 for 1 hour.

CUSTARD PIE

3 eggs	½ tsp. salt
¾ cup sugar	1 tsp. vanilla
2 cups rich milk	½ tsp. nutmeg

Beat eggs, add sugar and salt, and beat again; scald milk and add slowly. Stir well. Add vanilla. Pour into pastry shell pre-baked about 5 to 10 minutes in hot 450° oven, place in moderately slow oven 325° about 15 to 30 minutes. When a knife stuck into the center comes out dry, baking is completed. Sprinkle with nutmeg and cool before serving.

If a thicker pie is desired, prepare a deeper shell and add another egg and ½ cup milk to recipe.

STRAWBERRY SHORT CAKE

2 cups flour	1 egg
4 tsps. baking powder	½ cup milk
1 tbsp. sugar	1 quart berries
½ tsp. salt	1 cup whipping cream
4 to 6 Tbs. shortening	

Sift together dry ingredients, and cut in shortening as for pie crust. Beat egg and milk until blended and stir in. Pat out dough into a square on floured board, to the thickness of ¼ inch. Brush half the top with melted butter.

Fold over other half, or cut dough into rounds for individual servings if preferred.

Bake cake on greased sheet in moderately hot 425° oven for about 10 to 20 minutes. Split cake.

Serve with sweetened strawberries between layers and over top. Garnish with whipped cream.

GRAPE PIE

4 cups blue grapes
¾ cup sugar
1 Tbs. quick cooking tapioca

1½ Tbs. lemon juice
1 Tbs. grated orange rind, or ½
 Tbs. grated lemon rind

Stem grapes and slip pulp out of skins. Cook pulp, covered, until seeds loosen. Press it through a coarse sieve to remove seeds. Mix strained pulp with skins, sugar, tapioca, lemon juice and rind.
Line a pie pan with pastry, fill with grape mixture. Cover with lattice or top crust. Bake in hot 450° oven 10 minutes, then lower heat to moderate 350° and bake until done—about 15 to 30 minutes longer.

OATMEAL DROP CAKES

1¼ cups sugar
1 cup shortening
1 cup raisins or dates
2 cups rolled oats
1 cup flour

5 Tbs. milk
2 tsps. cinnamon
¼ tsp. soda
2 eggs

Cream shortening, which may be butter, vegetable shortening, or a mixture of both, and cream sugar into it.
If shortening is used, add a little salt to taste. Add beaten eggs, chopped raisins, dates or figs. Add rolled oats mixed with flour. Add cinnamon, soda and milk, and mix thoroughly into fairly stiff batter. Drop by teaspoonfuls on well-greased pan or baking sheet. Space well to allow for spreading.
Bake 7 to 15 minutes in moderate 350° oven.

BUTTERSCOTCH PIE

3 egg yolks
1 cup brown sugar
6 Tbs. flour
2 cups milk
4 Tbs. butter

1 tsp. salt
1 tsp. vanilla
3 Tbs. syrup, caramel
½ tsp. nutmeg

CARAMEL SYRUP:
½ cup sugar
⅓ cup boiling water

Beat egg yolks with sugar, mix with flour a little water to make smooth paste, add the first mixture, add milk, salt and caramel syrup. Cook in pan until thick. Remove from fire; add butter and vanilla. Cool, add beaten whites of eggs or reserve for a meringue. Pour into baked crust. If meringue is used add 4 tablespoons sugar to stiffly beaten whites, spread on top, return to slow oven to brown. To make syrup, heat sugar in smooth dry skillet until golden brown, add boiling water, cook to cream, stir.

Maggie Nola Sloan
Goodlettsville, Tenn.

QUICK AND EASY FUDGE PIE

2 squares unsweetened chocolate
1 stick butter
1 cup sugar
2 Tbs. plain flour
2 eggs
½ cup walnuts or pecans
1 tsp. vanilla

Melt in saucepan. Stir vigorously and pour into floured and greased 9″ pie pan.

Put into cold oven.

Bake at 350° for 30 minutes.

231

FRESH STRAWBERRY PIE

Pastry for 9-inch double crust

1 quart sound ripe strawberries	2½ Tbs. cornstarch or 4 Tbs.
¾ to 1 cup sugar	flour
	Dash of salt
	1 Tbs. butter

Adjust rack 4 to 5 inches above bottom of oven. Start oven 10 minutes before baking; set to hot (450F).

Make pastry; roll out ½ of it and line a 9-inch pie pan, fitting well into angles; trim off even with pan rim. Roll out remaining pastry for top and cut design in center for wide-open steam vents; or cut strips for lattice. Cover pastry-lined pan and top pastry with waxed paper or damp towel. Wash berries, drain and hull, removing any bad spots. Cut large berries in half. Blend sugar, cornstarch or flour and salt; sprinkle 2 Tbs. over bottom of pastry-lined pan. Turn remainder over berries and mix gently, then turn into pan and spread evenly. Dot with butter. Moisten edge of lower pastry; lay on top pastry (or lay lattice strips without interlacing) and press edge gently to seal. Trim off pastry ½-inch beyond edge of rim; turn overhang under edge of lower pastry so fold is even with pan rim. Again press to seal, then crimp with tines of fork. Bake 15 minutes then reduce heat to moderate (350F) and bake 30 minutes longer, or until golden brown. Remove to cake rack to cool to lukewarm before serving. 6 to 7 servings.

CHERRY PIE

3 cups fresh cherries
Scant cup sugar
⅛ tsp. salt

2 Tbs. flour
1 Tbs. flour
½ tsp. cinnamon

Blend sugar, flour, salt and add cherries. Mix well. Pour mixture into unbaked pie crust, add dots of butter, top crust, cover edge well. Bake in hot oven about 15 minutes, then reduce heat and bake until done.

BETH'S CARROT CAKE

3 cups finely grated carrots
2 cups sugar
1½ cups cooking oil
4 eggs
¾ cup chopped pecans

3 cups sifted, all-purpose flour
2 tsp. baking powder
1 tsp. baking soda
½ tsp. salt
1½ tsp. cinnamon

Preheat oven to 300° F. Lightly grease bottom of a 10-inch tube pan. Combine carrots, sugar, oil, and eggs. Sift together dry ingredients. Add to first mixture. Mix well. Fold in pecans. Turn into prepared pan. Bake about 1½ hours or until done. Cool in pan about 15 minutes before turning out. Makes about 24 slices.

Beth Scott
Goodlettsville, Tenn.

MINCE MEAT FOR PIES

1 lb. seeded raisins	2 lbs. lean beef chopped
¾ lb. lemon cut fine	1 lb. beef fat chopped
1 cup molasses	5 lbs. sour apples chopped
Juice and rind of orange and lemon	2½ lbs. brown sugar
	2 Tbs. cinnamon
1 cup boiled cider	1 Tbs. spice
1 tsp. lemon extract	1 tsp. salt

Combine ingredients thoroughly and add enough boiled cider to make right consistency. Heat slowly to boiling point and simmer 1 hour. Add meat and 2 tablespoons raisin jelly.

PUMPKIN PIE

1 unbaked 9 inch pie shell

2 cans canned pumpkin	½ tsp. nutmeg
1⅓ cup sweetened condensed milk	¼ tsp. cinnamon
	½ tsp. salt
1 egg	½ tsp. ginger

In a large mixing bowl, blend together all ingredients. Turn mixture into pie shell. Bake in 375 degree oven until sharp bladed knife inserted near center comes out clean. 50 to 55 minutes. Cool. Refrigerate at least 1 hour before serving.

CARROT CAKE

4½ cups flour
2 cups sugar
2 cups grated carrots
3 beaten eggs
1 cup chopped walnuts
1 cup veg. oil

1 tsp. salt
1 tsp. cinnamon
1½ tsp. baking soda
1 tsp. vanilla
1 can 13½ oz. crushed
    pineapple (not drained)

Mix all at once pour into ungreased 11x14 inch pan. Bake 1 hr. at 350°. Sift powdered sugar over top or ice lightly with lemon or vanilla icing.

Louise Hand
Murfreesboro, Tenn.

SKILLET CAKE—(Upside Down Cake)
(Pineapple, Apricot, etc.)

¼ cup butter
¾ cup brown sugar
1 cup pecan meats (optional)

8 canned pineapple slices, or
    24 cooked apricots, drained

Melt butter in 9 inch skillet. Remove from the fire.
Sprinkle brown sugar and nutmeats over bottom. Arrange fruit on sugar. Prepare following batter:

2 eggs
¼ tsp. salt
1 cup sugar
½ cup rich milk

1 Tbs. melted shortening
1 tsp. vanilla
1 cup sifted cake flour
1 tsp. baking powder

Beat eggs until light. Add gradually, beating constantly, salt and sugar.
Heat milk to boiling point. Add butter. Beat into egg mixture. Add vanilla. Resift flour with baking powder, and add it to egg mixture. Beat quickly until blended.
Pour batter over fruit. Bake cake in moderate 325° oven for about ½ hour.
Turn out while warm. Serve upside down.

LEMON MERINGUE PIE

1½ cups sugar, divided
3 Tbs. flour
1½ cups hot milk
3 eggs, separated
Pinch of salt

½ tsp. water
¼ tsp. vanilla
3 Tbs. lemon juice
1 baked 9 inch pie crust

Mix 1 cup sugar and flour together. Add to hot milk, and cook over low heat until mixture has thickened. Beat egg yolks, salt and water with flour and add enough cooked custard to mix well. Return egg mixture to pan and simmer until egg is set, stirring constantly. Add vanilla, lemon juice, and lemon rind. Stir until mixture begins to bubble. Set aside. Make meringue by beating egg whites until fluffy. Add ½ cup sugar a little at a time until stiff. Remove one cup of meringue and stir into cooked custard. Pour into pie crust immediately. Spread remaining meringue over pie and brown in 425 degree oven approximately 5 minutes.

KEY LIME PIE

8 or 9-inch pastry shell
¼ tsp. grated lime rind, pkd.
½ cup lime juice and pulp from
   either Key or Persian limes

3 eggs separated
14 or 15 oz. can sweetened
   condensed milk
½ cup powdered sugar, pkd.
1 tsp. granulated sugar

Bake and cool pastry shell. Wash limes and grate off a little of the rind onto waxed paper; measure and fold into paper to keep moist. Squeeze juice, remove seeds. Beat yolks with rotary beater until light colored. Remove beater and wash. Use wooden spoon to stir in lime juice and rind. Then, the condensed milk, until smooth and noticeably thickened. Pour into pastry shell, spreading to make filling a little higher at rim. Beat egg whites until stiff, then add powdered sugar gradually, beating to a stiff shiny meringue. Spoon meringue lightly over filling; swirl top or spread smoothly and mark into 6 serving pieces with a long knife blade. Sprinkle the tsp. of sugar evenly over the top. Bake in moderate oven (350F) 15 to 17 minutes or until golden brown. Remove to cake rack to cool 2 to 3 hours before cutting. 6 servings.

Helen Clark
St. Petersburg, Fla.

FRESH PEACH PIE

PASTRY FOR 9-INCH DOUBLE CRUST

1 Tbs. fine dry white bread
   crumbs
2 to 2½ lbs. juicy ripe peaches
1 cup sugar
Dash of salt

2 Tbs. flour
4 drops almond extract
2 Tbs. butter

Adjust rack to 5 or 6 inches from bottom of oven. Start oven 10 minutes before baking; set to hot (450F).

Make pastry; roll ½ of it out and line a 9-inch pie pan, fitting well into angles; trim off even with pan rim. Roll out remaining pastry for top and cut design in center for wide-open steam vents. Sprinkle bread crumbs over bottom of pastry-lined pan. Cover lined pan and top pastry with waxed paper. Wash peaches, pare, cut in halves and discard pits. Cut halves into 3 or 4 lengthwise slices, dropping into quart measure. There should be a full quart. Blend sugar, salt and flour and sprinkle ¼ cup of mixture over crumbs. Add rest to peaches turned into a bowl, sprinkle extract over, and mix gently. Turn into pastry-lined pan, spread to make them moderately compact. Fruit should be very slightly rounded up in center. Dot with butter. Moisten edge of lower pastry, lay on top pastry, and press down gently around rim to seal. Cut top pastry off with scissors ½ inch beyond pan rim, then turn overhang under edge of lower pastry so fold is even with rim of pan. Again press down gently around rim and crimp with tines of fork or flute with fingers. Bake 15 minutes, then reduce heat to moderately slow (325F) and bake 25 minutes longer or until well browned and juice bubbles up thru vents. Remove to cake rack to cool 2 or 3 hours. 5 to 6 servings.

"PEACHES-AND-CREAM" PIE

Pastry for 9-inch single crust
2 Tbs. firm butter
1 cup 12% cream, half & half
2/3 cup sugar

1/4 cup flour
1/4 tsp. salt
1/8 tsp. nutmeg or 1/4 tsp.
   cinnamon
3 cups sliced fresh peaches

Adjust rack 5 to 6 inches from bottom of oven. Start oven 10 minutes before baking; set to moderately hot (425F). Make pastry and line a 9-inch pie pan, fitting well into angles. Let rest 5 minutes, then using scissors, trim pastry off 1/2 inch beyond pan rim. Fold pastry under so fold is even with pan rim, then finish edge in any way desired. Slice butter thinly over bottom of pastry. Measure sugar, flour, salt and nutmeg into small bowl and stir to blend well, then stir in cream until well mixed. Pare peaches, slice thinly, measure and turn into pastry-lined pan, spreading level. Then pour cream mixture over peaches, pressing slices down into cream with back of spoon. Bake 30 to 35 minutes or until pastry is nicely browned and peaches are tender. Remove to cake rack to cool to lukewarm before cutting. 6 servings.

PEACH COBBLER

8 medium peaches, peeled and
   thinly sliced
1 cup sugar
1/4 cup water

2 sticks margarine (1 cup)
1 cup flour
1 egg
1 cup sugar

Combine peaches, sugar and water in saucepan and bring to boil. Pour into 8-inch square pyrex dish. Mix margarine, flour, egg and sugar. Spoon over hot peaches. Put in 500 degree oven until light brown. Turn down to 250 degrees and cook for one hour or until thick.

HOT WATER PASTRY FOR A 9 OR 10-INCH 2-CRUST PIE

⅔ cup shortening
7 Tbs. boiling water

2½ cups all-purpose flour
1 tsp. salt

Step 1: Measure shortening into a 3-quart mixing bowl. Use measuring tbsp. to dip water from kettle that is actually boiling onto shortening.

Step 2: With a fork beat together until mixture is smooth, creamy and cooled.

Step 3: Sift flour, measure, resift with salt into the shortening- water mixture and with a fork stir until well mixed.

Step 4: Shape into a ball and proceed as for plain pastry for 2-pie crust, dividing pastry into 2 portions, one a little larger than the other, or divide in half for 2 single-crust pastry shells then follow steps for making the 2-crust pie or single-crust shells.

PECAN PIE-COLD FILLING METHOD

Pastry for 9-inch single crust

1 cup white corn syrup
½ cup brown sugar, pkd.
¼ tsp. salt
1 tsp. vanilla

2 tsp. lemon juice
3 eggs, slightly beaten
1 cup small pecans or large
   meats, broken

Adjust rack 4 or 5 inches above bottom of oven. Start oven 10 minutes before baking; set to moderately hot (425).
Make Pastry. Roll out and line 9-inch pie pan, fitting well into angles. Trim ½ inch from edge with scissors, turn overhang under so fold is even with pan rim. Flute or imprint with tines of fork. Do not prick. Combine next 6 ingredients and stir until well blended, then stir in nuts. Pour into pastry lined pan. Bake 10 minutes, then reduce heat to moderately slow (325) and bake 35 to 40 minutes longer or until crust is golden brown and filling is set. Remove to cake rack to cool until just lukewarm. Serve plain or with whipped cream. 6 to 8 servings.

PASTRY FOR DESSERT DUMPLINGS

2½ cups all-purpose flour	⅔ cup shortening
½ tsp. baking powder	½ cups ice water or cold milk
½ tsp. salt	
1 tsp. sugar	

Sift flour, measure and sift twice with next three ingredients, the last time into a 2-quart mixing bowl. Add shortening and cut in with pastry blender until particles are size of peas. Drizzle in water or milk and toss with fork to dampen in same manner as for pie pastry. Shape into a ball, then pat into a neat rectangular shape on a well-floured pastry cloth. Roll out carefully into a generous 12 x 21-inch rectangle. Trim off ragged edges. Cut rectangle in half lengthwise, then in thirds crosswise, making six 7-inch neat squares.

Note: For a fancy finish to dumplings, stack the trimmed-off pieces of pastry on top of each other and roll out. Cut out with a 1½ to 2-inch scalloped cookie cutter. Brush top of dumplings with egg yolks, wash, then lay cut-outs on top of dumplings. Prick or gash for steam vents.

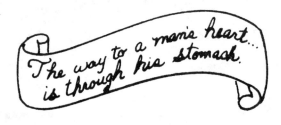

The way to a man's heart... is through his stomach.

BERRY DUMPLINGS

2 cups sifted flour	1 Tbs. sugar
4 tsp. baking powder	3 Tbs. shortening
½ tsp. salt	1 cup milk
Fruit	½ tsp. vanilla

Sift together flour, salt, and baking powder. Cut in shortening. Stir in milk to make stiff dough. Stir in cup of sweetened fruit and vanilla. Drop from tablespoon into rapidly boiling salted water. Cover and cook about 12 minutes. Drain well and serve with your favorite pudding sauce.

PEARL'S PECAN PIE

⅓ cup Crisco
½ cup brown sugar
½ cup milk
1 cup chopped pecans

3 eggs
½ tsp. salt
1 cup corn syrup (Karo either
    light or dark)
½ tsp. vanilla

Cream Crisco and sugar. Add remaining ingredients and blend. Pour into unbaked pie shell. Bake in hot oven 425F 10 minutes. Then at 350 for 25 or 30 minutes. Beat the whole eggs together before you add them and they mix better.

  *So easy to make it will amaze you how good it is.

                              Annie Pearl Matthews
                              White House, Tenn.

BROWNIE PECAN PIE

⅔ cup sugar
⅛ tsp. salt
1 cup light corn syrup
1 pkg. German sweet chocolate
    broken in pieces
3 Tbs. margarine

3 eggs, slightly beaten
1 tsp. vanilla
1 cup coarsely chopped pecans
1 unbaked 9 inch pie shell
Whipped cream to garnish

Combine sugar, salt and corn syrup in a saucepan. Bring to a boil over medium heat. Stirring until sugar dissolves. Boil 2 minutes. Remove from heat, add chocolate and butter and stir until melted. Cool. Gradually pour chocolate mixture over the eggs, mixing well. Add vanilla and pecans. Pour into pie crust and bake at 350 degrees for 50 minutes, cool. Serve topped with whipped cream. Serves 6 to 8.

DIXIE PECAN ROLLS

1 jar marshmallow cream	1 package assorted vanilla &
1 package powdered sugar	chocolate caramels
1 tsp. vanilla	3 Tbs. water
	1 cup chopped pecans

Combine marshmallow, powdered sugar and vanilla; mix well with hands, shape mixture into 5 rolls each 1 x 4 inches, chill 3 hours. Melt carmels and water in top of double boiler or in microwave. Dip rolls in melted caramel and roll each in pecan. Chill 1 hour and cut into slices to serve. Yields 5 rolls.

CURRIED FRUIT BAKE

1 large can peach halves	1 large can pineapple slices
1 large can pear halves	5 maraschino cherries
⅓ cup butter	¾ cup light brown sugar,
4 tsp. curry powder	packed

Drain fruit well; pat dry with paper towels. In a flat casserole arrange fruit; pineapple slices on bottom, peach and pear halves on top of pineapple. There will be peach and pear halves left over. Just tuck them in and around the stacked fruit. Place the cherries here and there in peach or pear centers. Melt butter; add brown sugar and curry. Mix well. Spoon mixture over the fruits. Bake for 1 hour, uncovered, at 325 degrees. Refrigerate, preferably overnight. Thirty minutes before serving reheat fruit in a 350 degree oven for 30 minutes. Serve warm with turkey, ham or any cold meat.

BLACK BOTTOM PIE

10-inch pastry shell

Filling-dark part:

4 tsp. cornstarch
½ cup sugar
¼ tsp. salt
2 cups milk
4 egg yolks, well beaten
1½ cups semi-sweet chocolate
   chips, 1½ pkgs
½ tsp. vanilla
Dash of salt

Filling-light part:

2 tsp. plain gelatin softened in
   ¼ cup cold water 5 minutes
3 egg whites
⅓ cup sugar
1 tsp. rum flavoring
½ cup whipping cream
1 Tbs. sugar
Sweet chocolate bar for shaving

Bake and cool pastry shell. Filling dark part: Blend first 3 ingredients in top of double boiler, using wooden spoon. Stir in milk. Cook and stir over medium heat until smooth and thick as whipping cream. Place over boiling water (top part should not touch water), cover and cook 10 minutes, stirring occasionally. Quickly stir about ⅓ cup of hot mixture into egg yolks; return to hot mixture and cook and stir 2 minutes longer. Remove from heat. Quickly measure 1¼ cups hot custard into bowl that held yolks. Stir softened gelatin into rest of custard and let stand. Stir chocolate into hot custard in bowl; let stand and stir until chocolate melts. Stir in vanilla and dash of salt. Spread smoothly in baked pastry shell. Cool at least 15 minutes.
Filling light part: Beat egg whites to stiff foam, then beat in ⅓ cup sugar gradually to form a stiff shiny meringue. Stir rum flavoring into gelatin mixture, then lightly but thoroughly fold in meringue. Pour over chocolate filling, swirling out level. Chill until firm, 2 to 3 hours. Then spread with the cream whipped until stiff and sweetened with the 1 Tbs. sugar. Sprinkle with shaved chocolate. Again chill for an hour. Serve same day. 8 servings.

Beth Scott
Goodlettsville, Tenn.

APPLE CUSTARD PIE

CRUST:
1½ cups flour
½ tsp. salt
1 stick butter

FILLING: 1 egg
3 apples, peeled and sliced thin   1 cup evaporated milk
⅔ cups sugar
1 tsp. cinnamon

For crust, mix flour, salt and butter with fork until mixture resembles
coarse meal. Press firmly on the bottom and sides of a buttered pie
plate. Place sliced apples on crust. Sprinkle with ⅔ cup sugar and
cinnamon. Bake at 375 degrees for 20 minutes. Beat egg, ½ cup
sugar and milk. Pour over apples and return to oven to bake 30
minutes longer. Serves 6 to 8.

   *Unusual and very good.

APPLE PIE

6 cups tart apples, sliced   ⅛ tsp. salt
6 Tbs. flour   ¼ tsp. cinnamon
1 cup sugar   9-inch pastry for double shell
¼ tsp. nutmeg   pie, unbaked
1 tsp. lemon juice   2 Tbs. cream
2 tsp. butter

Preheat oven to 425 degrees. Mix ingredients. Arrange in pastry shell
and cover with a top crust. Seal top crust to bottom crust. Make
several gashes in top crust. Brush with cream. Bake for about 40
minutes.

GRANNY'S EASY CHERRY COBBLER

Cream together until light and fluffy:

¼ cup soft butter
½ cup sugar

Stir into shortening and sugar:

1 cup flour
2 tsp. baking powder
½ cup milk

Grease pan and add mixture. Pour juice off can of cherries packed in water and add ½ cup sugar to juice.

Place cherries on top of batter and then pour juice over batter. Cook 55 minutes in 8 x 8 cake pan at 375 degrees.

*This is easier than it looks. This has been handed down for generations.

Ann Horan
Nashville, Tenn.

NO BAKE FRUIT CREAM PIE

2 large containers cool whip
1 can eagle brand milk
1 cup nuts

1-8 oz. can crushed pineapple, drained
½ cup lime juice

Mix well all ingredients together. Bake pie crust and after cooling fill pie pan. Leave in refrigerator at least 2 to 5 hours before serving. Will fill 3 pie crusts.

*These can be frozen for later use.

Nell McClung
Murfreesboro, Tenn.

WASHINGTON CREAM PIE

⅓ cup butter	3 tsps. baking powder
¾ cup sugar	¼ tsp. salt
2 eggs, beaten	½ cup milk
1½ cups sifted cake flour	1 tsp. vanilla

Cream butter and sugar and beat in eggs. Combine and sift flour, baking powder and salt, and add, alternately with the milk, to butter mixture.

Beat batter well, add vanilla and bake cake in greased pans in two layers in moderate 375° oven for 12 to 25 minutes.

Place filling between layers and sprinkle top with powdered sugar. Spread whipped cream, a cooked cream filling (adding cocoanut to it, or other nuts), jam, jelly or fruit between layers.

CRANBERRY PIE

2 cups cranberries	½ cup cold water
2 Tbs. flour	2 Tbs. butter
½ tsp. salt	¼ tsp. nutmeg
2 cups sugar	

Cut cranberries into halves. Mix together flour, salt and sugar and sprinkle 2 tbsps. of this mixture into unbaked pie shell. Add remaining sugar mixture to berries with water. Pour into pie shell. Dot with butter and sprinkle with nutmeg. Cover with lattice top and bake in hot 450° oven about 7 to 15 minutes. Reduce heat to moderate 350° and bake until done-about 20 to 35 minutes longer.

For Mock Cherry Pie add 1 cup seeded raisins to cranberries and use only 1 cup sugar.

LEMON SNOW BARS

CRUST:
½ cup butter, softened
⅓ cup all-purpose flour
¼ cup sugar

FILLING:
2 eggs
¾ cup sugar
2 Tbs. all-purpose flour
¼ tsp. baking powder
3 Tbs. lemon juice
Confectioners sugar

In 1 ½ qt. mixing bowl, combine crust ingredients. Mix on low speed until blended, about one minute. Pat into ungreased 8" square pan. Bake near center of oven at 350 degrees for 15 to 20 minutes, or until brown on edges.

EGGNOG CHIFFON PIE

9-inch pastry shell

2 tsp. plain gelatin
2 Tbs. cold water
1 cup milk
3 egg yolks, beaten
½ cup sugar
½ tsp. salt/scant

1 Tbs. rum or 2 tsp. rum
    flavoring
¾ cup whipping cream
3 egg whites
¼ cup plus 3 Tbs. water
¼ tsp. nutmeg or
2 Tbs. chopped pecans or
    pistachios

Bake and cook pastry shell. Sprinkle gelatin over cold water to soften 5 minutes. Blend next 4 ingredients thoroughly in top of double boiler. Place over boiling water and cook and stir with wooden spoon until mixture just thickens. Remove from heat, stir in gelatin until dissolved; stir in rum. Chill until thick like syrup. Beat cream until thick but still smooth; remove mixture from refrigerator and fold in with rubber scraper. Quickly beat egg whites to stiff foam; gradually beat in remaining sugar until stiff and shiny. Fold meringue quickly but thoroughly into gelatin mixture; quickly pour into pastry shell. When filling settles, sprinkle with nutmeg or nuts; if both are desired, fold nutmeg into filling along with rum. Chill until set, 2 to 3 hours.

OATMEAL CAKE

1¼ cups boiling water
1 cup uncooked oats
½ cup margarine
1 cup white sugar
1 cup brown sugar
¼ tsp. ground nutmeg

3 eggs
1 tsp. vanilla
1½ cups sifted all-purpose flour
1 tsp. baking soda
½ tsp. salt
¾ tsp. cinnamon

Preheat oven to 350° F. Grease and lightly dust with flour a 9-inch square pan. Pour boiling water over oats. Cover and let stand for 20 minutes. Cream butter. Add sugars gradually. Continue beating until light and fluffy. Blend in eggs and vanilla. Add oats mixture. Mix well. Sift together flour, soda, salt, and spices. Add to creamed mixture, mixing well. Pour into prepared pan. Bake 50 to 55 minutes or until done. Do not remove from pan.

Topping

¼ cup melted butter or margarine
¾ cup shredded coconut
½ cup brown sugar

3 Tbs. light cream
½ cup chopped nuts

Combine all ingredients. Spread over baked cake. Broil until topping is bubbly. Serve warm or cold. Makes 9 to 12 servings.

JEFFERSON DAVIS PIE

½ cup butter or margarine
2 cups brown sugar
4 eggs yolks
2 tsp. all-purpose flour
½ cup chopped pecans
1 large unbaked pastry shell

1 tsp. cinnamon
1 tsp. ground nutmeg
½ tsp. ground allspice
1 cup light cream
½ cup dates
½ cup raisins

Preheat oven to 350° F. Cream butter and add sugar, creaming until light and fluffy. Add egg yolks. Mix well. Combine flour and spices. Add to creamed mixture. Stir in remaining ingredients. Pour into unbaked pastry shell. Bake 35 to 40 minutes or until set. Cool. Top with whipped cream or ice cream. Makes 8 to 10 servings.

ICE CREAM CAKE

1 cup butter, cream well
2 cups granulated sugar
3 cups sifted flour
3 tsp. baking powder

⅛ tsp. salt
1 tsp. almond extract
1 tsp. vanilla
1 cup milk
7 egg whites, beaten stiff and
    added last.

Beat the sugar into the well creamed butter. Add the well sifted dry ingredients alternately with the milk. Add the flavoring and fold in the stiffly beaten egg whites. Bake in 3, 9-inch buttered layer cake tins 25 minutes in a 375 degree oven. Add your favorite frosting.

OLD TIMERS COCONUT CAKE

1 cup butter
2 cups sugar
3 cups sifted cake flour
½ tsp. salt
½ tsp. almond extract

3 tsp. baking powder
4 eggs
1 cup milk
1 tsp. vanilla

Cream butter, adding sugar gradually. Beat with electric mixer for 10 minutes. Sift dry ingredients. Add eggs one at a time to creamed mixture, beating well after each addition. Add flour mixture alternately with milk, almond and vanilla extract. Pour batter into 3 greased 9-inch pans, lined on bottoms with paper. Bake at 350 degrees for 25-30 minutes. Cool in pans for 10 minutes; remove from pans and cool on racks. Frost with seven-minute icing and grated fresh coconut.

BAKED APPLE

Wash and core firm apples. Add butter, sugar, mixed with raisins, dates, nuts, canned peaches or pineapple, diced marshmallows, or any combination of these. Bake in buttered pan with little water. Add little butter, nutmeg or cinnamon.

DATE BUTTER

1 cup dates, finely cut
½ cup sugar

¼ cup water
½ cup nuts, coarsely cut

Combine dates, sugar and water. Cook until dates are soft, stirring frequently. Add nuts. Cool slightly.

COFFEE SPICE CAKE

2 cups flour, sifted
4 tsp. baking powder
¼ tsp. salt
½ cup sugar
2 eggs, beaten

4 Tbs. butter
¾ cup milk
¼ tsp. cinnamon or nutmeg
1 tsp. vanilla

Sift the flour, baking powder and salt together. Beat the egg, add the melted butter, vanilla and stir in the sifted dry ingredients alternately with milk. Cover with following blended mixture:

1 Tbs. flour
6 Tbs. light brown sugar
1¼ tsp. butter

¼ tsp. cinnamon
½ tsp. vanilla

Blend the flour, sugar, cinnamon with melted butter and spread over the cake. ¼ cup chopped nuts may be added with the sugar and flour. Bake about 25 minutes in a 375 degree oven.

COFFEE CAKE

1 beaten egg
½ cup milk
1 cup flour
½ tsp. salt

½ cup sugar
2 tsp. melted shortening
2 tsp. baking powder

Combine egg, sugar, milk and shortening. Add flour sifted with salt and baking powder. Mix and put in 8 inch greased pan. Cover with following and bake in moderate oven at 375 degrees 20 or 25 minutes.

TOPPING:
¼ cup brown sugar
½ cup nuts
1 tsp. melted butter

1 tsp. cinnamon
1 Tbs. flour

TENNESSEE MUD

2 sticks margarine
2 cups sugar
⅓ cup cocoa
4 eggs
1½ cups flour
1 tsp. vanilla
1 cup chopped pecans
Dash salt

1 jar marshmallow cream
1 stick melted margarine
½ cup evaporated milk
1 box powdered sugar
chopped pecans, optional
½ cup cocoa
1 tsp. vanilla

Cream margarine, sugar and cocoa; add eggs and vanilla; mix, add flour, nuts and salt. Beat two minutes. Bake in a greased 9 x 13 inch pan at 350 degrees for 35 minutes. Spread marshmallow cream on hot cake and cool. Melt one stick of margarine and add milk and vanilla. Stir in powdered sugar and cocoa until smooth. Spread on top of marshmallow cream. May be sprinkled with more chopped pecans, if desired.

BLACK WALNUT CAKE

½ tsp. salt
2 cups brown sugar
3 tsp. baking powder
½ cup butter
1 tsp. vanilla

1 cup finely chopped black
  walnuts
3 eggs
2 cups all-purpose flour
⅔ cups milk

Preheat oven to 350 degrees. Grease a pan. Cream butter and sugar; add egg yolks and nut meats. Add sifted dry ingredients alternately with milk. Add vanilla. Beat egg whites until stiff. Fold into cake mixture. Bake for 1 hour. Frost.

JELLY ROLL

5 eggs
1 cup sugar
⅓ tsp. salt
1 tsp. vanilla

2 cups flour sifted
½ cup sweet cream
4 tsp. baking powder

To the well-beaten eggs, add salt, cream, sifted dry ingredients. Pour into well-buttered tin, bake about 20 minutes in moderate oven. Turn on damp cloth. Spread with jelly, whipped cream, or apple butter and roll. Wrap towel around roll until ready to serve, sprinkle with powdered sugar.

LEMON LAYER CAKE

½ cup soft butter
3 eggs
1¼ cups sugar
2½ tsp. baking powder
½ cup milk

2 cups sifted flour
⅛ tsp. salt
½ tsp. vanilla
½ tsp. lemon juice

Cream butter, add sugar, beat well. Add egg yolks. Sift dry ingredients, add alternately with milk. Beat thoroughly, add beaten egg whites, add vanilla. Bake in 2 well-greased tins in oven 375 degrees about 25 minutes.

SOUTHERN CHOCOLATE FUDGE CAKE

2 cups flour
2 cups sugar
1½ tsp. baking soda
¼ tsp. salt
½ Cup cocoa
1 cup oil
1 cup buttermilk
2 eggs, beaten
3 tsp. vanilla

¾ cups hot water
6 Tbs. milk
1 stick butter
1 box (1 pound) powdered sugar
1 Tbs. vanilla
1 cup chopped pecans, optional

Sift together flour, sugar, soda, salt and cocoa. Add oil, buttermilk, eggs, vanilla and hot water; mix well. Bake in greased 9 x 13 inch pan at 350 degrees for 30 to 40 minutes. For icing, make a paste of the cocoa and milk in a saucepan. Add butter and bring to a boil, stirring constantly. Remove from heat and add powdered sugar and vanilla. Beat well. Add pecans. Pour over still hot cake in baking pan.

MAHOGANY CAKE

2 cups sifted flour
1 tsp. baking soda
½ tsp. salt
½ cup butter, shortening
1 cup sour milk

1 cup water
1 egg, well beaten
½ cup cocoa
⅓ cup water
1 tsp. vanilla

Sift flour once, measure, add baking soda and salt and sift together three times. Work butter with spoon until creamy. Add sugar gradually, beating after each addition until light and fluffy. Add egg. Add water to cocoa slowly, mixing until a smooth paste is formed. Add to creamed mixture, blending well. Add flour, alternately with milk, a small amount at a time, beating until smooth after each addition. Add vanilla. Turn into greased loaf pan. Bake in moderate oven for 50 minutes. Spread with date butter and top with chocolate frosting.

REFRIGERATOR CHOCOLATE CAKE

2 tsp. vanilla
1 cup whipped cream
2½ doz. lady fingers

10 Tbs. cocoa
10 marshmallows
½ cup cream
½ cup hot water

Dissolve cocoa in hot water, blend together until smooth. Cook, add whipped cream and vanilla. Line oblong loaf pan with thin layer of chocolate. Add layer of vanilla wafers or sponge cake cut one fourth inch thick or lady fingers, then layer of chocolate; wafers, until chocolate mixture is used. Top with wafers, chill in refrigerator 10 hours. Cut in slices, serve with whipped cream.

BROWN BETTY

2 cups bread crumbs
¼ cup butter, melted over hot
   water
1 quart sliced apples
¾ cup sugar, brown or white

¼ tsp. nutmeg
Grated rind and juice of ½
   lemon
½ cup hot water
Almond or lemon flavoring

Mix crumbs and butter with fork. Cover bottom of buttered pudding dish with crumb mixture, cover with half the apples, sprinkle with half of sugar, nutmeg, lemon juice, cover with crumbs and remaining ingredients. Bake 40 minutes in moderate oven. Cover at first to prevent crumbs browning too rapidly. Serve with cream.

255

STRAWBERRY SHORT CAKE

2 cups sifted flour
4 tsp. baking powder
½ tsp. salt
¼ cup sugar

⅓ cup butter
¾ cup milk
Softened butter

One quart strawberries cut, add 1 cup sugar. Let stand 2 to 3 hours at room temperature.

Prepare as for baking powder biscuit. Roll ¼ inch thick, cut with floured cutter. Place one half of rounds in ungreased baking pan, spread well with melted butter. Cover with biscuit halves, brush top with butter. Bake in hot oven 450 degrees about 15 minutes and bake at meal time to serve hot. Separate halves, spread soft centers with soft butter. Cover bottom half with berries, place top with soft side up. Cover with berries. Pass sweetened whipped cream. FOR LARGE CAKE—Pat dough into 2, 8 inch ungreased layer cake tins, or bake in 1 pan, split dough, spread well with soft butter. Add berries.

STRAWBERRIES IN WHIPPED CREAM

1 pint sound ripe strawberries
9-inch pastry shell
1 cup whipping cream, chilled

1 Tbs. lemon juice
½ cup sugar
Dash of salt

Bake and cool pastry shell. An hour before serving time wash berries, drain well, then hull. Save 5 perfect berries for garnish. Cut rest of berries in 4 lengthwise slices or in quarters, dropping into a bowl. Place in refrigerator. Just before serving, whip cream until thick, then add lemon juice gradually and beat until very stiff, then beat in the sugar. Now fold in cold berries lightly and turn into pie shell, gently spreading out to level. Garnish with saved whole berries and serve at once. 5 servings.

PECAN DATE CAKE

1 lb. butter
2¼ cups white sugar
6 whole eggs

4 cups flour (sift 3 times) Plain
2 tsp. vanilla

Cream butter, sugar & eggs. Beat batter until smooth.

ADD:
1 lb. pecan halves
1½ lbs. candied cherries
1 lb. chopped pitted dates
1 box golden seedless raisins

Bake in large tube pan for 3 hours at 275 over pan of water.

* If recipes were rated by stars like restaurants, this would definitely be a FOUR STAR recipe.

SOCK IT TO ME CAKE

1 pkg. butter cake mix
½ cup sugar
8 oz. sour cream
2 tsp. brown sugar

¾ cup pure vegetable oil
4 eggs
½ cup chopped pecans
2 tsp. cinnamon

Mix cake mix, sugar and oil. Add eggs one at a time, add sour cream. Mix well. Stir in pecans. pour half of batter into greased tube pan. Sprinkle brown sugar and cinnamon over batter. Add remaining batter. Bake in moderate oven at 350 degrees for 60 to 65 minutes until cake is done.

GLAZE IF DESIRED; 1 cup confectioners sugar
                 3 Tbs. milk
                 Orange or lemon juice

Mix and pour over cake.

                                    Dot Casteel
                                    Madison, Tenn.

257

RAISIN BRAN COFFEE-DATE SKILLET BALLS

¾ cup butter or margarine
1 cup firmly packed brown sugar
1 package chopped dates
2 Tbs. instant coffee
1 egg slightly beaten
3 cups raisin bran
2⅔ cups coconut
½ cup chopped nuts

Melt butter in large heavy skillet. Stir in sugar, dates and instant coffee. Remove from heat; blend in egg. Cook and stir over medium heat until mixture comes to a full boil. Boil 1 minute, stirring constantly. Remove from heat; stir in cereal, 1⅓ cups of the coconut and the nuts. Let stand 10 minutes. Shape into 1 inch balls. Roll in remaining coconut. Makes 5 dozen.

Delicious and different.

GRANDMA'S POUND CAKE

2 cups flour sifted
2 cups granulated sugar
1 cup butter
4 eggs

½ tsp. cream of tartar
1 tsp. vanilla
1 cup grated lemon

Cream butter, slowly add sugar and mix thoroughly. Then add whole egg, one at a time stirring constantly. Sift together flour, cream of tartar and salt. Add to first mixture, beat well. Add vanilla. Bake in well buttered greased loaf tins about 1 hour in 325 degree oven.

ORANGE SPONGE CAKE

1 cup sifted flour
¼ tsp. baking soda
¼ tsp. salt
3 egg yolks, beaten until thick
   & lemon colored

¾ cup sugar
¼ tsp. grated orange rind
¼ cup orange juice
1 Tbs. lemon juice
3 egg whites, stiffly beaten

Sift flour once, measure, add baking soda, and salt and sift together four times. Add sugar gradually to egg yolks beating thoroughly after each addition. Add rind and fruit juices. Beat egg whites until stiff but not dry. Fold in egg yolk mixture. Fold in flour, a small amount at a time. Turn into ungreased tube pan. Bake in moderate oven 45 minutes. Invert pan one hour or until cold before removing cake.

NO EGG ORANGE SPICE CAKE

¾ cup butter
2 cups granulated sugar
4 cups sifted flour
2 tsp. baking powder
½ tsp. cinnamon
½ cup walnuts

½ tsp. nutmeg
1 cup boiled coffee
1 tsp. soda dissolved in
1 cup sour milk
1½ tsp. vanilla extract
½ lb. orange slices

Cream butter thoroughly, slowly beat in sugar. Sift dry ingredients three times and add alternately with sour milk and coffee. Add flavoring. Add finely cut orange slices and nuts blended with a little of the flour. Pour into greased, lightly floured loaf pans and bake about 55 minutes to 1 hour in a 350 degree oven. Will make 2 loaf cakes.

HARVEY WALLBANGER CAKE

1 box yellow cake mix
1 small box vanilla instant
  pudding
½ cup oil
4 eggs

¼ cup vodka
¼ cup Galliano liqueur
¾ cup orange juice
powdered sugar optional

GLAZE:

1 cup sifted powdered sugar
1 Tbs. orange juice

1 Tbs. vodka
1 Tbs. galliano

Mix cake mix, pudding, oil, eggs, vodka, galliano, orange juice and beat for 4 minutes. Pour batter into greased and floured tube pan. Bake at 350 for 45 to 50 minutes or until toothpick clean. If desired, dust with powdered sugar or frost with glaze made from powdered sugar, orange juice, vodka and galliano.

Lynda Woodard
Goodlettsville, Tenn.

PLAIN BUTTER CAKE

½ cup shortening (butter)
1 cup sugar
2 eggs
⅔ cup milk
2 cups flour (sifted)

3 tsp. baking powder
¼ tsp. salt
1 tsp. vanilla

Cream shortening, add sugar gradually, blend thoroughly. Beat eggs well, add to first mixture. Mix, sift flour, salt and baking powder, combine alternately with milk. Lastly, add vanilla. Bake in buttered layer tins, 25 minutes, 375 degree oven.

TENNESSEE APPLE CAKE

Batter

1¼ cup liquid oil
2 cups sugar
3 eggs
1 tsp. baking soda
1 tsp. salt
3 cups flour
3 cups peeled and chopped or grated apples
1 cup chopped nuts
2 tsp. vanilla

Blend oil and sugar well. Sift dry ingredients and add to oil and sugar mixture. Beat eggs slightly and add to batter. Add vanilla. Fold in apples and nuts. Grease and flour large tube or Bundt pan. Bake at 250° for 1½ hours. Cool and invert. Add topping.

Topping

1 cup brown sugar
1 stick butter or margarine
¼ cup evaporated milk
1 tsp. vanilla

Cook above ingredients to a full boil. Beat and cool. Spread on apple cake.

Lynda Woodard
Goodlettsville, Tenn.

DELICATE GINGER CAKES

1½ cups sifted flour
¾ tsp. baking soda
¼ tsp. salt
½ tsp. cinnamon
½ tsp. ginger
¼ tsp. cloves
½ cup butter or shortening
½ cup boiling water
¾ cup molasses
1 egg, well beaten

Sift flour once, measure, add baking soda, salt and spices, and sift together three times. Pour boiling water over butter, and stir until blended. Add molasses. Add egg. Add flour mixture. Beat only until blended. Turn into greased, small cup cake pan. Bake in moderate oven 18 minutes. Makes 24 cakes.

CHARLENE'S APPLE CAKE

2 cups flour
2 tsp. soda
1 tsp. salt
4 eggs

2 cups sugar
2 tsp. cinnamon
1½ cups vegetable oil
2½ cups peeled and grated
    apples

Sift together dry ingredients, add cooking oil and eggs. Mix well then add grated apples. Cook in 3 layer pans for 30 minutes at 350 degrees.

ICING:

1 8-ounce pkg. cream cheese
½ stick oleo
2 tsp. vanilla

1 box powdered sugar
1 cup chopped nuts

Mix together well, and spread on cooled cake.

Charlene Johnson
Houston, Texas

POOR MANS SPICE CAKE
(No Eggs)

1 cup brown sugar
1 cup boiling water
1 cup raisins
⅓ cup shortening
¼ tsp. nutmeg
1 tsp. cinnamon
1½ tsp. vanilla

1½ cups flour
⅛ tsp. cloves
¼ tsp. ginger
¼ tsp. allspice
½ tsp. salt
1½ tsp. baking powder

Boil sugar, water, shortening, raisins together about 3 minutes until sugar is well dissolved. Put aside until cold. Sift flour, baking powder, spices together, add to above mixture, add flavoring. Bake in moderate oven. Use small square pan.

LAYER SPICE CAKE

2 cups brown sugar
½ cup butter
2 egg yolks
2¾ cups flour sifted
1½ tsp. baking powder
1 tsp. vanilla

1 tsp. cinnamon
½ tsp. allspice
½ tsp. nutmeg
1 cup sour milk
1 tsp. soda

Cream butter, beat in sugar, add beaten egg yolks. Add vanilla. Add sifted dry ingredients and milk. Mix thoroughly, bake in 375 degree oven. Add beaten egg whites. Cover w/white frosting.

OLD SOUTH SWEET POTATOES WITH CARAMEL SAUCE

4 Cups cooked, peeled, mashed sweet potatoes
¾ cup brown sugar
1 tsp. vanilla
1 cup pecans
½ cup cream (half & half)

After creaming potatoes, add sugar, vanilla and cream. Put in greased casserole dish. make a "well" in the center and sprinkle with pecans. Bake at 350 degrees until hot and just before serving, pour sauce over, filling the "well".

Sauce: Melt one cup butter and one cup sugar together in iron skillet until golden. Slowly pour in ½ cup cream and cook about two minutes, adding a pinch of salt and one teaspoon vanilla.

*This is a "must" with every Thanksgiving and Christmas dinner.

Pearlie Scott
Goodlettsville, Tenn.

RUM CAKE

½ to ⅔ cup dark sweet rum
1 oz. unsweetened chocolate,
  melted

1 3¾ oz. package vanilla
  flavored pudding and pie
  filling mix
2 egg yolks

Prepare sponge cake batter, but divide among 3 eight inch layer pans lined with wax paper. When cake layers are cool, sprinkle each generously with rum. Prepare filling by preparing vanilla pudding and pie filling according to directions on package; when thickened, beat pudding mixture into egg yolks. Stir over low heat about 3 minutes. To ⅓ of the custard mixture, add melted chocolate. Spread plain custard over first layer of cake, chocolate over second, plain custard over third. Chill in refrigerator over night.

Frosting:

3 cups granulated sugar
½ cup evaporated milk
⅛ tsp. salt
4 oz. unsweetened chocolate

4 Tbs. butter
1 tsp. vanilla, or 1 Tbs. rum

Place sugar, milk, salt and chocolate in saucepan. Cook and stir over medium heat until sugar is dissolved; cook, stirring constantly, until mixture boils; cook until a little dropped in water forms a soft ball-about 5 minutes longer. Add butter and vanilla; cool until lukewarm. Beat until frosting is creamy and spreads easily. Immediately spread sides of cake.

APRICOT ICE BOX CAKE

½ lb. vanilla wafers
1 cup powdered sugar
⅓ cup butter
2 eggs, beaten
1 med. sized can apricots
   drained

1 cup whipped cream
½ tsp. vanilla
2 Tbs. sugar to cream

Crush the wafers with a rolling pin and line the bottom of a pan with half of the crumbs. Cream the butter and slowly beat in the sugar. Add the beaten eggs and mix thoroughly. Spread this mixture over the crumbs in the pan. Place the apricot halves on top and cover with the sweetened whipped cream. Sprinkle with the remaining crumbs and let stand in a cool place 24 hours. Cut in squares. Will serve 8.

  *Strawberries or drained canned pineapple may be used instead of apricots.

APPLE CAKE OR DRIED PEACH CAKE

4 eggs beaten
1 cup sugar
1 cup butter, cream well
1 cup sour milk
3 cups cake flour, sifted
2½ tsp. baking powder

½ tsp. soda
1 tsp. cinnamon
½ tsp. cloves
½ tsp. nutmeg
Lemon extract or flavoring to
  taste

Soak 3 cups dried apples in as little water as possible overnight. Chop the apples fine and boil 30 minutes in 2 cups sugar. Cool. Add rest of ingredients as for any cake mixture. Heat oven to 350 degrees. Bake in buttered lightly floured sheet pan or in 2 deep 9-inch layer tins for 40 minutes. Cover with thick boiled frosting. This cake will keep moist and delicious.

OLD-FASHION DARK FRUIT CAKE

2 lbs. currants
2 lbs. seedless raisins
2 lbs. chopped candied
   pineapple
½ lb. chopped candied cherries
1 lb. chopped candied citron
2 cups fruit juice
2 cups shortening
2 cups sugar
1 cup grape jelly

12 eggs
4½ cups flour
½ tsp. salt
1 tsp. cinnamon
2 tsp. alspice
½ tsp. nutmeg
2 tsp. cloves
1 lb. chopped blanched
   almonds
1½ lb. broken pecans
2 tsp. vanilla

Combine fruit, add fruit juice, cover and let stand over night. Sift flour, spices and salt together 3 times. Cream shortening and sugar together until fluffy. Add jelly and mix thoroughly. Beat eggs and add to creamed mixture alternately with flour mixture. Add nuts and fruit, a small amount at a time. All flavoring. Bake in a greased paper lined loaf pan in a slow oven 300-325 degrees. Bake large cakes 3 hours. Cook cakes in a pan. When cook-glaze and garnish. Yields 20 lbs.

* This is a very old and very good dark fruit cake. It can be made 3 to 4 weeks before Christmas. Wrap in cloth soaked in wine or grape juice and it will be more delicious at Christmas then when it was fresh baked.

Pearlie Scott
Goodlettsville, TN

COCA COLA CAKE

Mix together and set aside:

2 cups plain flour	2 cups sugar

Mix and bring to a boil;
2 sticks oleo, 3 tsp. of cocoa and 1 cup coca cola

Pour over sugar and flour, then add:
½ cup buttermilk, 2 eggs beaten, 1 tsp. soda
1 tsp. vanilla and 1½ cups of miniature marshmallows

Cook in a greased sheet cake pan at 325 degrees for one half hour.

ICING:

1 stick oleo	3 tsp. cocoa
6 Tbs. coca cola	1 box confectioners sugar
1 cup chopped nuts	

Combine margarine, cocoa, coca cola and bring to a boil and pour over 1 box confectioners sugar. Mix well. Add nuts, blend well. Pour over cake as soon as you take the cake from the oven.

Dot Casteel
Madison, Tenn.

CHOCOLATE DATE CUP

2 whole eggs	2 or 3 Tbs. milk
¼ cup sugar	1 tsp. vanilla
½ cup dates	2 cups milk
½ cup chopped walnuts	½ cup shredded coconut
2 heaping tsp. chocolate dessert	Pinch salt

Beat eggs two or three minutes. Add sugar, dates (pitted and cut) walnuts (not chopped too fine) chocolate dessert mixed with milk and vanilla. Put in buttered baking dish, bake in slow oven 35 to 45 minutes. Serve with whipped cream, sprinkle with shredded coconut. Serves 4 to 6.

GRANNYS LEMON PIE

Juice and grated rind of 1 lemon
3 Tbs. milk
1 cup sugar
1 8-inch unbaked pastry shell

2 tsp. cornstarch
3 eggs slightly beaten
2 Tbs. butter or margarine

Preheat oven to 375° F. Combine all ingredients except butter. Pour into unbaked pastry shell. Dot with butter. Bake about 30 to 35 minutes or until brown. Makes 6 servings.

"SUGAR CREEK" CHESS PIE

½ cup butter or margarine
1½ cups sugar
3 eggs, beaten
1 8-inch unbaked pastry shell

1 Tbs. cider vinegar
1 Tbs. vanilla
¼ tsp. salt

Preheat oven to 300° F. Combine butter and sugar in a saucepan over medium heat. Cook, stirring constantly, until very smooth. Remove from heat. Add eggs. Mix thoroughly. Stir in vinegar, vanilla, and salt. Beat to blend ingredients. Pour into pastry shell. Bake about 50 minutes. Makes 6 servings.

JEWISH APPLE CAKE

6 peeled apples sliced thin
3 tsp. sugar
2 tsp. cinnamon

Mix together and set aside.

Batter:

3 cups flour
2½ cups sugar
1 cup Crisco oil
4 eggs

½ tsp. salt
⅓ cup orange juice
2⅓ tsp. vanilla
3 tsp. baking powder

Mix above ingredients together. Mix most of the apples into the batter, and place balance of apples on top.

NOTE: If you use self rising flour, omit baking powder and salt.

*This receipe came South from Maryland and quickly won a loyal following. Very good and stays moist for days.

The way to a man's heart... is through his stomach.

TWINKIES CAKE

9 or 10 twinkies cut in half
6 or 7 bananas sliced
1 small can crushed pineapple
1 large instant vanilla pudding (Mix according to directions)
1 medium cool whip

Place twinkies in cake plate add bananas, and pudding. Add cool whip. Chill for several hours.

Ann Fitzhugh
Murfreesboro, Tenn.

DRIED APPLE STACK CAKE

3 eggs
4 cups uncooked dried apples
2 cup brown sugar-packed
1 tsp. soda
1 tsp. salt
½ tsp. nutmeg

1 tsp. vanilla
3 cups plain flour
2 cups soft butter
½ tsp. cinnamon
½ tsp. cloves

Cook dried apples until very tender. Drain. Mash until smooth. Add 2 cups sugar, and spices. Set aside. Cream butter and brown sugar. Add eggs one at a time and beat until lightly mixed. Combine sifted flour; soda and salt. Add flour mixture to the egg, butter and sugar mixture. Beat until smooth. Spread very thin in greased and floured regular size round or square cake pans. Will make 5 or 6 thin layers. Bake 25 minutes in 350 degree oven. Stack layers with generous quanity of apple mixture between each layer and on top of cake. Let stand 6 hours before serving.

*This receipe was passed down through the generations of the McClung family. The McClung family of East Tennessee has passed this receipe from generation to generation for at least 100 years. This copy was among the receipes left by Nancy McClung, mother of Vince McClung of Murfreesboro, Tennessee. It's a rare taste of the past and delicious.

BANANA CAKE

½ cup butter
1½ cups sugar
3 eggs
2¼ cups sifted cake flour
½ tsp. baking powder
¾ tsp. soda

½ tsp. salt
1 cup mashed or riced bananas
1 tsp. vanilla
¼ cup sour milk

Cream butter and sugar. Beat in eggs one at a time. Resift flour with baking powder, soda and salt.

Add vanilla to milk. Stir sifted ingredients into butter mixture alternately with milk and bananas. Beat batter until smooth after each addition.

Bake the cake in two greased 9-inch cake pans in moderate 350° oven 15 to 30 minutes.

Place sliced bananas between layers. Ice top of the cake with uncooked lemon icing.

PLUM PUDDING

1 lb. suet, chopped
1 lb. seeded raisins
1 lb. currants, washed and dried
1 lb. citron, chopped
½ cup flour
1 nutmeg, grated
1 Tbs. cinnamon
½ Tbs. mace

1 tsp. salt
7 egg yolks
6 Tbs. sugar
4 Tbs. cream
½ cup brandy or sherry
3 cups grated bread crumbs
7 egg whites, stiffly beaten

One-half cup orange juice and 2 tbsps. grated orange rind may be substituted for brandy.

Prepare first four ingredients and dredge with flour. Add remaining ingredients in order given. Place batter in greased mold. Steam pudding for 6 hours. Serve with hard sauce. Amount: 24 servings.

COCONUT DELIGHT

FIRST LAYER:
1 stick oleo (Melted)
1 cup flour
½ cup chopped nuts
¼ cup sugar

Mix & Press in 9x12 pan, bake 15 minutes at 350 degrees, cool.

SECOND LAYER:
1 8 oz. cream cheese
1 cup powdered sugar
1 cup cool whip

Mix with mixer and spread over 1st layer.

THIRD LAYER:
2 pkg. vanilla pudding mix
3 cup milk

Mix pudding mix and milk. When begins to thicken, spread over 2nd layer.

FOURTH LAYER:
Spread one cup cool whip over 3rd layer & sprinkle with Bakers canned coconut.

> **Grace Young**
> **Murfreesboro, Tenn.**

SEVEN-MINUTE WHITE ICING

2 egg whites (unbeaten)   ¼ tsp. cream of tartar
1½ cups sugar   1 tsp. vanilla
5 Tbs. cold water

Place ingredients, except flavoring in top of double boiler.
Beat until they are thoroughly blended. Use wire spiral egg whip or
dover beater. Place top over bottom of double boiler filled with
rapidly boiling water.
Beat icing for 7 minutes. Remove from fire and add flavoring.
The icing is then ready to be spread.

Variations of Seven-Minute Icing

Nut Icing: Add ½ cup chopped nut meats to cooked icing.
Lemon Icing: Use only 2 tbsps. water. Add 2 tbsps. lemon juice, ¼
tsp. grated lemon rind.
Orange Icing: Omit water, Add ½ tsp. grated orange rind, and ¼ cup
orange juice.
Sea Foam Icing: Substitute brown sugar for white. After 5 minutes
remove double boiler from fire. Beat 2 minutes longer. Place boiler
top in cold water, and beat for 3 minutes longer.
Chocolate Icing: Melt over hot water, then cool 3 oz. (squares)
chocolate. When icing is cooked, fold in vanilla and melted chocolate.
Raisin Icing: Spread cooked icing. Sprinkle with 1 cup seeded or
seedless raisins chopped.
Cocoanut Icing: Spread cooked icing. Sprinkle with shredded cocoanut.
Chocolate Coating over White Icing: When cooked icing is spread,
pour chocolate (melted over hot water) on it. Spread it lightly over
surface with broad knife. Permit chocolate to harden. Do not attempt
this in hot weather.

CHOCOLATE ICING

2 cups sugar
2 ozs. (squares) chocolate
2 Tbs. corn syrup

¾ cup milk
2 Tbs. butter
1 tsp. vanilla

Cook first four ingredients until syrup forms a ball when dropped into cold water (238°). Remove syrup from fire, add butter and place saucepan in cold water.
When icing is lukewarm, add vanilla and beat icing until creamy. If icing hardens too rapidly, add a few drops of hot water, or place saucepan in hot water.

SOUR CREAM ICING

1 cup sugar
1 cup sour cream
1 tsp. vanilla

½ cup nut meats, chopped

Boil sugar and sour cream until syrup forms a soft ball when dropped into cold water (238°).
Cool syrup until lukewarm, then beat until creamy. Add vanilla and nuts and spread icing.

CARAMEL ICING

2 cups brown sugar
1 cup milk or cream

3 Tbs. butter
1 tsp. vanilla

Boil sugar and liquid until syrup forms a soft ball when dropped into cold water (238°). Add butter, remove icing from fire and cool. Add vanilla and beat until thick and creamy.
If too heavy, thin icing with a little hot cream until right consistency to spread.

Maggie Nola Sloan
Goodlettsville, Tenn.

HARD SAUCE

⅓ cup butter
1 cup confectioners sugar

1 tsp. vanilla

Work butter with spoon until creamy. Add sugar gradually and beat until light. Add flavoring. Set in cool place until needed. Grated lemon rind, nutmeg or cinnamon to taste may be substituted for vanilla.

BOILED FROSTING

1 cup sugar
½ cup water

2 egg whites, beaten
½ tsp. vanilla

Cook sugar and water together, stirring only until sugar has dissolved. Continue cooking until syrup spins a thread when dropped from the tip of a spoon. Remove from heat. When syrup stops bubbling pour in stream over egg whites, beating constantly. Continue beating until frosting stands in peaks. Add vanilla. Makes enough frosting to cover tops and sides of two 9 inch layers.

SOFT CHOCOLATE FROSTING

1 cup confectioners sugar
1 egg slightly beaten
Dash of salt

2 squares unsweetened
  chocolate
½ tsp. vanilla

Add sugar gradually to egg, and beat until smooth and light. Add salt and chocolate and blend well. Add vanilla. Cool before spreading. Makes enough to cover tops and sides of a 6 x 10 loaf cake.

ORANGE BUTTER FROSTING

2 Tbs. butter
2 cups confectioners sugar
3 Tbs. milk

¼ tsp. grated orange rind
¼ tsp. orange extract
A few drops lemon extract

Work butter with spoon until very soft. Add sugar gradually, beating well, thinning with milk until of right consistency to spread. Add orange rind and flavoring. Makes enough frosting to cover tops and sides of two 8 inch layers.

MOCHA FROSTING

2 Tbs. butter 2 cups confectioners sugar
3 Tbs. strong coffee

Work butter with spoon until creamy. Add sugar gradually, thinning with coffee, until of right consistency to spread. Beat well. Makes enough frosting to cover tops of two 9 inch layers.

FLUFFY FROSTING

1 cup sugar ¼ tsp. cream of tartar
2 egg whites, unbeaten Dash of Salt
4 Tbs. cold water ½ tsp. vanilla

Combine sugar, egg whites, water, cream of tartar and salt in upper part of double boiler. Beat well. Place over boiling water and beat constantly with rotary beater seven minutes. Remove from heat and continue beating until frosting stands up in peaks. Add vanilla. Makes enough frosting to cover tops and sides of two 9 inch layers.

LEMON CHESS PIE

2 cups sugar
1 Tbs. all-purpose flour
1 Tbs. corn meal
½ cup melted butter or
   margarine

4 eggs
¼ cup lemon juice
2 Tbs. grated lemon rind
¼ cup milk
1 9-inch unbaked pastry shell

Preheat oven to 325° F. Combine all ingredients. Mix well. Pour into unbaked pastry shell. Bake about 35 to 40 minutes or until done. Top will be quite brown. Makes 6 to 8 servings.

FUDGE CAKE

2½ squares unsweetened
   chocolate
1 cup butter or margarine
2 cups sugar

5 eggs
1 cup sifted, all-purpose flour
1 tsp. vanilla

Preheat oven to 350° F. Grease and lightly flour a 9- x 13-inch pan. Melt chocolate over low heat. Cool slightly. Cream butter. Gradually add sugar, beating until light and fluffy. Add eggs one at a time, beating well after each addition. Stir in flour. Mix well. Add vanilla. Pour into prepared pan. Bake for 30 minutes. Cool. Do not remove from pan.

Refreshments

HOW TO DECORATE YOUR PUNCH BOWL

DECORATED ICE CUBES:
Arrange in each section of refrigerator tray a berry, red cherry, piece of lemon or orange slice, or a sprig of mint. Then fill tray with water and freeze as usual. Serve in fruit drinks.

FLAVORED ICE CUBES:
Freeze fruit juices or sparkling beverages in ice cube trays. Serve in cold fruit drinks or sparkling beverages of contrasting flavors.

OTHER GARNISHES:
Thin slices of lemon, lime or orange. Melon balls, strawberries, cherries, grapes. Scoops of lemon, lime, orange or pineapple ice cream.

FRUIT PUNCH

2 pkgs. Kool-Aid cherry and strawberry (2 each)
1 6 oz. can frozen orange juice
1 6 oz. can frozen lemonade
1 gallon water
3 cups sugar
1 pkg. red jello
1 46 oz. can pineapple juice

Combine jello with small amount of heated water first and then add all other ingredients. Will serve 50 people or makes about 7 quarts.

MINT JULEP

1 tsp. sugar	Water
2 to 3 sprigs fresh mint	Cracked ice
2 jiggers bourbon	Mint (for garnish)

Use just enough water to dissolve sugar thoroughly. Add mint. Fill a cup (preferable metal) with finely cracked ice. Add bourbon and stir gently. Add a little more cracked ice and allow to stand until cup is frosted. Garnish with mint.

APRICOT BRANDY

½ pound rock candy	1 pound dried apricots
1 quart vodka	

Mix and let stand in covered glass container for 6 weeks. (Remove rope from candy if it comes on it.) Yield: 1 quart. You may drink as is or serve as follows:

Apricot brandy Ices: In a blender, place 2 dips of vanilla ice cream and 1 ounce apricot brandy. Mix briefly. Serve in champagne glasses as an after dinner drink or dessert.

SPICED COFFEE

4½ cups water
6 Tbs. coffee
4 cinnamon sticks
8 whole cloves

8 whole allspice
½ cup heavy cream
Nutmeg
Whipped cream

Pour water into electric percolator. Place coffee and spices, except nutmeg, in basket; brew. Pour into small cups. Whip cream for topping (do ahead); place spoonful on top of each coffee and sprinkle with nutmeg. Serve with sugar, if desired. Yield: 8 servings.

*May be made with a coffee maker if spices are allowed to steep in coffee for at least 15 minutes after brewing. Strain before pouring into cups.

HOT CIDER

½ cup brown sugar
1 tsp. whole cloves
1 tsp. allspice
¼ tsp. salt

Dash of nutmeg
3 sticks of cinnamon
2 quarts cider
Orange wedges

Combine all ingredients except orange wedges in a saucepan; slowly bring to a boil. Cover and simmer for 20 minutes. Strain to remove spices. Pour cider into warmed glass pitcher over orange wedges studded with additional cloves. Serve in mugs with orange wedges. Makes 20 servings.

CRANBERRY CHRISTMAS PUNCH

1 3-ounce pkg. cherry flavored Jello
1 cup boiling water
1 6-oz. can frozen lemonade concentrate
3 cups cold water
1 quart bottle cranberry juice cocktail (chilled)
1 28-ounce bottle gingerale (chilled)

Dissolve cherry flavored gelatin in boiling water. Stir in lemonade concentrate. Add cold water and cranberry juice cocktail. Place in a large bowl with two trays of ice cubes or a mold ring. Pour the punch over ice slowly.

INSTANT SPICED TEA

2 cups Tang
½ cup instant tea w/lemon
1 tsp. cloves

4 cups sugar
½ tsp. cinnamon

Mix well and keep in closed jar or canister. Use 2 to 4 tsps. of mix to 1 cup hot water.

COCA COLA PUNCH

Juice of one dozen lemons
3 cups sugar
5 pints water
grated lemon rind

Mix and let stand over night. Strain and add 6 Coca Colas or Royal Crown Colas.

LIME DAIQUIRI

1 small can frozen limeade
1 small can pineapple juice
1 tsp. confectioners sugar
1 ounce rum

Combine ingredients in blender, mixing ice as you blend for 15 seconds. Pour into frosted glasses.

STRAWBERRY DAIQUIRI

2 ounces Strawberry de Bordeaux
1 ounce rum
1 tsp. lemon juice
½ cup frozen strawberries, partially thawed

Combine ingredients in blender, and whir at low speed for 15 seconds. Pour into stemmed glasses.

WEDDING PUNCH—SERVES 100

Juice of 2 doz. oranges
Juice of 2 doz. lemons
2 large bottles ginger ale

2 large cans crushed pineapple
1 large jar red cherries
½ gal. vanilla ice cream

2 qts. water
4 c. sugar

½ gal. peach ice cream (or any kind of sherbet)
50 lbs. crushed ice

Boil water and sugar and let cool.
Mix juices of lemons and oranges with sugar mixture (this can be done the night before). Add crushed pineapple, cherries (cut in half, if desired), ginger ale to first mixture and stir well. About ½ hour before serving, add ice cream and stir well. Just before serving, add some crushed ice. Keep plenty of ice in mixture as it is much better ICE COLD.

SPRING WINE

1 pkg. lemon-lime Kool-Aid
1 c. sugar

1 tall can pineapple juice
1 or 2 trays of ice

Mix together and serve ice cold.

HOT APPLE TODDY

5 qts. apple juice	1 tsp. whole cloves
1 tsp. whole allspice	1 lb. sugar
4 sticks cinnamon	1 qt. orange juice
1 lemon, sliced very thin	1 lg. can pineaple juice
4 lemons, juice	(optional)
2 qts. 100 proof whiskey	1 qt. apple brandy

Boil 2 qts. apple juice with the spices for 5 minutes. Add this to sugar, then drop in sliced lemon. Boil 1 minute. Cool. Add rest of apple juice, orange juice, lemon juice and pineaple juice (if used). Strain. Add whiskey and brandy to strained mixture. Seal in quart jars. When used, serve hot but do not boil. This is good to have on hand in winter months—especially for those suffering from colds.

MOCK WHISKEY SOUR

1 small can frozen lemonade	1 can dark rum
1 can light rum	1 can bourbon

Serve over crushed ice. Use lemonade can for measuring rum and bourbon.

DILL VEGETABLE DIP

1 large carton sour cream
1 Tbs. parsley flakes
2 tsp. dill weed

1 tsp. garlic powder
1 Tbs. onion powder
1 c. salad dressing
2 Tbs. mayonnaise

Mix all ingredients well and chill. Serve with round rye bread hollowed out center, use center of bread (cut up into pieces) to dip into dill dip. Also good with fresh vegetables.

JALEPENO PARTY CHEESE

1 pound velveeta
1 pound mild cheddar
1 pound sharp cheddar
1 pound hot country sausage
1 medium jalepeno peppers

Brown sausage and drain. Chop peppers. Remove seeds.

Grate cheese in a large pan and melt on low heat. Add sausage and peppers to cheese.

Add each of following to taste:
    Garlic salt
    Garlic powder
    Cayenne pepper

Mix well. Pour into an 8 inch square pan. Refrigerate. When completely cool. Remove from pan and cut into four sections. Wrap each secion in aluminum foil and freeze. Remove from freezer and allow full thawing before using.

PARTY CUCUMBER DIP

2 large unpeeled cucumbers
½ cup cider vinegar
2 tsp. salt
2 8 ounce packages cream
   cheese.

¾ cup mayonnaise
½ tsp. garlic salt
1 tsp. lemon juice

Wash and grate unpeeled cucumbers. Add vinegar and salt; stir, cover and allow to stand overnight in refrigerator. Next day, press out liquid. Blend garlic salt, cream cheese, lemon juice and mayonnaise; add cucumbers. Serve with potato chips. Yield: approximately 3 cups. This makes an excellent filling for cherry tomatoes and spread for cucumber sandwiches.

To prepare sandwiches, peel and thinly slice an additional cucumber. Soak cucumber slices in refrigerator overnight in solution of ½ vinegar and ½ ice water. Before serving, spread bread rounds with cream cheese mixture, top with drained, sliced cucumber and sprinkle with paprika.

PARTY CHIP DIP

1 (3 oz.) Philadelphia cream
   cheese
1 small can deviled ham

¼ c. milk
Salt and pepper
Dill Weed

Mix ingredients and let stand for a few hours before serving.

BRAN DATE BARS

1 cup flour, sifted
1/3 tsp. salt
2 tsp. baking powder
1 1/2 cups sugar
1/4 cup milk
1 tsp. vanilla extract

1 cup bran
1 1/2 cups chopped dates
1 cup chopped walnuts
4 eggs yolks and whites beaten
    separately

Beat egg yolks, beat in sugar. Add sifted dry mixture alternately with milk. Add dates, nuts and lastly, beaten egg whites. Turn into shallow greased baking pan and bake in moderate oven. When cool cut in strips and brush with powdered sugar.

CHOCOLATE BALLS

2 sticks margarine
1 1/2 cups graham cracker
    crumbs
1/2 cup chopped pecans
1 cup grated coconut
1 1-pound box powdered sugar
1 Tbs. vanilla

1 12-ounce jar crunchy peanut
    butter
1 6-ounce package chocolate
    chips (milk chocolate or
    semi-sweet)
1/2 cake paraffin wax (half of 1/4
    lb. size)

Melt margarine in a large saucepan. Stir in graham cracker crumbs, pecans, coconut, powdered sugar and vanilla. Add peanut butter and mix well. Roll into walnut-size balls and lay out on waxed paper. Melt chocolate and paraffin together in the top of a double boiler. Dip each ball into the mixture, returning balls to waxed paper. The balls will cool quickly.

GEORGIA PRALINE ICE CREAM PIE

1 cup flour
¼ cup brown sugar
½ cup margarine, melted

½ gallon vanilla ice cream, softened
1 jar caramel ice cream topping
½ cup chopped pecans

Combine flour, brown sugar, margarine and nuts. Spread in 9x12-inch pan. Bake at 350 degrees for 20 minutes, stirring occasionally. Sprinkle ¾ of crust mixture in bottom of two 8-inch or one 10-inch pie pan. Spoon softened ice cream on top of crumbs. Freeze until firm. Top with caramel and return to freezer for several hours. Sprinkle the remaining crumb mixture on top. This pie can be made several days ahead of time. Serves 12 to 14.

Helen Clark
St. Petersburg, Fla.

SOUTHERN PECAN PRALINES

1½ cups brown sugar
1½ cups white sugar
1 cup evaporated milk

2 Tbs. butter
2 cups pecans
1 tsp. vanilla

Cook sugars and evaporated milk until soft ball forms in cold water. Remove from heat and add butter. Beat until creamy. Add pecans and vanilla. Drop on waxed paper. Yields 30 pieces.

COCOANUT KISSES

1 can cocoanut
1 cup sugar
1 cup nuts

4 egg whites beaten stiffly
4 cups cornflakes

Add sugar to egg whites, then cocoanut, nuts and corn flakes. Bake in a slow oven on greased paper until delicately brown.

BUTTERSCOTCH BROWNIES

⅔ cup butter
⅔ cup light brown sugar
⅔ cup dark corn syrup
2 eggs

1½ cups flour
1 tsp. baking powder
1 cup chopped walnuts
1 tsp. vanilla

Cream butter; slowly beat in the sugar. Add syrup then the beaten eggs, sifted dry ingredients; nuts and flavoring. Pour well blended mixture into a buttered pan. Bake in a 325 degree oven about 20 to 25 minutes. Cut in squares.

BROWNIES

2 eggs
1 cup sugar
1 stick melted butter (½ cup)
2 squares Baker's chocolate
   (blue box), melted

1 tsp. vanilla
⅛ tsp. salt
½ cup flour
1 cup nuts

Preheat oven to 325 degrees. Melt chocolate and butter. In a mixing bowl beat eggs and sugar together. Add chocolate mixture, vanilla, salt, flour and mix until smooth. Add nuts. Pour into a greased 9x9-inch pan and bake for 25 minutes.

SAND TARTS

2 sticks margarine
2 cups flour
4 to 5 Tbs. sugar
Pinch of salt

1 cup finely chopped pecans
1 tsp. vanilla
granulated sugar

Melt butter in saucepan, add flour, sugar and salt; stir. Add nuts and vanilla; mix well. Form into balls, place on ungreased cookie sheet. Bake at 300 degrees for 30 minutes. Roll in granulated sugar while still warm.

CHARLENE'S PEANUT BRITTLE

3 cups sugar
1 cup white Karo syrup
½ cup water
3 cups raw peanuts

1 tsp. salt
1 tsp. soda
3 tsp. butter

Boil sugar, water and Karo until thread spins. Add peanuts and stir continuously after peanuts are added. Cook until it turns golden brown. Take from heat and add other three ingredients. Pour on buttered board.

Charlene Johnson
Houston, Texas

DIVINITY

4 cups sugar
1 cup white Karo

¾ cups water

Place in saucepan over low heat. Stir till sugar is dissolved. Then cook without stirring to 255 degrees or hard boil stage. Remove from heat and pour, beating constantly, in a fine stream. Add 3 egg whites, stiffly beaten. Continue beating till mixture holds its shape and loses its gloss. Add 1 tsp. vanilla and 1 cup broken nuts. Drop quickly from tip of spoon onto wax paper in individual peaks, or spread in buttered pan and cut into 1-inch squares when firm. Makes about 8 dozen pieces.

FIVE-MINUTE FUDGE

2 Tbs. butter
⅔ cup evaporated milk
1⅔ cups granulated sugar
½ tsp. salt
2 cups miniature marshmallows

1½ cups semi-sweet chocolate
   chips (1½ 6-ounce packages)
1 tsp. vanilla
½ cup chopped nuts

Combine butter, milk, sugar and salt in saucepan over medium heat. Bring to a boil; cook 5 minutes stirring constantly. Begin timing when mixture starts to bubble around the edge of the pan. Remove from heat; add marshmallows, chocolate, vanilla and nuts. Stir vigorously for one minute; until marshmallows melt and blend. Pour into an 8-inch square buttered pan. Cool. Makes 2 pounds.

FUDGE VELVET

1 large can evaporated milk
4 cups granulated sugar
1 jar marshmallow cream
1 pound nuts

18 ounces semi-sweet
   chocolate chips
10-12 plain Hershey bars—
   small
1 tsp. salt
1 tsp. vanilla

Mix the milk, sugar and salt in saucepan. Cook over low heat. Time for 6 minutes after the cooking process has started. Immediately pour this mixture over the other ingredients and stir until the chocolate and marshmallow cream have melted. Pour into buttered pan. Set in a cool place until firm enough to cut.

STRAWBERRY TARTS

6 individual pie shells baked
1½ cups ripe strawberries
1 cup sugar

1 cup water
4 Tbs. red currant jelly
1 Tbs. cornstarch

Make a rich pie dough, form pastry. Chill. Roll ¼ inch thick and cover inverted muffin tins. Prick several times with fork. Bake in 450 degree oven 12 to 15 minutes. Remove from tins. Cool. Boil sugar and water 3 minutes. Add currant jelly, add cornstarch dissolved in a little cold water. Stir constantly to boiling point. Then cook mixture over boiling water until it thickens. Cool. Fill pastry shells two thirds full of sweetened ripe berries, or cook berries in the hot syrup until tender then remove berries and cool. Cover berries with cold syrup and chill.

EGG NOG

3 eggs
$\frac{1}{3}$ cup sugar
3 ounces rum
7 ounces whiskey

10 ounces heavy cream
7 ounces milk
$\frac{1}{4}$ Tbs. vanilla
cinnamon

Beat egg yolks until light adding sugar and vanilla. Put in bowl and gradually stir in rum and then the whiskey. Let this mixture stand in your refrigerator for 24 to 48 hours stirring now and then. Add cream and milk. Beat egg whites and fold in half of them. Add a little sugar to the rest and spread on top of the egg nog swirling with a spoon. Sprinkle with cinnamon. Serves 10.

CARAMEL POPCORN

2 sticks margarine (1 cup)
2 cups brown sugar
$\frac{1}{2}$ cup corn syrup
1 tsp. salt

$\frac{1}{2}$ tsp. baking soda
1 tsp. vanilla
6 quarts popped corn

Preheat oven to 250 degrees. Melt margarine, add sugar, salt and syrup. Boil for 5 minutes without stirring. Remove from heat and add soda and vanilla. Pour mixture over corn in 2 shallow baking pans. Bake at 250 degrees for 1 hour, stirring every 15 minutes. Cool slightly and seal in an airtight container.

RICE KRISPY CANDY

$\frac{1}{4}$ cup margarine
1 package marshmallows
5 cups Rice Krispy cereal

Melt margarine in large saucepan over low heat. Add marshmallows and stir until melted and well blended. Remove from heat. Add Rice Krispies cereal, stir until well coated. Press mixture evenly into greased 13x9x2- inch pan. Cool completely. Yields 24 squares.

BUTTER COOKIES

1 cup butter
1 cup granulated sugar
1 tsp. cream of tartar
2 eggs

2¼ cups flour, sifted
½ tsp. soda
½ tsp. vanilla
½ tsp. lemon extract

Cream butter, add sugar and beat well. Add beaten eggs then sifted dry ingredients. Chill dough. Roll thin on lightly floured board. Cut, sprinkle with sugar, decorate with bits of cherries. Bake on greased cookie sheet 8 to 10 minutes in 375 degree oven. Keep in covered dish. Less flour used, more crisp the cookies.

BUTTER CRISP COOKIES

1 cup butter
2 cups sugar
3 eggs
4 cups flour

1 tsp. vanilla or lemon extract

Cream butter, slowly add sugar, beaten egg yolks. Fold in stiffly beaten egg whites and flavoring. Blend thoroughly. Chill. Roll on lightly floured board, brush dough with white of egg. Decorate dough with chopped nuts or shredded coconut, bake until light brown, 8 to 10 minutes, 375.

COCONUT MACARONS

2 egg whites
1 cup sugar
1 cup shredded coconut

2 cups corn flakes
½ tsp. salt
1 tsp. vanilla

Beat egg whites until they form stiff peaks. Blend all ingredients. Drop on well greased baking sheet, about 3 inches apart. Bake in 325 degree oven about 12 minutes to a light brown.

BROWN SUGAR COOKIES

2 cups sifted flour, less if
    possible
1½ tsp. baking powder
⅓ tsp. salt
½ cup butter

½ cup brown sugar, packed in
    cup
1 egg
1 Tbs. cream
1½ tsp. vanilla

Blend 1 cup flour, baking powder, salt. Cream butter, beat in sugar. Beat in egg vanilla and cream. Stir in flour, and enough more to make dough stiff enough to roll. Wrap in waxed paper, chill several hours. Place on lightly floured boards, roll ⅛ inch in thickness, use floured cutter. Place on ungreased baking sheet, sprinkle with granulated sugar. Bake about 8 minutes in 375 degree oven. When cold keep in covered dish.

VANILLA DROP COOKIES

2½ cups sifted flour
½ tsp. baking soda
½ tsp. salt
1 tsp. vanilla

½ cup butter or shortening
1 cup sugar
2 eggs, beaten
½ cup sour milk

Sift flour once, measure, add baking soda and salt, and sift together three times. Work butter with spoon until creamy. Add sugar gradually, beating after each addition until light and fluffy. Add eggs and blend well. Add alternately with milk, beating after each addition until smooth. Add vanilla. Drop by teaspoonfuls on ungreased baking sheet. Bake in hot oven 10 minutes or until brown. Makes 3 dozen cookies.

CONGO SQUARES

Melt 1½ cups butter
Mix with 1 box brown sugar and 3 eggs,
Add: 1½ tsp. baking powder
   1 tsp. salt
   2 ¾ cups flour

Mix well.

Fold in: 6 oz. bag semisweet chocolate chips
      1 cup nuts

Put in greased 13″ x 9″ x 2″ pan. Bake at 350 degrees 35 to 45 minutes until brown on top.

Chris Shultz
Murfreesboro, Tenn.

CHRISTMAS FRUITCAKE COOKIES

1 cup butter or margarine,
   softened
1½ cups sugar
3 eggs, separated
3 cups flour, divided
½ pound candied cherries,
   finely chopped
1 tsp. vanilla

½ pound candied pineapples,
   finely chopped
½ pound white raisins
1 qt. shelled pecans, finely
   chopped
1 tsp. ground cinnamon
1 tsp. ground nutmeg
½ tsp. salt
1 tsp. baking soda, dissolved in
   water

Cream butter. Add sugar, and then add beaten egg yolks. Sprinkle some of the flour over the fruit and pecans. Add spices and salt to the remaining flour. Combine butter, fruit and flour mixture. Add vanilla and baking soda. Beat egg whites until stiff, and fold in. Drop by scant teaspoons on greased cookie sheet, bake at 350 degrees for 10 to 15 minutes. Batter may be prepared and frozen several weeks ahead. Cookies freeze well before and after baking. Yields 125 to 130 cookies.

Bonnie Sloan
Hendersonville, Tenn.

ARIE ADAMS MOLASSES COOKIES

1 cup dark molasses
1 cup sugar
1 cup lard
1 Tbs. ginger

1 Tbs. vinegar
1 Tbs. soda dissolved in Tbs.
   water
Pinch salt
Pinch red pepper

Add enough plain flour to make a stiff dough. Add ingredients in same order listed. Chill for 15 minutes. Divide dough into three parts. Roll out ¼ inch thick. Cut with cookie cutter. Bake in moderate 350 degree oven until brown. About 10 minutes. Makes 100 to 125 cookies.

*Very old, very different receipe. Highly unusual to find lard and red pepper in a cookie receipe. This receipe belonged to my grandmother, Arie Adams of Murfreesboro, Tenn. It was passed on to her from members of the Adams family. Its at least 100 years old. Will keep for months without refrigeration.

Pearlie Scott
Goodlettsville, Tenn.

NUTMEG COOKIES

4 cups cake flour
¼ tsp. nutmeg
¾ cup butter or shortening
2 tsp. baking powder

2 cups granulated sugar
2 eggs, beaten
¼ cup milk
1 lemon grated rind
1½ tsp. vanilla

Mix and sift 3 cups of flour and nutmeg. Cream shortening with a wooden spoon, gradually beat in sugar, add eggs and grated rind. Stir in the flour alternately with milk then gradually add just enough remaining sifted flour to make dough stiff enough to roll. Chill the dough thoroughly, place on lightly-floured board, roll ⅛ inch thick and cut with floured cutter in desired shapes. Place on greased baking sheet and bake in moderately hot oven, 375 degrees about 12 minutes. Will make 4 dozen cookies.

BUTTER N' NUT COOKIES

⅓ cup butter
½ cup sugar
2 eggs
¾ cup chopped nuts

¾ cup flour
1 tsp. vanilla
1 tsp. baking powder

Cream butter, add sugar and well beaten eggs. Sift flour and baking powder together. Add to first mixture. Add vanilla and nuts. Drop on unbuttered pan with teaspoon, about one inch apart. Sprinkle with chopped nuts and bake in moderate oven.

OATMEAL COOKIES

1 cup butter, creamed
1 cup brown sugar
Add ½ tsp. soda dissolved in
½ cup hot water

2 cups ground oatmeal
2 cups sifted flour
3 tsp. baking powder
1 tsp. vanilla

Blend all ingredients. Chill dough, roll thin, cut dough, add filling, cover with dough. Bake in moderate oven.

FILLING:

1 package dates, cleaned
1 cup cold water

1 cup sugar
Vanilla

Cook mixture until quite thick. Cool, then spread one half of cookies with filling and cover with balance of thin dough. Cut into squares and allow to cool before serving.

CRISP BRAN COOKIES

1 cup sifted flour
½ tsp. baking soda
1 tsp. ginger
1 tsp. cinnamon
½ tsp. cloves
½ cup shortening

½ cup sugar
3 cups bran
2 eggs, well beaten
½ cup molasses
½ cup milk

Sift flour once, measure, add baking soda, spices, sugar and sift again. Add bran and mix well. Combine eggs, molasses, milk and shortening and add to bran mixture. Beat well. Drop by teaspoonfuls on greased baking sheet 2 inches apart. Bake in hot oven 425 degrees for 10 to 15 minutes.

TOLL HOUSE PAN COOKIE

2¼ cups unsifted flour
1 measuring tsp. baking soda
1 measuring tsp. salt
1 cup butter, softened
1 12-ounce pkg. (2 cups) Nestle semi sweet chocolate morsels

¾ cup firmly packed brown sugar
¾ cup sugar
1 measuring tsp. vanilla extract
2 eggs
1 cup chopped nuts

Preheat oven to 375 degrees. In small bowl, combine flour, baking soda and salt; set aside. In large bowl, combine butter, sugar, brown sugar and vanilla extract; beat until creamy. Beat in eggs. Gradually add flour mixture; mix well. Stir in Nestle semi-sweet real chocolate morsels and nuts. Spread into greased 15x10x1-inch baking pan. Bake at 375 for 20 minutes. Cool; cut into 2-inch squares. Makes 35 2-inch squares.

*Note: For one 6-ounce package recipe may be divided in half. Spread into greased 9-inch square pan. Bake at 375 for 20-25 minutes. Cool; cut into about 16 2-inch squares. FOR A CRISPER PAN COOKIE: Follow 6-ounce package directions but spread dough into greased 13x9x2-inch pan. Bake at 375 for 12-15 minutes.

ORANGE COOKIES

1 cup butter or other shortening
½ cup granulated sugar
½ cup light brown sugar
1 egg
3 Tbs. strained orange juice
2¾ cups flour, sifted

½ tsp. salt
2 tsp. baking powder
½ cup chopped nuts
1 Tbs. grated orange rind
½ tsp. lemon extract

Cream shortening, slowly beat in the sugar. Add the egg and beat thoroughly. Add the orange juice. Blend the mixture thoroughly. Sift 2¼ cups of the flour, salt, and baking powder together and add to the mixture. Then blend the nuts and orange rind with the remaining ½ cup of sifted flour. Add lemon extract. Form dough in a ball, wrap in wax paper and chill in the refrigerator several hours. Cut in thin slices, place on a well- greased cookie sheet and bake in a hot oven, 400 degrees, about 8 to 10 minutes.

FRUIT CAKE COOKIES

1 cup whiskey or rum
1 pound glazed pineapple,
   coarsely chopped
1 pound glazed red cherries,
   coarsely chopped
1 pound chopped dates
1 box white raisins
2 pounds pecans, chopped
1¼ tsp. cinnamon

1⅓ cups sugar
¾ pounds butter, softened
4 eggs
4 tsp. baking soda
4 tsp. milk
4 cups flour
1¼ tsp. cloves
1¼ tsp. allspice

In a large bowl, pour liquor over chopped fruits and nuts; marinate overnight. Cream sugar and butter; add eggs, one at a time and mix well. Dissolve baking soda in milk and add to mixture. Sift together flour and spices; stir liquid mixture. Mix batter with fruits and nuts. Drop by ½ teaspoonsful onto greased cookie sheet. Bake at 375 degrees for 12 minutes or until golden brown. Freezes well. Yields 18 dozen.

MOLASSES COOKIES

1 cup molasses
1 cup sour milk
1/2 cup lard and butter, melted
2 tsp. ginger
½ tsp. soda
2 tsp. baking powder

½ tsp. salt
2¾ to 3 cups flour sifted
1 tsp. cinnamon
1 tsp. vanilla
1 egg
½ tsp. nutmeg

Cream shortening, beat in sugar, molasses and egg. Sift together flour, soda, and baking powder. Add milk, shortening, cinnamon, ginger, salt, and flour. Chill thoroughly—roll. Add just enough flour to roll on lightly floured board. Roll ⅛-inch thick. Bake in 375 degree oven about 12 minutes. Keep in covered tin.

HARVEST SOFT MOLASSES COOKIES

4½ cups sifted flour
1 tsp. soda
2 tsp. baking powder
3 tsp. ginger
½ tsp. salt

1 cup butter
1 cup light brown sugar
2 eggs
¾ cup molasses
¾ cup sour milk
2 tsp. vanilla

Cream butter, slowly beat in sugar, beat thoroughly. Add beaten eggs and molasses. Add sifted dry ingredients, alternately with milk, beat after each additions. Chill 2 to 3 hours at least. Turn on lightly floured board. Roll ⅛ inch thick, cut, sprinkle with sugar. Bake in 375 degree oven about 12 minutes.

Maggie Nola Sloan
Goodlettsville, Tenn.

GINGER COOKIES

1 cup molasses
½ cup sugar
1 cup shortening
2 eggs

1 tsp. ginger
2 tsp. soda (add to flour)
1 tsp. salt

Cook molasses, sugar and shortening until it boils. Cool and mix with other ingredients, flour to roll and cut out.

OATMEAL FRUIT COOKIES

2½ cups flour
½ tsp. salt
½ tsp. allspice
1 tsp. soda
Then add 1 cup raisins rubbed
   with flour
½ cup shredded coconut
1 tsp. flavoring

2 tsp. baking powder
3 cups rolled oatmeal
½ tsp. cinnamon
Beat together 1½ cups
   granulated sugar
3 whole eggs
2 cups thick sour cream
1 cup walnuts

Mix thoroughly, drop from spoon and bake in a 375 degree oven.
Keep cookies in a covered dish.

OATMEAL COOKIES

1½ cups flour
1 tsp. cinnamon
½ tsp. baking soda
½ tsp. salt
1¾ cups uncooked oatmeal
1 cup sugar

½ cup raisins, optional
½ cup chopped nuts
½ cup shortening, melted
1 egg
¼ cup milk
2 Tbs. molasses

In a large bowl, combine first four ingredients; stir in remaining
ingredients. Drop by teaspoonsful on ungreased cookie sheet. Bake
at 350 degrees for 10 to 12 minutes. Yields 5 dozen.

MINCE MEAT COOKIE BARS

2 cups mincemeat
½ cup butter
1 cup light brown sugar
1 tsp. vanilla

1½ cups flour
2 tsp. baking powder
¼ tsp. salt
1¾ cups oats

Cream butter thoroughly, slowly stir in sugar, vanilla and flour, baking powder and salt sifted together. Add oats and mix thoroughly.
Take one half of the mixture and pat into a buttered, square pan.
Spread with a layer of mince meat. Crumble the remaining cake
mixture and sprinkle over the mince meat. Press gently in place.
Bake in a 325 degree oven about 25 minutes. Cut in two-inch bars
while warm and remove from pan. Keep in air- tight tin when cold.

ROLLED SUGAR COOKIES

3 cups flour
1/2 tsp. baking powder
1 cup butter
1/8 cup granulated sugar

1 egg, beaten
1 tsp. vanilla
2 Tbs. milk

Mix and sift 2½ cups of flour and baking powder. Cream butter, gradually beat in sugar, add egg, vanilla and milk. Gradually add just enough of the remaining flour to make the dough stiff enough to roll. Chill thoroughly and place on lightly floured board. Roll ⅛ inch thick and use a lightly floured cutter. Place on greased baking sheet and bake in a moderately hot oven, 375 degrees about 12 minutes.

SUGAR & SPICE COOKIES

1½ cups sugar
½ cup shortening
2 eggs
½ cup milk
3 cups flour, sifted
1½ tsp. baking powder
1 cup nuts

⅛ tsp. salt
¼ tsp. soda
1 tsp. cloves
2 tsp. cinnamon
1 tsp. allspice
1 cup raisins
1 tps. vanilla

Blend all ingredients thoroughly, drop with teaspoon on buttered pan. Bake 10 to 12 minutes in 375 degree oven. Frost to taste.

GINGERBREAD

1 cup granulated sugar
2 eggs
1 cup molasses
2 level tsp. soda
¼ tsp. cloves

½ cup butter
½ tsp. cinnamon
2 tsp. ginger
2½ cups flour, sifted
1 cup hot water

Cream butter and sugar, add beaten eggs, molasses, water. Add dry ingredients which have been sifted together. Mix thoroughly and bake in moderate oven 350 degrees about 45 minutes.

Peggy Warren
Smyrna, Tenn.

SCALLOPED PINEAPPLE

2 cups sugar
½ lb. butter
3 eggs, beaten

1-16 oz. can crushed pineapple
1 qt. white bread cubes

Cream together butter and sugar, add beaten eggs, stir well. Add pineapple and bread cubes. Bake at 350 degrees for about 1 hour. Yield 6 to 8 servings.

Grace Young
Murfreesboro, Tenn.

DATE AND NUT KISSES

2 egg whites
⅛ tsp. salt
1 cup sugar

½ tsp. vanilla
1 cup dates, chopped
1 cup nuts, chopped

Add salt to egg whites. Whip until stiff.
Whip in sugar a tablespoonful at a time. Beat constantly. Fold in other ingredients.
Drop batter from teaspoon onto greased paper. Bake kisses in very slow 225° oven until they will retain their shape.

HERMITS

¾ cup butter
1½ cups brown sugar
3 eggs
¼ tsp. cloves
¼ cinnamon
2⅓ cups flour

1 tsp. baking powder
Pour ½ cup boiling water over
1 level tsp. soda
1½ cups walnut chopped
1 cup raisins
1 tsp. vanilla

Cream butter, beat in sugar, add beaten eggs. Add sifted dry ingredients. Blend with fruit. Drop small amount of batter from spoon on greased bake sheet. Bake in 375 degree oven. Two cups of rolled oats may be used, and 2 cups less flour.

HOLIDAY SPICE DROP COOKIES

1 tsp. cinnamon
1 level tsp. nutmeg
¼ tsp. cloves
Pinch of salt
½ cup raisins
¼ cup lemon juice
1 tsp. vanilla

¾ cup light brown sugar
½ cup butter
1 egg, beaten
¼ cup milk
2 cups flour, sifted
½ tsp. soda
1 tsp. baking powder

Cream butter, beat in sugar. Beat in egg, vanilla. Add sifted dry ingredients rubbed with fruit, alternately with milk. Beat well. Drop from teaspoon on greased baking sheet. Bake 10 to 12 minutes in a 375 degree oven. ¾ cup chopped nuts may be added instead of fruit.

COCONUT CORN FLAKE COOKIES

½ cup butter
1 cup light brown sugar
1 egg
⅓ cup milk
1 cup shredded coconut
1½ cups flour

1½ cups corn flakes
1½ tsp. vanilla
½ tsp. salt
¼ tsp. soda
1 tsp. baking powder

Cream shortening, add sugar gradually, stirring all the time. Add well beaten egg, milk, corn flakes, coconut and vanilla. Mix and sift dry ingredients and add to the first mixture. Drop from a teaspoon on a well greased pan about 3 inches apart and bake in a moderate oven about 15 minutes. Will make 4 doz.

PERFECT SUGAR COOKIES

3 cups all purpose flour
1 cup sugar
1 tsp. baking soda
½ tsp. salt
1 tsp. cream of tartar

1 cup shortening
3 Tbs. milk
2 eggs
1 tsp. vanilla

Preheat oven to 350. Mix dry ingredients together; cut in shortening. Add remaining ingredients. Roll on lightly floured board; cut with cookie cutter. Bake until lightly browned. Sprinkle with granulated sugar before baking.

YUMMY PEANUT BUTTER COOKIES

2½ cups all purpose flour
½ tsp. salt
½ tsp. baking soda
1 cup shortening

1 cup sugar
2 eggs
1 cup peanut butter
1 tsp. vanilla

Preheat oven to 375. Mix flour, salt and soda; set aside. Cream shortening and sugar, add eggs, one at a time. Add vanilla; mix well. Add peanut butter and blend well. Add flour mixture; blend thoroughly. Shape into small balls. Place on cookie sheet and press each ball with the back of a fork. Bake 10-15 minutes.

SURPRISE DESSERT

1 Tbs. gelatin	1 cup fresh strawberries
¼ cup orange juice	1 cup heavy cream
¾ cup sugar	¼ cup orange cubes
½ cup crushed pineapple	¼ cup sliced bananas
½ cup shredded cocoanut	¼ cup blanched almonds
1 tsp. vanilla	

Dissolve gelatin in orange juice over hot water. Mix with sugar, cool, add well drained crushed pineapple, strawberries, orange cubes, sliced bananas cut fine, chopped almonds and flavoring. When mixture begins to thicken fold in 1 cup heavy cream, beaten stiff. Place mixture in hollowed out sponge cake, set in refrigerator to form. Before serving, cover cake with sweetened whipped cream, and little vanilla.

MOLASSES DROP CAKES

½ cup molasses	1½ tsps. baking powder
¼ cup sugar	¼ tsp. soda
¼ cup melted butter	1 tsp. cinnamon
¼ cup boiling water	½ tsp. nutmeg
1½ cups flour	½ tsp. allspice
½ cup bread crumbs	¼ tsp. salt

Mix molasses, sugar, boiling water and melted butter in order named. Sift and measure flour, add baking powder, soda, salt, and spices. Resift, and thoroughly stir into first mixture. Add bread crumbs and mix to stiff batter. Drop spoonfuls on well-greased tin, or baking sheet. Bake for about 5 to 12 minutes in moderate 350° oven.

DIXIE MOLASSES WAFERS

1 cup New Orleans molasses	3 cups flour
½ cup butter and shortening	3 tsps. ginger
	3 tsps. soda
	1½ tps. salt

Bring molasses to boil; add butter and shortening. Add ginger and salt. Add soda dissolved in a little milk.

Mix well, and add flour, stirring in gradually. Roll mixture, add flour and knead well. Roll thin, cut and bake in moderate 375° oven on greased tins.

Let cool without removing from pans.

If desired, they may be baked on greased heavy paper laid on bottom of pan; by sliding the paper onto a table or board, pan may be used while snaps are cooling.

MACAROONS

½ lb. almonds (or other nut meats) blanched and ground	3 egg whites
	⅛ tsp. salt
1 tsp. rosewater or vanilla	1½ cups powdered sugar

Add flavoring to ground nuts. Add salt to egg whites.

Whip until they are stiff. Fold in sugar 1 tbsp. at a time. Fold in almonds. Drop batter from a spoon onto greased baking sheet.

Sprinkle macaroons with sugar.

Bake in slow 300° oven until done (for about 10 to 20 minutes).

CHOCOLATE MACAROONS

Add grated sweet chocolate to recipe for macaroons.
Use 2 ozs. or more.

GINGER BOX COOKIES

1 cup shortening
1 cup white sugar
2 eggs
½ cup molasses
4½ cups flour
2 tsp. baking powder

1 tsp. cinnamon
½ tsp. soda
½ tsp. salt
2 tsp. ginger
1 tsp. lemon extract

Cream shortening, add sugar gradually and beat well. Add beaten eggs and molasses. Sift flour, salt, ginger, baking powder etc., and add to mixture. Add lemon extract form into rolls and place in refrigerator. Chill. Slice and bake on cookie sheet, about 10 minutes in 375 degree oven.

RICE PUDDING

2 cups boiled rice
1⅓ cups milk
2 eggs
⅛ tsp. salt
¼ cup sugar (scant)

1 tbsp. soft butter
1 tsp. vanilla
⅓ cup raisins
1 tsp. lemon juice, or nutmeg

Combine milk with rest of ingredients, and pour over rice. Mix well with fork.

Grease baking dish and cover bottom and sides with bread crumbs. Put rice in; cover top with bread crumbs. Bake pudding in moderately slow 325° oven until set. Serve hot or cold.

Crushed pineapple may be substituted for part of milk. Amount: 6 to 8 servings.

ORANGE DROP COOKIES

⅔ cup butter
1½ cups granulated sugar
2 eggs, well beaten
4 Tbs. orange juice
1 Tbs. grated orange rind

½ tsp. almond extract
3 cups pastry flour
¼ tsp. salt
1 cup seedless raisins
1 Tbs. water

Cream butter and sugar. Add eggs and beat well. Blend all ingredients thoroughly and drop by teaspoon on a buttered cookie sheet and bake in a moderate oven, 375 degrees about 12 minutes.

POTATO CHIP COOKIES

2¾ c. flour
½ t. soda
¾ c. shortening
2 eggs
2 c. brown sugar

2 t. vanilla
½ c. milk
1 c. crushed potato chips
1 c. chopped nuts

Mix together flour and soda. Cream shortening and sugar very thoroughly. Add eggs, one at a time, and beat well. Add vanilla. Add flour mixture and milk alternately to the creamed mixture. Fold in crushed potato chips and nuts. Drop by teaspoon on a geased cookie sheet. Bake in a 400 degree electric oven for 10-12 minutes. NOTE: Bacon drippings may be substituted for shortening.

MARTHA WASHINGTON CANDY

2 boxes confectioners sugar
1 stick oleo or butter
1 can sweetened condensed
  milk
1 block paraffin

1 tsp. vanilla
4 cup. chopped pecans
1 pkg. (½ lb.) bitter or semi-
  sweet chocolate squares

Cream first 5 ingredients. Add nuts. Roll into balls the size of a walnut. (Use powdered sugar to dip hands into as you roll balls) Melt the chocolate and paraffin over low heat. Dip balls into this mixture, one piece at a time with a toothpick. Drop on wax paper.

*This candy is moist inside and has a hard coating of chocolate. It stays fresh for several weeks.

Peggy Johnson Wonzer
Houston, Texas

ROCKS

1½ cups light brown sugar
1 cup butter
3 cups flour
3 eggs
1 cup raisins
1 cup nuts

Pinch of salt
2 tsp. baking powder
½ tsp. soda
1 tsp. cinnamon
Lemon extract
1 tsp. vanilla

Cream butter, slowly beat in sugar. Add eggs, one at a time, beat briskly. Rub fruit with part of sifted flour and add last. Blend entire mixture. Drop from teaspoon on buttered baking sheet, leave 1 inch to spread. Bake about 15 minutes in 350 degree oven.

CREAM CHEESE SANDWICHES

1 8 oz. and 1 3 oz. cream
  cheese
1 small can crushed pineapple,
  drained
6 Maraschino cherries, cut up
  fine

¼ cup Hipolite
½ cup nuts, crushed

Mix all ingredients, spread on 2 slices of whole wheat bread and 1 slice white bread. Cut into ribbon sandwiches.

Grace Young
Murfreesboro, Tenn.

LOUISE'S TEA CAKES

2 eggs, well beaten
½ cup sweet milk
2 cups sugar
1 tbs. flavoring

Sift several cups flour in bowl. 1 cup crisco or 1 stick butter. 2 tsp. baking powder if self rising flour is used, if plain flour add 4 tsp. baking powder and 1 tsp. salt.
Make up as biscuits. Roll on floured board and sprinkle with sugar. Roll lightly, cut and bake on greased baking sheet.

Louise Hand
Murfreesboro, Tenn.

GENERAL INFORMATION

HELPFUL TIPS:

Keep a toothbrush around the kitchen sink, you will find it useful in cleaning rotary beaters, graters, choppers and similar kitchen utensils.

Use paper cups as handy containers for your "drippings" in the refrigerator as they take up little room and can be thrown away when empty.

To whiten laces, wash them in sour milk.

Dip a new broom in hot salt water before using. This will toughen the bristles and make it last longer

Plant a few sprigs of dill near your tomato plants to prevent tomato worms on your plants.

Spray garbage sacks with ammonia to prevent dogs from tearing the bags before picked up.

You can clean darkened aluminum pans easily by boiling in them two teaspoons of cream of tartar mixed in a quart of water. Ten minutes will do it.

Fresh lemon juice will take away onion scent from hands.

Wash old powder puffs in soapy water, rinse well and dry thoroughly. Then use them for polishing silverware, copper and brass.

If a cracked dish is boiled for 45 minutes in sweet milk, the crack will be so welded together that it will hardly be visible, and will be so strong it will stand the same usage as before.

When your hands are badly stained from gardening, add a teaspoon of sugar to the soapy lather you wash them in.

Before emptying the bag of your vaccum cleaner, sprinkle water on the newspaper into which it is emptied, and there will be no scattering of dust.

COOKING TIPS

To preserve leftover egg yolks for future use, place them into a small bowl and add two tablespoons of salad oil. Then put into refrigerator. The egg yolks will remain soft and fresh, and egg yolks kept in this way can be used in many ways.

You may determine the age of an egg by placing it in the bottom of a bowl of cold water. If it lays on its side, it is fresh. If it stands at an angle it is at least three days old and ten days old if it stands on end.

To keep egg yolks from crumbling when slicing hard boiled eggs, wet the knife before each cut.

Bread crumbs added to scrambled eggs will improve the flavor and make larger helpings possible.

A tablespoon of vinegar added to the water when poaching eggs will help set the whites so they will not spread.

When cooking eggs it helps prevent cracking if you wet the shells in cold water before placing them in boiling water.

Add a little vinegar to the water when an egg cracks during boiling. It will help seal the egg.

Meringue will not shrink if you spread it on the pie so that it touches the crust on each side and bake it in a moderate oven.

When you cook eggs in the shell, put a big teaspoon of salt in the water. Then the shell won't crack.

Set eggs in pan of warm water before using as this releases all white from shells.

Egg whites for meringue should be set out to room temperature before beating, then they can be beaten to greater volume.

If you want to make pecan pie and haven't any nuts, substitute crushed cornflakes. They will rise to the top the same as nuts and give a delicious flavor and crunchy surface.

To prevent crust from becoming soggy with cream pie, sprinkle crust with powdered sugar.

Cut drinking straws into short lengths and insert through slits in pie crusts to prevent juices from running over in the oven and permit steam to escape.

Put a layer of marshmallows in the bottom of a pumpkin pie, then add the filling. You will have a nice topping as the marshmallow will come to the top.

If the juice from your apple pie runs over in the oven, shake some salt on it, which causes the juice to burn to a crisp so it can be removed.

Use cooking or salad oil in waffles and hot cakes in the place of shortening. No extra pan or bowl to melt the shortening and no waiting.

GENERAL INFORMATION

General Cooking Terms

(Baking and meat cooking terms are explained in respective chapters)

Au Gratin: Food (usually creamed) covered with bread crumbs and butter or cheese and baked until top is brown.

Baste: To moisten food being cooked with juices from pan or with additional liquid.

Blanch: To pour boiling water over a food, then drain and rinse with cold water.

Boil: To cook in boiling water (212° F.).

Brush: To spread very thinly with brush or small paper or cloth.

Cook until firm: Until food is firm when touched with finger.

Cook until tender: Until fork can be easily inserted. In case of vegetables and fruit use straw.

Fry: To cook in deep fat.

Garnish: To use one food to decorate another.

Grill: Same as Broil. See meat chapter.

Larding: To draw narrow strips of salt pork or bacon through meat. A needle is made for this purpose, but it can be done with a small sharp knife.

Marinate: To soak in French dressing, vinegar, or lemon juice.

Mince: To chop very finely.

Parboil: To cook partly—not to complete cooking.

Pulp or Purée: Pulp and juice of a vegetable or fruit that has been rubbed through a sieve or ricer.

Ragout: Being French, a deluxe concoction, but literally stew.

Roast: To bake meat or other food.

Sauté or Brown: To cook in small amount of fat.

Scald: To cover with boiling water.

Sear: To brown surface of meat by quick application of intense heat.

Shred: To cut into very thin slices.

Shortening: Any kind of fat suitable to baking.

Simmer: To cook slowly, without boiling, but with temperature just below the boiling point.

Soak: To immerse in liquid for a period of time.

Steam: To cook over boiling water.

Stew: To cook gently in small amount of liquid for long period.

Truss: To tie fowl or other meat so it will hold together.

Tryout: To heat fat slowly until melted.

Until set: Until liquid has congealed (usually refers to gelatins).

COOKING TIPS

Potatoes soaked in salt water for 20 minutes before baking will bake more rapidly.

Sweet potatoes will not turn dark if put in salted water (five teaspoons to one quart of water) immediately after peeling.

Let raw potatoes stand in cold water for at least half an hour before frying to improve the crispness of french fried potatoes.

Use a strawberry huller to peel potatoes which have been boiled in their "jackets".

Use greased muffin tins as molds when baking stuffed green peppers.

A few drops of lemon juice in the water will whiten boiled potatoes.

The skins will remain tender if you wrap potatoes in aluminum foil to bake them. They are attractively served in the foil, too.

If you add a little milk to water in which cauliflower is cooking, the cauliflower will remain attractively white

When cooking cabbage, place a small tin cup or can half full of vinegar on the stove near the cabbage, and it will absorb all odor from it.

It is important when and how you add salt in cooking. To blend with soups and sauces, put it in early, but add it to meats just before taking from the stove. In cake ingredients, salt can be mixed with eggs. When cooking vegetables always salt the water in which they are cooked. Put salt in the pan when frying fish.

It is easy to remove the white membrane from oranges, for fancy desserts or salads, by soaking them in boiling water for five minutes before you peel them.

You can get more juice from a dried up lemon if you heat it for five minutes in boiling water before you squeeze it.

If it's important to you to get walnut meats out whole, soak the nuts overnight in salt water before you crack them.

If the whipping cream looks as though it's not going to whip, add three or four drops of lemon juice or a bit of plain gelatin powder to it and it probably will.

For quick and handy seasoning while cooking, keep on hand a large shaker containing six parts of salt and one of pepper.

Table of Weights and Measures

The recipes in this book call for standard measuring cups and spoons. A standard measuring cup equals ½ pint (8oz.) All measurements given are level. Note abbreviations for teaspoon (tsp.) and tablespoon (Tbs.) which will be used hereafter throughout the book.

1 salt spoon	¼ teaspoon (tsp.)
3 teaspoons	1 tablespoon (Tbs.)
1 rounded tablespoon	1 tablespoon (Tbs.)
2 tablespoons	⅛ cup
4 tablespoons	¼ cup
16 tablespoons	1 cup
2 gills	1 cup
1 cup	½ pint
2 cups	1 pint
2 pints	1 quart
4 quarts	1 gallon
8 quarts	1 peck
4 pecks	1 bushel
16 ounces	1 pound
16 liquid ounces	1 pint (2 cups)
2 cups granulated sugar	1 pound
2⅔ cups powdered sugar	1 pound
2 cups solid meat	1 pound
5 eggs	about 1 cup
8 egg whites	about 1 cup
16 egg yolks	1 cup
2 cups butter	1 pound
Butter the size of an egg	¼ cup
1 square bitter chocolate	1 ounce
5 cups shelled walnuts	1 pound
4 cups shelled pecans	1 pound
4 cups shelled almonds	1 pound
5 cups cocoanut	1 pound
4 cups grated cheese	1 pound
1 cup rice, cooked	3 cups
1 cup noodles, cooked	1¼ cups
1 lemon, juiced	about 3½ Tbs.
1 orange, juiced	about 6 Tbs.
3 cups chopped figs	1 pound
2 cups chopped dates	1 pound
3 cups dried apricots	1 pound

2½ cups dried prunes......................1 pound
2½ cups seeded raisins ....1 pound
3 cups seedless raisins ....1 pound

EQUIVALENT MEASURES

Dash—less than ⅛ teaspoon
Pinch—approximately ⅙ teaspoon
3 teaspoons—1 tablespoon
2 tablespoons—⅛ cup or 1 oz.
4 tablespoons—¼ cup
5 tablespoons and 1 teaspoon—⅓ cup
8 tablespoons—½ cup
12 tablespoons—¾ cup
16 tablespoons—1 cup
2 cups—1 lb. granulated sugar
2 cups—1 pint
4 cups—1 quart
2 pints—1 quart
4 quarts—1 gallon
8 quarts—1 peck
4 pecks—1 bushel
16 ounces—1 pound

The following chart is sometimes helpful:

No. 1 can contains......................................1½ cups
No. 2 can contains......................................2½ cups
No. 2½ can contains.....................................3½ cups
No. 3 can contains...................................... 4 cups
No. 10 can contains ....13 cups

Table of Fat Equivalents

When substituting fats other than butter for shortening
1 cup butter—⅔ cup chicken fat, clarified
1 cup butter—⅞ cup bacon fat, clarified
1 cup butter—⅞ cup cooking oil
1 cup butter—⅞ cup lard
1 cup butter—½ cup suet
1 cup butter—1 cup vegetable shortening

Oven Temperatures

	Degrees Fahrenheit
Slow oven...	250 to 325
Moderate oven	325 to 400
Quick or hot oven	400 to 450
Very hot oven..	450 to 550

EQUIVALENT AMOUNTS

almonds.............	⅘lb. shelled	1 cup chopped
apples...............	1 lb...................	3 cups sliced
apricots	1 lb...................	6 cups cooked
beans, dried	½ lb..................	1 cup
butter	1 lb..................	2 cups
cheese, American....	½ lb..................	2 cups grated
cheese, cream	3 oz.	6 tbsp.
chocolate............	1 oz.	1 square
egg whites...........	8 to 10	1 cup
egg yolks	14 to 16	1 cup
flour	1 oz.	4 tbsp.
flour, all purpose.....	1 lb..................	4 cups sifted
flour, cake...........	1 lb..................	4½ cups sifted
flour, whole wheat ...	1 lb..................	3½ cups
lemon juice..........	1 medium	3 tbsp.
lemon rind	1 medium	1 tbsp. grated
marshmallows	¼ lb..................	16
meal	1 lb..................	3 cups
meat	1 lb..................	2 cups diced
nuts.................	¼ lb..................	1 cup
orange juice	1 medium	⅓ cup juice
orange rind	1 medium	2 tbsp.
pecans	1 lb..................	4 cups
potatoes, white	1 lb..................	3 medium large
raisins...............	1 lb..................	3 cups
rice	1 lb..................	2½ cups raw and 3½-4 cups cooked
sugar, brown.........	1 lb..................	2½ cups
sugar, confectioners..	1 lb..................	2½ cups
sugar, granulated.....	1 lb..................	2 cups
tomatoes	1 lb..................	3 medium
walnuts, black	5½ lbs. unshelled....	4 cups

SUBSTITUTIONS

2 tbsp. flour—1 tbsp. cornstarch

1 cup butter—1 cup hydrogenated fat and ½ tsp. salt.

1 oz. chocolate—3½ tbsp. cocoa and ½ tbsp. butter.

1 cup sour milk—1 cup sweet milk and 1⅓ tbsp. vinegar or lemon juice.

1 tbsp. baking powder—¼ tsp. soda and ½ tsp. cream of tartar.

Chart for Deep Fat Frying

Time	Temperature	
Doughnuts and other raw dough mixtures..........................	360° to 370°	Until brown
Croquettes and other cooked food mixtures..........................	390°	Until brown
French Fried Potatoes	395°	4½ minutes

CONTENTS OF CANS

Size	Avg. Contents
6 oz.	¾ cup
8 oz.	1 cup
No. 1 (picnic)	1¼ cups
12 oz. (vacuum can) ...	1½ cups
No. 300..............	1¾ cups
No. 1 tall	2 cups
No. 303..............	2 cups
No. 2	2½ cups
No. 2½	3½ cups
No. 3	4 cups
No. 5	7 cups
No. 10 12to 13 cups...	1 gallon

Oven Temperature Chart

Slow—250° to 325° F.

Moderate—325° to 400° F.

Hot—400° to 450° F.

Very Hot—450° and above.

MY FAVORITE RECIPE FOR

_____

Name

MY FAVORITE RECIPE FOR

_____

Name

MY FAVORITE RECIPE FOR

_____

_____
Name

MY FAVORITE RECIPE FOR

_____

Name

INDEX

BREADS

CANNED GOODS

INDEX

MEATS

REFRESHMENTS

SALADS

VEGETABLES

INDEX